Y0-AAC-933

Hancock 2015

Christianity
after christendom

Harding
plus 250
graphic
more fun

Green Shoots
out of Dry Ground

Green Shoots
out of Dry Ground

Growing a New Future for the Church in Canada

JOHN P. BOWEN, EDITOR

WIPF & STOCK · Eugene, Oregon

GREEN SHOOTS OUT OF DRY GROUND
Growing a New Future for the Church in Canada

Copyright © 2013 John P. Bowen. All rights reserved. Except for brief quotations in critical publications or reviews, no part of this book may be reproduced in any manner without prior written permission from the publisher. Write: Permissions, Wipf and Stock Publishers, 199 W. 8th Ave., Suite 3, Eugene, OR 97401.

Wipf & Stock
An Imprint of Wipf and Stock Publishers
199 W. 8th Ave., Suite 3
Eugene, OR 97401
www.wipfandstock.com

ISBN 13: 978-1-61097-862-0
Manufactured in the U.S.A.

All scripture quotations, unless otherwise indicated, are taken from the New Revised Standard Version Bible, copyright 1989, Division of Christian Education of the National Council of the Churches of Christ in the United States of America. Used by permission. All rights reserved.

For
Abigail
Owen
Oliver
and those as yet unborn
—the next generation

Blessed are those who trust in the Lord, whose trust is the Lord. They shall be like a tree planted by water, sending out its roots by the stream. It shall not fear when heat comes, and its leaves shall stay green; in the year of drought it is not anxious, and it does not cease to bear fruit.

—JEREMIAH 17:7–8

And for all this, nature is never spent;
There lives the dearest freshness deep down things;
And though the last lights off the black West went
Oh, morning, at the brown brink eastward, springs—
Because the Holy Ghost over the bent
World broods with warm breast and with ah! bright wings.

—GERARD MANLEY HOPKINS, *GOD'S GRANDEUR*

Contents

Acknowledgments xi
List of Contributors xiii
Introduction xv

PART 1: THE LAY OF THE LAND 1

1 Why Mission? Why Now? Why Here? 3
   John P. Bowen

2 Canada's Ever-Changing Contexts:
   Mission in a Radically Pluralistic Society 21
   Robert C. Fennell

3 Church Planting in the 1950s: A Historical Perspective 35
   Reginald Stackhouse

   Green Shoots 1: Brave New Bloom 43
   Little Flowers, Winnipeg MB
   Diana Swift

PART 2: NURSERY GARDENS 47

4 New Shoots from Old Roots: The Challenge and Potential
   of Mission in Rural Canada 49
   Cam Harder

   Green Shoots 2: A Christian Community for the Broken 63
   Uptown Church, Fredericton NB
   Diana Swift

5 Discovering God's Heart for the City 67
   Cam Roxburgh

6 Church Planting by Immigrant Christians—
   And What The Rest of Us Can Learn 79
   Connie denBok

Contents

Green Shoots 3: Artistic Sensibility Meets Christian Spirituality 93
Artisan Church, Vancouver BC
Diana Swift

7   What's a Missionary Doing in Canada?
The Story of Greenhills Christian Fellowship 97
Narry F. Santos

Green Shoots 4: Transforming Communities 111
Neighbourhood Life Ministry, Edmonton AB
Diana Swift

8   "To All Nations"
The Distinctive Witness of the Intercultural Church 115
Sam Owusu

9   The Surprising and Improbable Mission of God
among the Indigenous Peoples of Canada 127
Mark MacDonald

Green Shoots 5: Anglican—and Aboriginal 142
Standing Stones, Edmonton AB
Kristin Jenkins

10   Where Have All the Young People Gone?
What Drives Them Away and What Helps Them Stay? 147
Erika Anderson

Green Shoots 6: Being Church, not Going to Church 163
Emerge, Montreal QC
Kristin Jenkins

11   Creation Care as Christian Mission 167
Leah and Markku Kostamo

PART 3: A GARDEN THAT WILL LAST 181

12   What Kind of Leaders Do We Need? 183
Alan J. Roxburgh

Green Shoots 7: A Fellowship of Urbanites 196
reConnect, Toronto ON
Kristin Jenkins

13   The Ancient Paths: Spirituality for Mission 201
            Constance Joanna Gefvert

     Green Shoots 8: A Free-Spirited Francophone Mini-church 215
     L'Ecclésiole Franglican, Trois Rivières QC
            Kristin Jenkins

14   Reading Your Community: Towards an Authentic Encounter
            with a Canadian Context 219
            Glenn Smith

     Green Shoots 9: Matching Church to the Needs of Young Families 239
     Messy Church, St John's NF
            Kristin Jenkins

15   Risky Business: Shaping a Diocese for Mission 243
            Jane Alexander

     Green Shoots 10: The Church Has Left the Building! 259
     Destination Church, St Thomas ON
            Diana Swift

16   Help! Where Do I Go from Here? Resources for the Journey 263
            Jenny Andison

     Afterword 279
            Colin R. Johnson

Acknowledgments

ANYONE WHO THINKS THAT a book is the product of a single mind must never have tried to write one. A book of essays above all is the product of a community. But the writers are only the tip of the iceberg of the community that enabled this book to come into being.

I am grateful firstly to the Principal and Board of Wycliffe College, where I have taught since 1997, for the privilege of a sabbatical in the winter of 2012 to undertake this work. Most people in the world never have a sabbatical, and I do not take it for granted.

Projects like this always need money, and I am greatly indebted to the Stanford Reid Foundation for their generous and enthusiastic support of this project.

My most substantial thanks must go, of course, to the contributing authors to this book—all nineteen of them: Jane Alexander, Erika Anderson, Jenny Andison, Connie denBok, Rob Fennell, Constance Joanna Gefvert, Cam Harder, Kristen Jenkins, Colin Johnson, Leah and Markku Kostamo, Sam Owusu, Mark MacDonald, Alan Roxburgh, Cam Roxburgh, Narry Santos, Glenn Smith, Reg Stackhouse, and Diana Swift. Here words fail me—almost. All are outstanding reflective practitioners of mission in Canada, and I am honoured and humbled that they agreed to carve out time in their busy schedules to write their chapters. Not only that, they responded, sometimes more than once, and (more often than I deserved) with a good grace, to my pernickety editing suggestions. The King of Assyria once boasted, "Are not my commanders all kings?"(Isa 10:8). I know how he felt.

The book covers a wide waterfront and includes many topics of which I know little. I therefore recruited a number of "second readers," people with some degree of expertise and experience in each area. In this regard, I want to thank very warmly Stephen Andrews, Nick Brotherwood, Robert Cousins, Connie denBok, Kevin Livingstone, Bill Mous, Barry Parker, James Penner, Don Posterski, Preston Pouteaux, Chris Schoon, Glenn Smith, Dan Sheffield, Karen Stiller, and Phil Wagler for their insights.

Having said that, this is not a book intended for experts. It is meant for that useful but mythical creature, "the average Christian reader"—

committed, thoughtful, literate, and concerned about the future of the church as we know it. Fortunately, mythology can take human form, and I want to thank the following friends very sincerely for being "third readers" of these chapters: David Anderson, Kevin Block, Julie Burn, Tracy Butt, Maggie Norman, Karen Isaacs, Graham McCaffrey, Naila Parsons, Jeff Stone, Mags Storey, and Rosalee VanStaalduinen. Not one of them could be said to be "average."

On the editing front, where I am a novice, I had invaluable advice from two friends who are seasoned professionals in the field: Karen Stiller and Kristin Jenkins. Thank you, friends, for your patience, your wisdom, and (not least) your unfailing good humour. Kate Merriman, as usual, has been a painstaking copy editor (more than one author made a point of thanking her for her excellent work). I told Kate that on my bucket list is, "Send Kate a file that needs no corrections." I am not there yet, but I live in hope. Late in the process, Marie Versteeg took Kate's place, and I am very grateful to her for filling in at short notice, not least while she was also nursing the newborn Anneke.

In the background have been other many friends and advisors: Michael Knowles, my prayer partner; Nick Brotherwood, my colleague at the Institute of Evangelism; and the annual "Think Tank" of the Institute—Jenny Andison, Peter Mason, Judy Paulsen, Ryan Sim, and my faithful administrative assistant, Judith Purdell-Lewis. My deep thanks to all.

The staff at Wipf and Stock have once again been friendly, efficient, and readily available—exactly what an author needs. In particular, I want to thank Christian Amondson and the staff of Wipf and Stock for their helpful advice and guidance.

The Second Cup coffee shop (Canadian, of course) in Westdale, Hamilton, has been a great place to work, and I am grateful to the staff there who have helped make it a not just a coffee shop but a community, including Georgina, Mark, and Dali. I have particularly appreciated Kyle for remembering my regular order (small dark roast in a china mug and a Belgian chocolate biscotti: marvellous). A number of the regulars there have encouraged me in my work, not least the self-confessed atheists and apostates (their words, not mine), who have gently but firmly reminded me of the cultural realities that surround the subject of this book.

And above all, as always, my best thanks to Deborah, for your love, partnership, support, patience, friendship, and humour for more than forty years. "Many women have done excellently, but you surpass them all" (Prov 31:29).

John Bowen
The Feast of St Aidan of Lindisfarne 2012

Contributors

Jane Alexander is Bishop of the Anglican Diocese of Edmonton in Alberta.

Jenny Andison is the Rector of St. Clement's Anglican Church, Toronto. She was previously the Archbishop's Officer for Mission for the Diocese of Toronto.

Erika Anderson is a grade 5 and 6 teacher in Grassy Lake, Alberta, and is a research associate of James Penner.

John P. Bowen is Professor of Evangelism and Director of the Institute of Evangelism at Wycliffe College in Toronto.

Connie denBok is lead pastor at Alderwood United Church in Toronto, and Adjunct Professor at Wycliffe College, Toronto.

Robert C. Fennell is Associate Professor of Historical and Systematic Theology at Atlantic School of Theology in Halifax, Nova Scotia.

Constance Joanna Gefvert is a member of the Sisterhood of St. John the Divine in Toronto, and Adjunct Professor at Wycliffe College, Toronto.

Cameron Harder is Professor of Systematic Theology at Lutheran Theological Seminary in Saskatoon, and Executive Director of the Centre for Rural Community Leadership and Ministry (CiRCLe M).

Kristin Jenkins is Director of Advancement at Albert College in Belleville, Ontario. She was previously editor of *The Anglican Journal*.

Colin R. Johnson is Bishop of the Anglican Diocese of Toronto and Metropolitan (Archbishop) of the Ecclesiastical Province of Ontario.

Markku and Leah Kostamo are on the staff of A Rocha Canada, based in Surrey, British Columbia. Leah is A Rocha's lead writer and editor, while Markku serves as A Rocha's Executive Director.

Mark MacDonald is National Indigenous Bishop of the Anglican Church of Canada.

Contributors

Sam Owusu is Senior Pastor of Calvary Worship Center in Vancouver, British Columbia, and Adjunct Professor at Trinity Western University.

Alan J. Roxburgh is Director of The Missional Network, and Adjunct Professor at Fuller Seminary in Pasadena, California.

Cam Roxburgh is the National Director of Forge Canada, Vice-President of Missional Initiatives for the North American Baptists, and Senior Pastor at Southside Community Church in Vancouver, British Columbia.

Narry F. Santos is Senior Pastor of Greenhills Christian Fellowship-Toronto, and Adjunct Professor at Tyndale Seminary in Toronto.

Glenn Smith is the Executive Director of Christian Direction in Montréal, Quebec, and Professor of Urban Missiology at the Institut de théologie pour la francophonie in Montréal and the Université chrétienne du nord d'Haïti in Limbé, Haïti. He is also Adjunct Professor of Mission at the Montréal School of Theology at McGill University.

Reginald Stackhouse is Principal Emeritus and Research Professor at Wycliffe College, Toronto.

Diana Swift is a writer for *The Anglican Journal,* and editor-in-chief of *Canadian Health/Santé canadienne* magazine.

Introduction

THE GOD OF CHRISTIAN tradition is the God of new things: a new covenant, a new birth, a new commandment, new wine in new wineskins, and ultimately a new creation. Of course, this is not newness for the sake of novelty: this is newness in the supreme cause of God's mission in Jesus Christ to renew "all things." Undoing the effects of sin and evil inevitably means change and newness. The mission of God is never static, always moving forward.

At the same time, the newness will be recognizable as the authentic work of God because it resonates with what God has done in the past. God has always been doing new things towards the redemption of the world. When the prophet Isaiah is trying to convince the people of Judah that God will do "a new thing" by taking them out of their exile in Babylon, he has to remind them that this is not actually as new as it seems. God has done this kind of thing before: do they not remember the exodus out of Egypt, centuries before? To Isaiah, the artist's style is distinctively recognizable in the two works of art. But it is not immediately obvious to all that the new is the work of God. So Isaiah asks, "Do you not perceive it?" (Isa 43:16–19). *This now* is like *that then*. Of course, recognizing the new as the work of God does not make it any less disruptive, but it does give grounds for faithful obedience.

This is a book about the church, by the church, and for the church. Specifically, it is a book about the mission of the church in Canada in the twenty-first century. And it is about newness in mission.

In many ways, Canada feels like "dry ground" for the church. During times of drought, plants and animals tend to wither and die. They lack the water, and the nutrients the water carries, that they need in order to thrive. They no longer burgeon with new life. Growth is difficult, and reproduction happens less and less. There is not always someone to blame—"climate change" is as good an explanation as any—but it happens all the same. The parallel is obvious. The picture of overall numerical decline in the church across Canada, particularly in mainline denominations, is clear and disturbing, and the book's authors write against this background. Hence the imagery of "dry ground" seems appropriate.

But this is also a book of immense and surprising hope. Writer after writer speaks of "new things"—things the book's title calls "green shoots"—which are springing up in church life across the country, and which defy the statistics. Some may seem strange to traditional Christians—"What do you mean, the Gospel relates to the lifecycle of the salmon? What on earth is a Gospel jamboree? And why does Canada need missionaries from overseas?"—and it will require the kind of discernment Isaiah commends in order to see that this is the same missionary God at work in new ways—new ways that, despite superficial differences, actually resonate with God's work in the past. The style of the artist is the same.

Another aspect of this "missional newness" is the intriguing blend of unity and diversity among the book's writers. There has been a healthy development in church life over recent decades: instead of differences between Christians being grounds for separation and suspicion, churches are coming to have a stronger appreciation for the fact that those differences can actually make a contribution to the mission of God. And alongside that appreciation has come a fresh emphasis on the things that Christians have in common—which, as it happens, are the very things that inspire mission. Might this renewed appreciation of diversity and unity be one of God's new things, intended to renew the church's sense of mission? I would not be surprised.

Here is how I see the unity and diversity working together in these pages:

Diversity

The church will always be diverse—and that is a good thing. We may speak about "the unity of the church," but that will never be at the expense of its diversity. Unity is not uniformity. Not that diversity is always comfortable. Diversity, especially when it takes forms we have never encountered before, can be unsettling, and cause fear and anger.

The diversity in this book takes several forms. To begin with, there is a range of denominational voices: Anglican, Baptist, Christian Reformed, independent, Lutheran, Mennonite, and United (to put them in alphabetic order).[1] I am aware that half of the authors are Anglican, mainly because that is the denominational "tribe" I know best, but hopefully those voices

---

1. The scope would have been wider, but at least ten potential authors had for various reasons to turn down the invitation to contribute.

do not speak with such a strong dialect as to make the book puzzling for others.

The writers also reflect the diverse geography of Canada: East, West, Central, and North, and most of the provinces. The variety of ethnicity is rather less, but the book does include Nigerian, Philippino, and First Nations voices, as well as the inevitable writers of Caucasian descent (though even here there are some seldom-heard voices, including Finnish, Swedish, and Welsh).

Some of the authors write like poets, others like scientists. Some tell stories, others offer statistics, yet others are heavy on the Bible. Some share a lot of autobiography, others almost none. Writers of some traditions use masculine language for God, while others try to be more neutral. Some are cautious in their proposals, others more radical. (Interestingly enough, liberal theology does not always mean radical ideas, nor does conservative theology always mean conservative ideas. Indeed, the opposite is sometimes the case.) You will detect differences of theology, attitudes to the Bible, and perspectives on church history, even between writers of the same denomination. There are some surprising convergences of opinion from divergent points on the spectrum, and there are startling differences of opinion even among authors from the same tradition. Sometimes the authors may contradict one another.

I have deliberately done nothing to iron out these differences, preferring to let them stand and provoke readers to make their own responses.

As a result, I can guarantee that you will enjoy some of these chapters more than others. Some will encourage you and warm your heart; others will irritate you and cause your hackles to go up. Some authors will use language that is comfortable for people of your tribe and makes you feel at home; others will use language that makes you roll your eyes because it is the language of a different tribe—maybe one you have previously had little time for.

This then is the diversity. Does it trouble us? Well, guess what: welcome to church! Welcome specifically to the Canadian church! Church is diverse by nature. Not that this is really news. Most of us encounter that diversity in microcosm every Sunday morning in our own congregations, not to mention across our own communities or denominations. What we are encountering in these pages is exactly the same thing, simply magnified onto the macro scale of the church across the country.

And, by the mysterious chemistry of God, it may be that we will be more blessed by the chapter that at first grates on us than by the one that makes us "feel good." If we make the effort to listen to the troubling voice, it may actually turn out to be the voice of Jesus—speaking with an unfamiliar accent.

Unity

What then of the unity? I guess I have assumed a kind of unity by saying that this is a book about "the church in Canada." But the unity is more than that, as will become clear. If I had to pinpoint the exact nature of that unity, I would point to several convictions that crop up time after time in these chapters—convictions that generate mission whenever they are rediscovered. For example, each of the authors, whatever their background, is convinced of these things:

- The Christian church still has something unique to offer to the world which is rightly called good news—the Gospel! I cannot help noticing that these authors all take a positive attitude to church and its mission, and this is why: they are passionate about the Gospel. I should warn you that the authors have little or no interest in finding ways to get more people inside the doors of the church so that the institution can survive. If that is what you are looking for in this book, you will be disappointed. These authors know that at the heart of the church is something more important than "getting bums in pews." What is central is the Gospel—a message that is both timeless and timely, a message that will survive the ups and downs of church life because it is the message of God. And it is a message the world badly needs to hear.

- At the heart of this good news is the person of Jesus. In the attempt to "make the church more relevant," there have been various attempts over the years to sideline Jesus. Harold Percy tells the story of a clergyman who told him somewhat apologetically, "I am okay talking about God in my church, but I feel a bit uneasy about talking about Jesus." Such reservations are perfectly understandable. Jesus is after all—as well as being compassionate—demanding, outspoken, and impossible to categorize. If you invited him to a dinner party, there was always a good chance he would embarrass you. Basically, Jesus would not have fitted the traditional Canadian stereotype. Yet all these authors unhesitatingly use "the J word." Why? As Harold replied to his colleague, "When you go to Canadian Tire and ask for a wrench, are they embarrassed to talk about wrenches?"[2] Without Jesus—his incarnation, death, resurrection, and ascension—there is no Christianity, no good news, and certainly no church.

- The word "disciple" needs to be reintroduced into the church's vocabulary. Sometimes the term is seen as the exclusive property of evangelical churches, but it needs to be reclaimed by churches of all stripes. The word encapsulates a new understanding of what it means to be a Christian. Or, rather, it is a very ancient understanding—in fact, the oldest understanding there is. There is a common realization among these authors that the next phase of the church's existence will not have much room for passengers—the curious, yes; enquirers, yes; catechumens, yes—but not for people who want a spiritual fix for the week, or a religious veneer to their lives. Being a Christian in post-Christendom Canada and engaging in the mission of Jesus will simply demand too many sacrifices, and require too many counter-cultural attitudes, for it to be attractive for anyone except the committed—and those considering commitment. Christians will be those who are working daily to figure out what it means to live as followers of Jesus in the many perplexing and challenging situations they face. This is why Jesus, as he set out on his mission, summoned men and women, not to be his admirers or his fan club, but first and foremost to be his disciples.

- There is a need for change. All the writers acknowledge that Canadian culture has changed and are not afraid to take the next step and say, therefore the church should change—unlike the church member who said, "I hope they don't start bringing culture into the church." Certainly we need to be cautious: change is not automatically a good thing, and it may sometimes turn out to be destructive. But the opposite—a kneejerk reaction against change—can be equally unhealthy. The discerning eye knows that "God" and "cultural change" are not incompatible terms and will seek to discern God's "new thing" in changing circumstances.

Good leaders are those who help people distinguish between, on the one hand, aspects of church life that have been shaped by a culture that has passed away—and may therefore be abandoned without fear—and, on the other, what is essential to maintain for the sake of the integrity of the Gospel and the church. That is what these authors seek to do. Naturally,

2. Personal conversation, May 2012.

they come to varying conclusions about what "the Spirit is saying to the churches"—there is the diversity again—but the underlying conviction is the same.

THE ECOLOGY OF THE KINGDOM

Jesus tells more parables about farming than about any other area of life, starting with his first parable: "A sower went out to sow . . ." Presumably the imagery appealed to him because he knew that the work of the Kingdom is often parallel to what happens in the natural world. After all, the same Creator is at work in both. Thus: the work of the Kingdom is gradual and takes time. The work of the Kingdom has different phases, often involving different kinds of work and even different workers. The work of the Kingdom is mysterious, unpredictable, and beyond our control.

Thus, in a book about mission, it seemed appropriate to use that same kind of imagery. Hence the title of the book: *Green Shoots out of Dry Ground*. Hence, too, the subtitles of the three sections to the book.

Section one is called "The Lay of the Land." Three chapters lay foundations for what is to follow: my own piece on a theology of mission, Rob Fennell's overview of Canadian culture, and Reg Stackhouse's story of church planting in the 1950s.

Section two is called "Nursery Gardens." Here eight authors look at different aspects of new developments in the church's mission in Canada. Perhaps it is in this section in particular that the book's diversity-in-unity is clearest.

The final section, "A Garden that will Last," offers clues as to how these "green shoots" of mission can be nurtured to maturity, and how they can become not just isolated shoots but a whole field of sustainable new growth—or perhaps a whole new ecosystem!

Sprinkled throughout the book are ten stories of specific "green shoots" of mission from across the country and across the denominational landscape. These serve as a reminder that this is not primarily a book of theory (though theory is certainly present) but a book whose ideas are already taking root in Canada and growing in unexpected ways, unlikely places, and surprising profusion. (It was a problem limiting the stories to ten because there were many more to choose from.) For some readers, these will undoubtedly be the highlight of the book.

WHAT IS MISSING

Inevitably, a single volume cannot do everything. Some readers will doubtless complain that the book is not traditional enough, or liberal enough, or evangelical enough, or progressive enough. Or maybe your particular area of concern is not addressed. "How on earth could anyone write a book on mission in Canada today and not address the crucial topic of X?" So let me be upfront and admit that, in an ideal world, the book would have included chapters about such things as mission and: social media; the university; children; the arts; church and parachurch; ecumenicity; theological education; seniors; the poor; those with disabilities; other religions; and what we learn from the church in the rest of the world. It would also have included an even broader spectrum of points of view. But the challenge of those topics will need to be picked up by others.

Finally, this book is not an academic exercise. The goal of those who have contributed to this volume is to play some small part in equipping the church in Canada for the work of mission in today's world. That is, after all, the very work for which God has brought the church into existence. In particular, we want to address the specificity of the church's mission in this country, this culture, this generation. We are aware of not being the first or the only ones to be doing this but rather of entering into an ongoing stream of conversation. But if these chapters can add some fresh and vigorous currents to that stream, the book will have achieved its purpose.

PART 1

The Lay of the Land

As a TEENAGER I loved maps—reading them, following them, and even drawing them. Part of their fascination, I suspect, was their variety—how you could view the same territory from radically different points of view. Most maps, of course, simply show you the roads for getting from A to B. Topographical maps, however, go a step further, and show you the contour lines, the hills and the valleys, and (if you are lucky) the trails: much more useful if you happen to be a hiker. If you are a geologist, on the other hand, you will need those wonderful multi-coloured maps that show you the different strata that lurk under the surface of the land. In spite of the differences, all these maps are true (at least we trust so), and the truths they tell are complementary. The three chapters in this section are complementary maps of the Canadian scene—theological, cultural, and historical. The intention is to give us "the lay of the land" before we zoom in and begin to explore the landscape in more detail to see what is growing across the country.

If the church in Canada died out in the next fifty years, would it make much difference in the long run? The answer depends on what story we are living out of. After all, each of us lives out of a particular story or stories. Christians claim that in Jesus Christ and in the pages of the Bible in which we learn about him, we are given a glimpse into the story God is writing of our world: its origins, its joys and problems, and its goal. If this is truly the story of God, then every other story either finds its fulfillment here or fades into insignificance in its light. Those who seek to be followers of Jesus urgently need to be familiar with that story, not least when there are so many other powerful and competing stories seeking to shape our world. And that story will tell us what the church is for and what its future might look like.

1

Why Mission? Why Now? Why Here?

John P. Bowen

MISSION IS A BIG word. It can mean a peace mission, or a trade mission, or a mission to the moon. When the word is used in the church, however, it means something rather different: mission means love.[1]

Of course, over the centuries, that basic meaning has often been encrusted with other meanings: mission as imperialism, mission as assimilation, mission as violence. Where those alien meanings came from is a matter for historians to research and for Christians to mourn.

In fact, however, the heart of mission is something else, because mission is God's idea, and God is love. Or, to put it another way, "the mission of God" is a shorthand way of saying that God's love is at work in the world, putting right everything that is wrong—sin and evil and suffering—and restoring joy and wholeness to the world.

The Book of Ezekiel pictures the love of God as a river, flowing out from the temple in Jerusalem into the whole world, bringing life wherever it goes. Fish (and fishermen!) multiply. Trees grow up on either side of the river and "bear fresh fruit every month" because they are well watered by the river. The leaves of the trees are used for healing. Indeed, "everything will live where the river goes" (Ezek 47).

Of course, if God is really like that, a river of life for the world—and that is what Christians have always believed—then that is good news, very

---

1. Lesslie Newbigin, *The Gospel in a Pluralist Society* (Grand Rapids: Eerdmans/ WCC 1989), 127.

good news indeed, for us and our world. No wonder the phrase "good news" has been central to Christianity from the beginning. The first thing Mark's Gospel says of Jesus' public ministry is that "Jesus came to Galilee, proclaiming the good news of God." And his first recorded speech ends with the words, "believe in the good news!"

This is what Jesus is about: announcing God's good news—the Gospel—and showing what it means: healing the sick, raising the dead, feeding the hungry, welcoming the marginalized, and confronting the powers of oppression. He says in effect, "I bring good news about God"—and then he shows what difference that good news makes in people's lives. This is what he calls "the kingdom"—the state of affairs where the Creator's love is expressed in everything, overcoming evil and creating wholeness. Jesus embodies the kingdom in his words and his deeds. He channels that river of life. If you want to know what God at work in the world looks like, look at Jesus. Which is not surprising, of course, since he is the king of this kingdom.

JESUS AND THE MISSION OF GOD

Why Jesus? It's a long story. The Gospel of Luke hints at the story by tracing Jesus' family tree back to Adam. Jesus is the fulfillment of all that humankind was meant to be, a second Adam who gets it right instead of swerving off track. The Gospel of Matthew reminds readers of the story by tracing Jesus' family tree back to Abraham. Jesus is the fulfillment of all that ancient Israel was called to be. He is a new Israel who lives in seamless harmony with God and shows the world what it means to be fully human.

To put it another way, with the coming of Jesus the work of God in the world took a quantum leap forward. His amazing life—what he did, what he said, and the way he did and said it—was part of it, but only a part of it. The achievement of his life cannot be separated from the achievement of his death. It is strange to think of someone's death "achieving" anything, but Christians have always believed that Jesus' death was not just an unfortunate martyrdom, the untimely end of a beautiful young life. Instead, it was the Creator striking a deadly and accurate blow at the heart of evil, from which it would never recover. Paul summarizes the mystery as "Christ died for our sins" (1 Cor 15:3). Something was accomplished by the crucifixion of Jesus which could not have been brought about in any other way.

Then there is his resurrection. The resurrection is not a hopeful clue to the search for personal survival after death. It is much bigger than that, much bigger. This is the first demonstration of the reality of the new world that God has in mind. The resurrection jolted the world on its axis and even the constellations cried out in surprise: it was that big. As C.S. Lewis says, it was "the first movement of a great wheel beginning to turn in the direction opposite to that which all men had hitherto observed."[2] The resurrection is a foretaste of the glories of the End.

lovely!

THE TRADE SCHOOL OF JESUS

But Jesus does not act alone. As soon as he had announced the good news, he started calling people to join him. His words "repent and believe" have an old-fashioned ring to us, but their meaning is simple: stop whatever you are doing and throw your lot in with me. The fishermen who were the first cohort of disciples were probably not any more "sinners" in need of repentance than anyone else. My guess is that they worked hard, supported their families, attended synagogue, and were faithful to their wives. Jesus' call is not a demand that they give up cheating on their income tax (or the first-century equivalent), which we might consider a suitable subject for repentance. That would be easy compared to what he is actually asking. His abrupt "Follow me" is a call to a radically new life. What is important now is not in the first place family, work, and synagogue, but joining in with God's new work in the world.

In the language of the church, we are used to calling these followers of Jesus "disciples." But that word has little meaningful content in our world. Maybe a better word for their role would be "apprentices." Jesus is like a master craftsman in the work of the kingdom, and the disciples are his apprentices, learning kingdom trades by watching him at work, asking him questions, and gradually being initiated into the work themselves.

Once we see that, at its heart, "church" consists of the spiritual descendants of those disciples—Jesus' first apprentices—this realization triggers a whole new way of imagining church. Baptism is all about our own response to Jesus' call to "repent and believe." Baptism is a commitment to reconfigure our lives in order to put God's kingdom first. That is why baptismal promises often have two halves: first the negative, the "repenting" (what we turn away from) and then the positive, the "believing" (what

2. C.S. Lewis, *Miracles: A Preliminary Study* (1947; London: Collins Fontana Books, 1974), 150.

we turn to).[3] When we are baptized, we are saying yes to God's invitation to set aside our own petty agendas and dreams for our lives and to enter into the work of God's new world—the work of the Gospel. By baptism we commit to live as apprentices of Jesus. But this makes it sound as though it is all something we do. Not so. Baptism is basically a gift of God, and in baptism we are welcomed by him into his school to be taught by his Spirit. As missiologist Lesslie Newbigin says, to be baptized is "to be baptised into [God's] mission."[4]

HOW THE EUCHARIST SACRAMENTALIZES THIS

If baptism speaks of mission, what about that other sacrament central to every Christian tradition[5]—whether we call it Eucharist, Holy Communion, Mass, or the Lord's Supper? Certainly in liturgical traditions, before the actual communion there is what is called the Prayer of Consecration, which tells once again the history of God's mission: the story of creation, the story of how we flouted God's way, the story of Jesus' coming to our world. And then it speaks of how we have been drawn into that work of God: the mission has reached us and turned us around in baptism so that we become not just recipients of grace but also in our turn bearers of grace. The river of God flows into this narrow place of the Eucharist, catches up in its flow all those who participate, and then flows out again to bring life and love to the world.

John Stott has said: "People need two conversions: one *from* the world to Christ, and the other with Christ *into* the world."[6] And at the hinge between those two movements stands the Eucharist, to which we are drawn *by* the mission of God, and from which we are sent *for* the mission of God.

EVERYTHING CONNECTS WITH EVERYTHING ELSE

Mission, Gospel, Jesus, discipleship, baptism, church, and Eucharist are thus links in a golden chain. (See figure 1.) *Mission* is God's determination

---

3. *The Book of Alternative Services of the Anglican Church of Canada* (Toronto: Anglican Book Centre, 1985), 154.

4. Newbigin, *The Gospel in a Pluralist Society*, 117.

5. The Salvation Army is an exception to this general rule.

6. I have been unable to find the source of this quotation.

to renew, restore, and redeem all things in our world. The *Gospel* is the announcement of the good news that this is so—that God still loves us, that God has not given up or forgotten us, that God in *Jesus Christ*—his life, death, and resurrection—is going to make all things new, something we could never have guessed at or expected in our wildest dreams.

Mission—the redeeming work of God

Gospel—the good news of that work

Jesus—God's work as "Kingdom "

Discipleship—apprenticed to Jesus in his work

Church—the community of disciples

Baptism—entry into discipleship

Eucharist—renewing us in God's mission

But when we say, "God is at work," it is not just a general statement. God's work is also personal and specific. God offers us forgiveness of our sins and the gift of the Holy Spirit not just for our personal benefit (though it certainly is that) but also in order that we can join God in God's work by being apprentices of Jesus. As C.S. Lewis says, God "seems to do nothing of Himself which He can possibly delegate to His creatures."[7] Thus we are invited to become *disciples or apprentices* of Jesus and to learn from him what it means to live as God's people in God's world in God's way. *Baptism* seals our welcome into God's mission. And *church* is the community of Jesus' apprentices who gather to be re-formed by their story and to be nurtured in the *Eucharist*. They then scatter to the four winds, to wherever

7. C.S. Lewis, "The Efficacy of Prayer," in *Fern-Seeds and Elephants* (London: Collins/Fountain Books, 1977), 102.

their Lord takes them, to engage once again in his *mission*. This is our story.

WHY NOW? WHAT CHANGED?

The way I have described church is not how most people think of it. In everyday speech, "church" more often than not means the decaying Victorian building on the corner where religious folk gather on Sundays. Or "church" can mean the institution with its complex hierarchies, archaic ceremonies, and quaint dogmas—as in "the church should stay out of politics" or "the church is behind the times." But the buildings and the hierarchies can hide what is really at the heart of church. Anglican Bishop Victoria Matthews, commenting on the earthquake damage to the cathedral in Christchurch, New Zealand, in 2011, put it this way: "We are . . . aware that the church is people and not buildings. The proclamation of the Gospel and the ministry and mission of the Kingdom are carried out by people empowered by the Spirit of God."[8]

The buildings and the hierarchy and everything else can be helpful in supporting and energizing what church is about: "the proclamation of the Gospel and the ministry and mission of the Kingdom." They are a scaffolding to support the true work of the church—a means to an end, not an end in themselves. When William Tyndale translated the New Testament into English in 1525, he translated the word for church as "congregation." A lot of confusion and heartache might have been avoided if later translations had stuck to that word instead of reverting to "church." The church itself is people, the congregation, the community—people who are committed to the Gospel of who God is, and to the mission of God's love in the world.[9]

Why has this theme of mission come to the fore in recent years? Because things have changed. The church used to fit snugly at the centre of society, a hub of ideas and activity. A lot of societal traffic went through the church. Most people would go to church at least a few times a year. Most marriages were celebrated in church; most children would be baptized or dedicated in church and would attend Sunday school, at least for a time; most funerals would be conducted by a clergyperson. Many cemeteries were reserved for members of particular churches. Civic leaders would

8. Diana Swift, "Christ's mission is done by people, not buildings," *The Anglican Journal*, 16 February 2012.

9. The text of Tyndale's New Testament may be downloaded free here: http://books.google.ca.

attend church on important occasions like Remembrance Day. The views of bishops and other church leaders were considered worth reporting in the media.

During these centuries, "mission" was something that happened elsewhere, usually overseas where (presumably) it was needed. Of course, there were also "missions" here at home, but those were usually in city centres and served the needy and homeless. That was the extent of it. The church and missions were two different things. As Newbigin says, "The one is conceived to be a society devoted to worship, and the spiritual care and nurture of its members. It is typically represented by a large and ancient building. The other is conceived to be a society devoted to the propagation of the Gospel, passing on its converts to the safe keeping of 'the Church.'"[10] Church came first, and missions were simply one expression of the church's life, as and where they were needed. They were a minority interest, on the fringes of most churches' lives, and occupying a small line in the annual budget.

So what was church actually for in that world? Once we had lost sight of the idea that the church exists to be an agent of God's mission, we had to figure out other reasons to justify the church's existence. Thus the church was often seen as "teaching good values" or "Christian morality." The church's role was assumed to be crucial to the formation of good people or responsible citizens, necessary for keeping crime rates down and strengthening family life. For others, the church was simply there to offer a spiritual dimension to life for those who felt their lives were lacking a little something. The role of the church in that world is clear from the comment Warren Lewis made when his brother, C.S. Lewis, went public about his atheism: "No useful purpose is served by endeavouring to advertise oneself as an Atheist. . . . [I]t is obvious that a profession of Christian belief is as necessary a part of a man's mental make-up as a belief in the King, the Regular Army and the Public Schools."[11]

But these are all Christendom interpretations of church, far from the spirit of the New Testament. And, somewhere along the way, the world changed—for complex sociological and philosophical reasons. People discovered that they could be good without God, and have "good values" independent of church, and have their spiritual needs met (if they actually believed in such things) in a thousand other ways, and that society did not

10. Lesslie Newbigin, *The Household of God: Lectures on the Nature of the Church* (London: SCM Press, 1953), 144.

11. C.S. Lewis, *Spirits in Bondage: A Cycle of Lyrics* (New York: Harcourt Brace, 1984), xxxvii–xxxviii.

collapse and the sky did not fall if people gave up believing. So where did that leave the church? For many, it quickly became marginalized and "irrelevant," and no longer had any reason to exist—except for people who, for odd personal reasons, continued to "like that kind of thing."

To put it another way, the church was left with an identity crisis. Brian McLaren tells the story of the Choluteca Bridge in Honduras. It was once a busy thoroughfare and an essential means of getting around. Then in 1998 came Hurricane Mitch, and the river moved, leaving the bridge literally high and dry. One reporter wrote at the time, "The graceful arches of the New Choluteca Bridge stand abandoned, a white, concrete sculpture far from shore, linking nothing to nowhere. . . . The Choluteca Bridge itself is perfect, the Japanese engineers [who built it] said—except that it now straddles dry land."[12] Now the bridge is no more than a curiosity for tourists.

In the same way, the relation of church and society has changed. For many, church has not changed: but the river of society has moved away. So what now is church and what is it for? Is it just a historic relic of an earlier age?

This kind of question has provoked many Christian leaders and thinkers, teachers and writers, to go back to basics and to bring to the surface the long-submerged truth that the basic job of the church is to be involved in the mission of God to the world. In fact, unless the church is the servant of God's work, it has little reason to exist.

WHY HERE?

The scope of God's mission is universal—as universal as God's love for all of creation throughout all of time. And so, in one sense, the job of the church is always the same: to follow the lead of our missionary God and to put our energies into the things that God cares about. Mission is not what the church does in the world. It is about what God is doing in the world, with which we are commissioned to co-operate.

At the same time, that mission is always rooted somewhere in a specific context and a particular culture, among local people in ordinary neighbourhoods. This is the model that Jesus' incarnation gives us: not becoming "human" in a generic sense or appearing to "the world" in general: but appearing in a specific place with a particular culture in a dateable

12. Peter Muello, "Honduras faces critical job of rebuilding 94 bridges." *The Indiana Gazette*, 16 November 1998.

calendar year. Thus there is a macro mission and there is a micro mission. This is the theological equivalent of "think globally, act locally."

What then is the church's mission in Canada—for the here and now of Jesus' followers in this country? That is the subject of this book. By its very nature, the book is for Canadian Christians. People of other nationalities may read it (and they are welcome, of course!), but mission is always related to context, and not everything is readily translatable across national or cultural borders. The Five Marks of Mission were formulated by Anglicans in the 1980s to provide a "checklist" for mission activities, but they are true for every Christian tradition when they say that "All mission is done in a particular setting—the context. So, although there is a fundamental unity to the good news, it is shaped by the great diversity of places, times and cultures in which we live, proclaim and embody it."[13]

SO HOW DOES THE CHURCH ENGAGE IN MISSION?

Here, then, are some dimensions of mission to consider. They are not mutually exclusive, and will often be expressed in ways that overlap and enrich one another.

The Church, Gathered and Scattered

The church exists in two modes, sometimes called "the gathered mode" (which generally happens on Sundays) and "the scattered mode" (the rest of the week). It is easy to think the gathered is more important simply because it is more obvious. The gathered church tends to meet in a special building and is usually staffed by trained professionals. The gathered church often advertises its services to the public. It is difficult to miss it.

By contrast, the scattered church does not meet in a fixed place at a regular time, led by religious professionals. It is largely the work of amateurs. Much of the time, nobody is aware it even exists. But the scattered church is no less important just because it is invisible.

The relationship between worship and the rest of the Christian life is much like that between sex and marriage. Sex in marriage is important

[handwritten margin notes: worship = sex. What a comparison!]

13. http://www.anglicancommunion.org/ministry/mission/fivemarks.cfm. The five are to proclaim the Good News of the Kingdom; to teach, baptize, and nurture new believers; to respond to human need by loving service; to seek to transform unjust structures of society; to strive to safeguard the integrity of creation and sustain and renew the life of the earth.

(some would even say sacramental), yet couples who have been married any length of time know well that their relationship during the rest of their lives is just as important. A healthy relationship in the rest of life enables good sex, and good sex nurtures the marriage the rest of the time. So with worship: it is important but it is not all. And there is a healthy symbiosis between good worship and the way life is lived in the rest of the week.

And so it is right and good that the scattered church becomes the gathered church, and then returns to its scattered mode. That scattering begins as soon as the members leave the building and the door closes behind them. Many churches have a sign over the exit saying, "You are now entering the mission field," and that is true. At 12:15 pm on a Sunday, the church does not cease to exist until next Sunday morning. School is not out, with the students on holiday for the rest of the week. Indeed, weekdays are the time when some of the hardest assignments have to be done. Church members go as Jesus' apprentices "into all the world" as representatives of his kingdom, to speak his truth and to act his love. A Christian bank teller turns down a promotion in order to continue giving her attention to those the bank considers little people—retired people with scant savings, the working poor, teenagers trying to save for college. A Christian businessman sets up a laundromat as a safe place for mentally challenged young people to find their first employment. A Christian professor is surprised at her students' comment that she is the only teacher who remembers their names.

I love the way Albert Wolters explains this aspect of mission, and how it connects to God's desire to restore everything: "If Christ is the reconciler of all things . . . then we have a redemptive task wherever our vocation places us in his world. . . . In the name of Christ, distortion must be opposed everywhere—in the kitchen and the bedroom, in city councils and corporate boardrooms, on the stage and on the air, in the classroom and in the workshop. Everywhere creation calls for the honoring of God's standards. Everywhere humanity's sinfulness disrupts and deforms. Everywhere Christ's victory is pregnant with the defeat of sin and the recovery of creation."[14]

This aspect of mission is easily overlooked, and yet it is the basis of everything else. Unless "scattered" Christians are "out there," living their faith with integrity and compassion, risking themselves in relationships with those who believe differently, there can be no other kind of effective mission.

14. Albert M. Wolters, *Creation Regained: Biblical Basics for a Reformational Worldview* (Grand Rapids: Eerdmans, 1985), 60.

Three Mission Emphases

But the scattered church is only one facet of mission: there are more. What constitutes the "more" has often been understood differently by different groups within the church. As each group seeks to be faithful to the mission of God, it has something with which to challenge the whole church. But in that it is only one group with one emphasis, there is also the danger of imbalance. Three examples will suffice.

Some stress that the mission of the church is to be *an inclusive community* where all are welcome, especially the poor and the marginalized. This certainly reflects the character of a God whose love overflows to the whole world, a God whose love works in precisely the opposite direction from the (sinful) human tendency to divide and exclude and feel superior to others. Jesus incarnates God's love in this respect by inviting all manner and conditions of people to eat at his table, whether or not they are "approved" by society or religious culture. His dinner parties are a foretaste of the new kind of world God is building. Thus, when we are inclusive, we represent our welcoming God more truly. Canadian Anglican Patricia Bays sums this up: "An inclusive church that has learned to live together with great variety and diversity is well placed to be an instrument of the Gospel in today's world of rapid change, economic dislocation and great diversity."[15]

What is easy to forget is that alongside this inclusiveness we have to set the invitation to discipleship. The tax collector was certainly a welcome guest (and, in one case at least, the host) at Jesus' table. He heard Jesus' parables, the stories of God's inviting love, and the challenge of the Gospel. But he would have heard, too, that discipleship means a radical reordering of priorities. He would have understood that to be a disciple would require putting first the kingdom of God. Matthew the tax collector made those changes, and became the Apostle Matthew; my guess is that others, of whom we hear less, were not so willing.

The truth of the need for an inclusive church needs to be balanced by the call to radical discipleship.

Others in the church stress that the Gospel is about *social justice*. This too contains a much-needed truth. One of the ways the love of God works in the world is on behalf of those who do not enjoy a share of the Creator's good gifts—the exploited, the oppressed, the marginalized, and the excluded. As the World Council of Churches explains it, "social justice is when people

---

15. Patricia Bays, *Anglican Diversity: Challenges for the 21st Century* (Toronto: Anglican Book Centre, 2001), 29.

enjoy universal access to common goods. It is when 'peace and justice kiss' (Psalm 85)."[16] This understanding of mission begins in the Old Testament, but finds its clearest expression in the work of Jesus for the dignity of all people and his promise of "abundant life"—which is not limited to spiritual abundance, but is the full life of God's restored world (John 10:10).

Social justice makes for strange bedfellows. One Baptist pastor I know puts it this way, that charity is meeting someone's need: social justice is dealing with the things that created the need in the first place. Dom Helder Camaro (1909–1999), a Roman Catholic Archbishop in Brazil, once said, "When I give food to the poor, they call me a saint. When I ask why they are poor, they call me a communist."[17] The universality of this concern across the church, from Baptist to Roman Catholic, speaks of its importance.

Yet at the same time, this focus too can become unbalanced, though for the best of motives. The need to forge alliances with other organizations, not necessarily Christian, can lead to a watering down of Christian distinctiveness. The determination to engage in societal transformation can mean an avoidance of even low-key, relational forms of evangelism. Likewise, the desire to do good can mean that churches move straight to action without taking time to build trusting relationships with those seeking justice. And the need for a quick and flexible response to emerging justice issues can lead to a fragmentation of action.

A third group in the church sees *evangelism* as the key to the church's mission. They understand that inclusiveness and social justice are important, but observe how they can distract the church from its calling to announce the Gospel and invite men and women to repent and believe. It is not that those who argue this way are indifferent to the needs of society. They merely point out that if more people were seeking to follow Christ and serve him in the world, many of the world's problems would solve themselves.

It is true that the first thing Jesus is recorded as doing is preaching the Gospel (Mark 1:14), and equally true that the hearing and reception of the Gospel have always had an amazing and transformative effect on the lives of individuals and societies.

Yet this approach can become one-dimensional and fail to represent the full Gospel. Bill Blaikie, long-time NDP MP and United Church

16. World Council of Churches, "Social Justice and Common Goods," *The Ecumenical Review* 63, Issue 3 (October 2011): 330–43.

17. Quoted in John Dear, *Peace Behind Bars: A Peacemaking Priest's Journal from Jail* (London: Sheed and Ward, 1995), 65.

minister, parodies this view: "if we get Jesus into the hearts of the poor, they will get themselves out of the slums." He counters by citing the Old Testament prophets: "Did Jeremiah, Hosea, Amos and other biblical prophets bemoan the spiritual life of the orphan, the widow, the stranger and the needy, and say that if only they returned to God, they would be alright? Or did they address the inadequacies and injustices of the king, and the elite, and the court prophets who told the powerful what they wanted to hear?"[18]

Blaikie is right. The division of words from action is both dangerous and ineffective. Dangerous because talk of love without loving actions smells suspiciously like hypocrisy. And ineffective because "a hungry man has no ears."[19] There is also the simple challenge of Jesus, for whom words and actions were a seamless web. He speaks and he acts: his acts prove the truth of his words (yes, the kingdom really is here), and the words explain what he does (no, it is not by Beelzebub that I cast out demons). For him, evangelism was front and centre ("believe the Gospel!") but never in isolation from holistic mission.

Fresh Expressions of Church

One aspect of mission that is being rediscovered these days is that of church planting. Of course, that phrase needs explaining. For some, it means buying a piece of land in a new subdivision, putting up an A-frame church building, appointing a full-time pastor, and putting out a sign advertising service times, in the sure knowledge that "if you build it, they will come." Of course, it never was quite as simple as that, as Reg Stackhouse's chapter on Anglican church planting in the 1950s makes clear.

Nevertheless, the world has changed. In Western countries like Canada, where the number of those with no religious affiliation and no church background grows with each passing year, especially among the young, it is more often the case that "if you build it," they will neither notice nor care.

Of course, there are exceptions. I think of a Coptic Orthodox Church in Toronto that is attracting hundreds of young people whose background is neither Coptic nor Orthodox, but that makes few concessions to Western culture (except that services are in English, and the length of the

18. Bill Blaikie, *The Blaikie Report: An Insider's Look at Faith and Politics* (Toronto: United Church Publishing House, 2011), 68–69.

19. Quoted by John R.W. Stott, *Christian Mission in the Modern World* (Downers Grove: InterVarsity Press, 1975), 28.

service is something over an hour). Some of this may be attributed to a postmodern fascination with mystery, ritual, and tradition. More may be due to the perennial power of a friend's invitation, "Hey, come with me. You might just like it."

But in many cases, church planting in a post-Christendom world is more likely to arise from the grassroots, seeded by Christian involvement in a particular community. One young Canadian church planter told me, "We're not setting out to plant churches. We're just setting out to be witnesses to the Gospel. But where the Gospel takes root through that witness, new churches will be the result." One might ask, where people begin to respond to the Gospel, why can they not simply get involved in existing churches, and maybe help revive them? The answers are sad but not hard to find. Not infrequently, the problem is the existing church, which is unwilling to be flexible in order to accommodate the new believers—which is rather as if a family should refuse to change its way of doing things in order to accommodate the needs of a newborn baby.

In any case, there is an argument to be made that new churches multiply the diversity within the Body of Christ—which is always a good thing. In theological terms, the diversity displays the many-faceted glory of God more clearly. And on a pragmatic level, it enables the church to reach out to more and more diverse populations who would otherwise never hear the good news. Newbigin anticipated this over thirty-five years ago: "We ought to expect that there is brought to birth . . . , outside the walls of the church as it is now, a community which is the first-fruit of the Gospel in that place. It should have its own proper character as distinct from that of the community from which the mission came."[20]

So how do new churches begin today if not with a building and a paid pastor? There is a methodology (if that is not too formal a word for what is really an intuitive strategy) emerging among young church planters. It begins not with a building but with relationships; with serving rather than with leading services; and with discerning where God is already at work rather than with a program. Often these new ventures are led by lay people. Not infrequently those who begin them are bivocational—working at a part-time job in order to support their church planting. And many of these new communities will not be recognizably "church-like" in the early stages—which may last several years. Hence the phrase that they are "fresh expressions of church." Bishop Steve Croft offers what I think is the

---

20. Lesslie Newbigin, "What is 'a local church truly united'?" *The Ecumenical Review*, 29, Issue 2 (April 1977): 123.

clearest definition: a fresh expression of church, he suggests, is "the attempt to go to where people are, listen carefully to the context and through service form new communities of faith which have the potential to grow into church in their own right."[21]

All these dimensions of mission are, and will continue to be, facets of the church's mission in Canada: ordinary Christians seeking to be salt and light in their communities—what Roman Catholics call "the apostolate of the laity"; a passion for inclusiveness, social justice, and evangelism, which together form a Christ-honouring synthesis; and increasing freedom to pioneer fresh expressions of church.

HOPE FOR THE CHURCH'S FUTURE

My hope is that this book will help open our eyes to see what the church is and what the church can be in Canada in these early years of a new millennium. There is hope for the church, but it is not the hope of a return to a central place of power and influence and huge numbers in Canadian society. That will likely never happen, and although Christendom brought the opportunity to do much good, the temptations to idolatry and unfaithfulness and compromise that go with such a position are difficult to resist, and we should probably heave a sigh of relief that those days are over, and thank God for it.

Our hope is, at the same time, more modest than that—and more grandiose. What we may realistically hope for is that we will once again find our place in the work of God in Canada. What better future could we possibly pray for? The church began on the Day of Pentecost as a witness to the work of God in the world, and that is where the church will always finds its direction, its energy, and its destiny.

For the foreseeable future, the church in Canada is likely to be small and on the fringes of society, but so be it. Why does that matter? The fringes are where God seems to like to work. When God chose the people of Israel, they were "the fewest of all peoples"[22] and quite insignificant in the world of the Middle East. The fringes of society are where Jesus spent most of his life. Paul understood this when he said that "God chose what

---

21. Unpublished lecture, May 2011. Quoted with permission.

22. "It was not because you were more numerous than any other people that the Lord set his heart on you and chose you—for you were the fewest of all peoples" (Deuteronomy 7:7).

is foolish in the world to shame the wise."[23] On the edge is a good place to be because God is there. That is what the authors of this book are writing about.

When I say there is hope for the church, however, do not misunderstand me. I do not mean there is hope that the church as we presently know it will "survive"—as though the main goal of church is to survive. Survival is not the most important thing. Indeed, according to Jesus, it is not a thing that should even be on our agenda: "Those who want to save their life will lose it, and those who lose their life for my sake, and for the sake of the gospel, will save it" (Mark 8:35). He warns that if we spend our energies on saving our lives—and many congregations are doing just that—that is the surest way to guarantee our extinction. We will die out—and it will be no more than we deserve. We will have missed the whole point of church. Whereas, if we give our lives away—our time, our resources, our love—to the work of Jesus and his kingdom, that is how we will save our lives, even if it is not in this world.

The hope we then find is something rather different: it is, as Paul expresses it, "the hope promised by the gospel" (Col 1:23), that same good news of the love of God. Not a vague, wishful-thinking kind of hope for something which might or might not come to pass if we are lucky—but a sure and certain hope that God will accomplish all God has promised us in Jesus Christ. Authentic Christian hope is the expectation that in the end—God's end—"all manner of things shall be well." It is the promise of scripture that there will be "a new heaven and a new earth" where God wipes away every tear and all things are made new. I love the way Eugene Peterson describes this in his translation of Colossians chapter 1:

> We look at [Jesus Christ] and see the God who cannot be seen.
> We look at this Son and see God's original purpose in every-
> thing created. For everything, absolutely everything, above
> and below, visible and invisible, rank after rank after rank of
> angels—everything started in him and finds its purpose in him.
> He was there before any of it came into existence and holds it
> all together right up to this moment. And when it comes to the
> church, he organizes and holds it together as a head does a body.
> He was supreme in the beginning, and, leading the resurrection
> parade, he is supreme in the end. From beginning to end he's

23. "God chose what is foolish in the world to shame the wise; God chose what is weak in the world to shame the strong; God chose what is low and despised in the world, things that are not, to reduce to nothing things that are" (1 Corinthians 1:27–28).

18

there, towering far above everything, everyone. So spacious is he, so roomy, that everything of God finds its proper place in him without crowding. Not only that, but all the broken pieces of the universe—people and things, animals and atoms—get properly fixed and fit together in vibrant harmonies, all because of his death, his blood that poured down from the cross. (Col 1)

Is this just pie in the sky when you die? No: Christian hope for the future is anchored securely in an event in the past, the resurrection of Jesus Christ from the dead. The restoration of all things in the future is just as certain as the resurrection of Jesus in the past. Indeed, God's past is also a foretaste of God's future. In the resurrection, God has lifted a corner of the veil that hangs over the end of time and given us something to hope for that is not dependent on us and our ups and downs, but is dependent on the God of Jesus Christ, who is faithful and therefore may be trusted.

If God became a human being in the world of first-century Palestine, then culture matters. And the mission of God in any culture will affirm and strengthen that culture on the one hand, and challenge and refine it on the other. As Lesslie Newbigin puts it, "We have to say both 'God accepts human culture' and also 'God judges human culture.'" [1] *All this means that we need to understand cultures, because the mission of God will look different in twenty-first-century Canada from how it appeared in nineteenth- or even twentieth-century Canada. The mission of God in Canada will also look different from the form it takes in the United States or Europe or Africa. This chapter helps us find our bearings in the worlds that make up Canada today.*

1. Lesslie Newbigin, *The Gospel in a Pluralist Culture* (Grand Rapids, MI: Eerdmans/WCC, 1989), 195.

2

Canada's Ever-Changing Contexts

Mission in a Radically Pluralistic Society

Robert C. Fennell

THE LAST TIME I took a plane all the way across Canada, from the west coast to the east coast, I was amazed by the scope and scale of this gigantic country. We saw the edges of two immense oceans; crossed through five times zones; and flew above mountains, lakes both Great and small, rivers, prairies, wilderness, and huge metropolitan areas—all in a matter of hours. In a nineteenth-century horse and wagon, that cross-country journey would have taken months! Canada is enormous, rich, and diverse in its population, and embraces a vast range of geographies and cultures. It is a beautiful panorama of God's creation, both human and non-human. For centuries and millennia, it has been experienced as a place of opportunity, challenge, and hope. It remains such a place for God's people today as we discover and explore the emerging landscapes of Christian mission in this country.

I am going to "fly" over some of those amazing, diverse, particularly Canadian realities in an effort to see as clearly as possible the cultural matrix in which Christ's mission, working through the Canadian church, takes place. First, I will consider some of the major shifts in Canadian society as they have unfolded in the past twenty years or so. Then, second, I will suggest some ways that Christian communities might respond to Canadian society in our shared task of living and proclaiming the Gospel of Jesus Christ.

WHICH CANADA? CANADIAN SOCIETY
AT THE HINGE OF THE CENTURIES

Before getting into the ways Canadian society has changed in the last two decades, I want to note how, in broad terms, the cultural landscape of Canada is both *pluralistic* and *consumerist*. What I mean by *pluralistic* is that there is a spectrum of norms and values that often have little to do with each other. There is no single, distinctive, cultural value that makes us "Canadian." My neighbour's cooking, style of dress, family norms, religious practices, and so on, might be totally unlike mine, but neither of us is any less Canadian. Whether it is on the bus, at a summer picnic in a city park, or on a Sunday morning (or a Wednesday evening) at church, the richness and wonder of our differences is striking. Surface differences—skin colour, tattoos, piercings, or the partners at our sides—are just the tip of the iceberg. Below the surface is the incredible diversity of God's created order—and sometimes the raging strangeness of various disorders in our inner lives. Politics, populations, economics, relationships, institutions, and religion are all aspects of the increasingly pluralistic Canadian society we share.

Years ago, Canadians used to talk about "peace, order, and good government" as cultural hallmarks of this country. Politeness, industriousness, and earnest sincerity might also have been near the top of that list. But now it would be very difficult indeed to describe a "typical Canadian." Not only are we found scattered across a huge physical territory, but we are also wildly diverse in our languages, habits, jobs, religious and moral values, and backgrounds. Pluralism is something we take for granted these days, even if it can produce unsettling feelings for some. Pluralism is the new normal.

As for being *consumerist,* I find sometimes that people are a bit shocked when I talk about this. I have even had someone ask me, "We're *supposed* to buy stuff, aren't we?" The society around us certainly seems to think so. From the opening up of shops and malls on Sundays to the obsession with gadgets and "stuff," Canadians, like many others in the world today, love to buy things. Fair enough. What concerns me, however, is the way we are being shaped to think that consuming is the heart of our *identity* as human beings. Even our everyday language about ourselves is shifting. Once we spoke of being "citizens" as our main identity; now we seem to be "taxpayers" and, even worse, mere "consumers." Rapid communication through various media and the internet is overwhelming us day by day with advertising, to the point where it seems obvious that "to be" has come to mean "to buy." This reality is not limited to Canada, of course. A couple of years ago I noticed a billboard on a Pittsburgh train platform. It showed a model with windswept hair and the logo of a local mall. The large caption displayed across the breadth of the billboard read, "I am what I shop." I have to admit I was shocked and amused at the same time. Are we really just animals that "consume"—one way or another? In *The Consuming Instinct,* Gad Saad argues that to consume is natural and indeed *essential* to what it means to be human. Four evolutionary forces drive this: survival, reproduction, kin selection (preferring one's own clan to others), and mutual altruism (the habit of doing nice things for people who do nice things for us). Each of these, he says, is genetically programmed into us, and each one of these forces (on their own and in combination) drives us to consume.[2] Reading this, I wondered, are we then helpless before these powers? Or is there more to life than this? Is there more to being human? The Christian account of reality says that there is indeed more, and that we are therefore not helpless. We are made in God's image, made to love and glorify God: we are not merely consumers.

How, then, has Canadian culture changed in the past twenty years?

In that time, Canadian *political culture* has changed. Two new and major political parties arose from populist movements: the Reform Party and the Bloc Québécois. The Bloc, limited to seats in the province of Quebec, enjoyed tremendous success at the ballot box in several elections, and at one point had enough members elected to form the official opposition in Ottawa. The irony of an opposition dedicated to the separation of one province from rest of the nation was obvious. Reform, although at first a largely regional party based in Western Canada, eventually merged with the historic Progressive Conservative party. The resulting national Conservative Party took several years to coalesce and gain a mandate from Canadian voters. Claiming both economic and social conservatism as their platform, the Conservatives displaced the governing Liberal Party, which had held power for thirty-three of the previous forty-three years, in 2006. The 2011 majority victory for the Conservatives was accompanied by a huge surge in the popularity of the left-of-centre New Democratic Party (currently the official opposition), the near-eradication of the Bloc Québécois (reduced to four seats in Parliament), and the worst-ever showing for the Liberal Party. Some say that these years reveal a noticeable shift toward a more politically and socially conservative Canadian population.

2. Gad Saad, *The Consuming Instinct: What Juicy Burgers, Ferraris, Pornography, and Gift Giving Reveal about Human Nature* (New York: Prometheus Books, 2011).

Others say it is simply the party in power needing to move pragmatically to the centre of the spectrum to gain and retain popular support. Still others would note that Canada tends to have long pendulum swings when it comes to elections, so it is possible that the more centre-left parties may experience resurgence in the near future. In any case, the emergence of new political movements and the formation of a new government have dramatically shifted the landscape of Canadian politics.

In terms of *population,* since 1990 Canada has grown from approximately 27.5 million to 34.5 million. A little over 40 percent of our growth today is due to immigration.[3] Canadians claim more than two hundred different ethnic origins, defined in terms of our ancestry. Eleven of those ethnic groups have more than one million members each (Canadian, English, French, Scottish, Irish, German, Italian, Chinese, North American Aboriginal, Ukrainian, and Dutch).[4] There are also ever-increasing numbers of persons immigrating from south Asia, the Middle East, and Africa. Immigrants as a percentage of the total population have increased from 17 percent to nearly 20 percent, and First Nations have grown from 2.8 percent to almost 4 percent. In every province, cities have increased in size, while rural areas are depopulating. We are also aging as a society, as the number of retired Baby Boomers increases. Canada as a whole has fewer persons in the under-eighteen age bracket than we did in 1990. Fewer couples have children of any age (59 percent in 1996 but 54 percent in 2006). These trends seem to be accelerating.

New awareness of Canada's First Nations peoples has emerged in recent years. The media coverage of the lawsuits, hearings, and settlements connected to the Indian Residential School system, run jointly by the federal government and Christian churches, has brought a painful chapter from Canada's history into the open. The Canadian Truth and Reconciliation Commission, which began in 2008, and the educational processes accompanying it, have made many personal histories of abuse and victimization more accessible than ever. Recent publicity about the appalling conditions in many First Nations communities—substandard housing, poverty, and inadequate school facilities—do not name new realities: rather, public awareness seems at last to be catching up to these problems. Other aboriginal faces and voices are increasingly seen in the public eye: screen

3. Statistics Canada, "Canada's Population Clock," http://www.statcan.gc.ca/ig-gi/pop-ca-eng.htm Accessed 22 May 2012.

4. Unless otherwise noted, the statistics in this chapter are drawn from Canada's 2006 or 2011 Census results, available online from www.statcan.gc.ca.

actors, politicians, artists, and others are making connections between First Nations peoples and other Canadians in a new way.

Canada's *economic life* has also changed. Overall unemployment has dropped slightly in the last twenty years, as the value of the Canadian dollar has risen and our natural resources (especially oil and minerals) become increasingly valued around the world. As part of the G8 group of nations, we remain one of the largest economies in the world. However, there are fewer permanent jobs and fewer full-time jobs, resulting in increased insecurity about careers and the ability to meet long-term financial goals such as buying a house. Many young adults continue (or return) to live at home for economic reasons, sometimes for years. At the same time, personal debt levels are soaring. Canada has seen a rise in two-income families, as both partners choose to work. While this is often seen as a necessity, it is also a matter of desiring to maintain a particular standard of living. Tax rates have decreased in most jurisdictions (excluding local property taxes), but user fees have increased for public services. Since 2008, global pressures on credit have depressed economic activity nearly everywhere, and Canada has also felt the effects of this. Market instability and credit crises no longer seem to be temporary problems.

Socially in Canada, *relationship patterns* continue to evolve. We are more likely to count as part of our "networks" people who live thousands of kilometres away, not necessarily relying on our physical neighbourhoods to form the core of our relational world. The advent of Facebook and other social media platforms is currently transforming how we become and stay connected to those we call "friends."

The domestic scene has shown both change and stability. Just as the non-Anglo and non-French immigrant populations of Canada have increased, so also have the number of friendships and marriages across lines of race, ethnicity, and religious tradition. The 2006 Census reported that there were 33 percent more such "mixed unions" (marriages and common-law partnerships) than in 2001. After Canadian law changed in 2005 to permit marriage between partners of the same gender, same-sex unions also increased (some 90,000 were reported in 2006). The proportion of persons who identified themselves as "single" remained consistent between in 1996 and 2006 (around 27 percent of the population), and the total percentage of marriages or common-law partnerships was steady at around 58 percent. Yet fewer couples are seeking marriage within the context of a local church, as most local church records will show. One-person households have risen from 24 percent to 26 percent of the population.

Finally, public opinion about sex before marriage has altered dramatically. While in the past it was taboo and rarely discussed, today it is often assumed to be a normal form of bonding in adult dating relationships and partnerships. This is true even as more and more overt expressions of sexuality find their way into such media as prime-time television and print advertising; and the prevalence of pornography on the internet is well known.

Canadians are becoming increasingly *distrustful of authority and institutions.* The web of connections that used to be very strong among the triad of individual citizens, community, and institutions (such as church and government) was reinforced by elements like the school system, Scouting and Guiding, 4-H Clubs, and of course Sunday schools and churches themselves. But that "social compact" has deteriorated. The suspicion of institutions that became so prominent in the 1960s counter-culture has endured into the present. Most recently it has taken shape within the Occupy movements in most Canadian cities and of course around the world. There are good reasons to call for social change (economic inequities and unfair tax laws, for example), yet we know we cannot function effectively as a society without some healthy institutions. We still need schools, hospitals, police services, and so on; and as I will argue below, we still need church communities.

Finally, Canada's *religious landscape* is ever-changing. Unsurprisingly, given the shape of Canadian society as it has been described thus far, secularization has been a major force in the religious landscape. The fastest-growing category of response to the question of one's religious affiliation in recent censuses has been that of "No Religion." Roughly 20 percent of the Canadian population today currently identifies itself in this way (up from 12 percent in 1991). This group is not necessarily all atheists, but it is difficult to be more precise about what "No Religion" means without speaking to individuals one-on-one. New religious movements (such as Wicca, Scientology, and various New Age groups) have also had higher profiles in recent years. There has been an especially sharp rise in popularity in meditation and private spiritual practices that individuals undertake on their own, apart from faith communities. This is the cohort that might say, "I'm spiritual, but not religious."

On the other hand, some argue that the trend toward secularization or a "non-religious" society is actually waning, and we are entering a "postsecular" age. Non-Western immigrants to Canada, in particular, do not necessarily make the same assumptions about the relationships between religion and culture as many established Canadians have done in the last forty years or so. New Canadians are often more likely to bring their religious identities openly into play, and to expect that others will do the same. As Connie denBok has noted, "Faith as a private personal practice is so last century, so insensitive to our changing culture and so un-Canadian."[5] One of the happy effects of this faithfulness among many immigrant groups is that they are actively starting up new churches. Some are very small; some are growing rapidly. Quite often, the powerful community cohesion and commitment within these new faith communities is the seedbed of very significant mission and ministry, within and beyond their own circle. (The importance of this often unnoticed change is suggested by the fact that three chapters in this book address the subject of immigrant churches.)

Beyond this, it is well known that participation in mainstream Christian communities is declining in Canada (see figures 1 and 2).[6]

At the same time, membership in other major world religions (Islam and Hinduism in particular) is gradually increasing. These days, about 9 percent of the Canadian population claims membership in such faith communities. Some majority-culture Canadians have reacted strongly to this trend, with letters to newspaper editors and open hostility to new neighbours. In isolated cases, there have been acts of vandalism. In more than one community, work to build a new mosque has been met with vocal and strident opposition.

Less obvious, and more common, are the quieter suspicions and misgivings among many majority-culture Canadians toward non-Christians. This is often described as Canada's "quiet racism." In the mid-2000s, the attempt to introduce Sharia law (traditional Muslim family law) into Ontario's legal system failed. This was partly a matter of law and policy, but I would suggest the provincial government's rejection of Sharia was in many ways a response to objections from the wider public. Curiously, Ontario has permitted the Catholic, Mennonite, and Jewish communities to organize faith-related mediations in place of legal processes for at least two decades. This is true in other provinces as well.

---

5. Connie enBok, "White-Collar Work," *The United Church Observer* 75, no.4 (November 2011): 32.

6. These charts are based on Colin Lindsay, "Canadians Attend Weekly Religious Services Less Than 20 Years Ago" (*Statistics Canada Catalogue no. 89–630-X,* June 2008). The graphics were adapted by Rick Hiemstra of The Evangelical Fellowship of Canada. See also Brian Clarke and Stuart Macdonald, "How are Canada's Five Largest Protestant Denominations Faring? A Look at the 2001 Census," *Studies in Religion/Sciences Religieuses* 40, no. 4 (Dec 2011): 511–34.

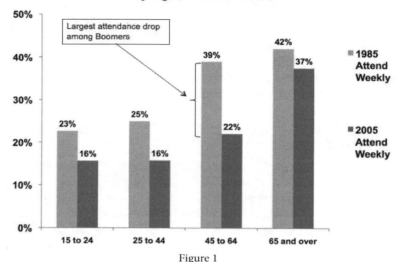

Figure 1
Source: Colin Lindsay, "Canadians attend weekly services less than 20 years ago."
Statistics Canada 2008. Catalogue no. 89-630-X.

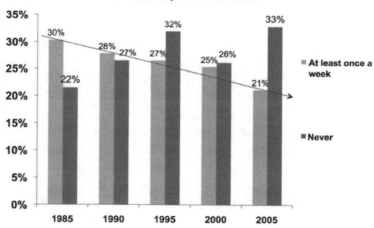

Figure 2
Source: Colin Lindsay, "Canadians attend weekly services less than 20 years ago."
Statistics Canada 2008. Catalogue no. 89-630-X. Note: The category "less frequently"
includes "at least once a month," "a few times a year," and "at least once a year."

Of course, there are also moments of resistance toward Christianity in the public sphere. Recently, the congregation of St. John's United Church in Halifax, Nova Scotia, began the task of replacing the crumbling physical structure of their church building. When they proposed a multistory facility that would both house low-income seniors and provide a new worship space, an outspoken group of local residents filed their objections with the city council. The neighbours were not just hostile to this specific project design, but were against *any* church building being constructed on that property. And this on a site where a Christian church has stood for nearly a century! Despite troubling local stories like this, Christians still retain a strong relative position of privilege within the Canadian religious and cultural environment.

SOMETHING TO SHARE? MISSIONAL RESPONSES

The gift that Christians in Canada have to offer this remarkable and remarkably diverse nation is the same treasure the Christian movement has always cherished: the Gospel itself. The good news of God's great love and transforming power in Christ who is "the same yesterday and today and forever" (Heb 13:8) is something that our local faith communities and every faithful Christian is called to bear into the world. The Gospel is a gift—freely given, freely offered—and it is a special grace entrusted to us to pass along to others. The mission to share the Gospel becomes especially important when we realize that we cannot rely on (so-called) "Christian Canada" to share the Gospel in its systems and institutions. "Christian Canada" is a thing of the past. Sharing the Gospel is a vocation for today's activist Christians, inspired Christians, missional Christians. It is not the general work of a society that is vaguely imagined to be "more or less Christian."

The changes in the rapidly evolving Canadian cultural landscape highlighted above present both problems and opportunities for churches committed to mission and to sharing the Gospel. The pluralism that now characterizes Canada is, perhaps surprisingly, a new gateway for Christian witness, because Christian voices (while no longer holding a place of privilege) can claim an equally legitimate place in the mosaic of a plural society. The challenge is to find a way to be heard in the midst of the competing voices that also strive for public attention, and to find the clear, compelling word of hope that is at the heart of the Gospel of Jesus Christ. In our shared task of living and proclaiming the Gospel, local Christian

communities have many gifts to offer as we respond faithfully and generously to our neighbours. Here are some examples of the gifts the church
has received and is called to share—gifts that we often take for granted but
that actually offer a taste of God's good news to our world.

To those who experience loneliness and isolation, churches can *provide authentic friendship and a place to belong.* Being "church" in a truly
welcoming way—whether as an authentically open local parish or as authentic, loving friends to others in our everyday lives—is so urgent. Yet this
is hard work! To be God's commissioned agents of grace, as we gather or as
we are dispersed, takes deep commitment and a whole lot of Holy Spirit.
Whether it is in our places of work, in community groups, over coffee after
worship, across the back fence or the apartment corridor: wherever we
find ourselves, we need to let down our guard with those we do not know
yet, and to be open to new relationships with people who may be different
from us. Mutual trust and care take time to develop, and this mutuality
transforms both persons. Perhaps our prayer needs to be that God would
shape us and even prod us to take the first (and second and third) step in
reaching out with care, a smile, or an invitation to a meal.

In our congregations, we are called to soften our grip on "doing
church" our own way and to make room for newcomers, who are also
beloved of God and often deeply in need of a loving, transformative community. Our acceptance and inclusion of "strangers" is a special grace, as
we practise genuine hospitality and an ethic of loving friendship (John
13:34). This is so much more powerful than mere tolerance. And when
it comes to sharing our faith, of course, relationships are foundational to
good evangelism.

Churches can also provide *true citizenship* in a world where diversity
and pluralism leave many of us with our heads spinning. Political and
economic ups and downs put us on a rollercoaster of responses. Signals
from the media, and often from our peers, can develop in us a terrible fear
of being imperfect. Youth, beauty, wealth, health, height, weight, status,
nice house, perfect kids, boat . . . what if I don't measure up? Into all this,
churches have a word of grace to share: "our citizenship is in heaven" (Phil
3:20). That is, within a local congregation or among a circle of committed,
faithful friends, we learn to discover that we truly belong to Christ and his
people. We have a home, now and for all eternity.

Sharing the sacraments reinforces this for us: we are not merely individual units of consumption, as the "Buy! buy! buy!" culture tries to tell
us. Baptism and communion remind us that we are beloved children of
God, the family of God, a holy nation, accepted and welcomed, just as

we are—and just as we are becoming—by the grace of God. This lies at the heart of the Gospel—the good news about what God has done and is doing for us in Jesus Christ through the power of the Holy Spirit. Chosen, redeemed, and empowered, we receive those gifts God chooses to pour through us to bless the world around. With those gifts of the Spirit, we are sent into the world to be salt and light, bearers of hope, ordinary people with an extraordinary message. It is a high and holy calling. So much for being a mere consumer!

Amid the changing tides of history, the uncertainties of employment and economy, and a rapidly transforming society, churches can also *proclaim the good news that God's love provides stability*. Whether it is because of the often-distressing headlines we read, or at times when we experience troubles within our own families, we need the reliable testimony of other believers who can help us tune into the stories of the faith. We hear those stories through scripture and through the history of the church. Even among friends and co-workers, those stories and references can find their way into our ordinary conversation. And there is great hope in that witness because—odd and counter-cultural as this is—Christians have a narrative about grace and love to share, a narrative that runs counter to the selfishness and individualistic consumerism of our age. Most importantly, this narrative tells us again and again that God, who has been with us faithfully in the past, is with us now and will be with us in the days to come. These stories ground us in an alternative reality, one that is eternal and secure in God's faithfulness, which endures forever.

We do not need to be miracle workers. We do have a calling, however, to reach out with joyful care and clear speech and action that testify to God's great love. It will take real dedication to discover how to express our faith in ways that are culturally appropriate and that make good sense to regular people. In particular, our challenge is to connect with the increasing numbers of people who say they have "No Religion"—but who are *very* likely to say they are "spiritual." Their hunger and need for God's grace is just as real as anyone's. But they may not listen if (for instance) we insist on speaking in "Christian code," using jargon terms that make sense only to church insiders. Secular language and even secular values, however, are the "ambient noise" around the Gospel; they form the soil into which the seed needs to fall. Effective Christian witnesses can use all kinds of secular examples as rich raw material for the proclamation of the Gospel. If the Gospel is too foreign to people's experiences, they just ignore it. Speaking in plain language about the joy we find in Christ is a gift we can offer our neighbours and friends.

Finally, committed Christians at this moment in history have an amazing opportunity to be part of *new and emerging forms and communities of faith.* From the classic "church plant" to "pub church," from "Messy Church" to spiritual conversation groups, and the hundreds of other ways we might imagine this, the call of the Holy Spirit at this time seems to be pushing us onto and beyond the frontiers of how to "do church." This missional heart, a heart that reaches out to the wider community and lets go of (at least some) old forms of traditional church, seems to be the new gift God is giving us at this time. It is erupting across Canada and around the world.

For generations, new Canadians have been, and today continue to be, ready and eager to start church communities in private homes, not waiting for huge buildings to be built before getting on with mission and ministry. That kind of daring, faithful, sometimes risky venture among "immigrant" faith groups can inspire all of us to trust in God's great love and transforming power in Christ. We need now more than ever to trust in the Gospel, rather than only in the familiar and tested pathways, some of which may be coming to the end of their fruitfulness. New fruit, new wine, new hope is always the Holy Spirit's work. The clear, compelling word of hope with which we are entrusted *will* bear fruit.

To reach out with love toward this changing, wildly diverse, and exciting Canadian culture, we will need our best imaginative work and a humble reliance on the Holy Spirit. The great Christian writer, Evelyn Underhill, once said, "The only thing that counts, and proves the presence of Divine Life in us, is total dedication to God, total dependence on Him. The small, helpless child at the font with new life in it, not the successful preacher in the pulpit, is the typical Christian; the last shall be the first, and the first last."[7]

That "new life" which most of us crave—immigrant or established resident, majority culture or minority, rich or poor or in-between—is a free gift, lovingly given by our gracious God. Learning to love, and witnessing to love, is perhaps our highest calling—in this or any culture.

---

7. Evelyn Underhill, *Fruits of the Spirit* [1942] (New York: Morehouse Publishing, 1989), 43.

Apart from the first church in Jerusalem, no other local church began on the Day of Pentecost. Every other church was begun at a particular date in history. Every church was once upon a time a church plant—a baby church, started by a group of pioneers with vision and hope. That is why many churches continue to celebrate "Anniversary Sunday" every year, and almost all churches celebrate when (and if) they reach one or more centuries. (A bishop in England told me he had recently been to two such celebrations—each marking nine hundred years.) So when people today talk about the need to create new Christian communities, this is not really a new idea. It is an idea going back to the very first century—having babies is in the DNA of the church—but it is an idea we have sometimes forgotten. Reg Stackhouse was a leader in the last wave of Anglican church planting in Canada in the 1950s, and here he tells us the story and his part in it. The impulse to reach out through church planting was the same as it is now, but the shape of that planting was determined by the cultural context—just as it will be today, in our own very different context.

3

Church Planting in the 1950s

A Historical Perspective

Reginald Stackhouse

MARY PRICE FELT GOOD when she put the telephone down. She had just received a call to join other wives in her neighbourhood for coffee at a home only two doors down the street—the same street to which she and her husband Don and their new baby had moved the week before. The invitation was one more sign that they already belonged. One of the first signs had been when the local Anglican rector had knocked on their door to invite them to church. That rector was me, and I hoped that my church would become their church.

When Mary told me about her new baby, I had immediately written down all the information for the baptismal register and invited her to bring him to the next baptismal service. Because there were so many new babies in this new neighbourhood, filled as it was with young parents, such services were held on the second Sunday of every month.

Mary loved it all. She loved owning her own house. She loved having neighbours she knew by name and being able to knock on their doors. And for the first time in her life, she felt she was going to belong to a church that had come looking for her, instead of waiting for her to show up. A little bit on the shy side, she appreciated when others took the initiative as her next door neighbours and the rector had.

What she did not know, but would have been pleased to learn, was that this good feeling was being enjoyed by people all over the suburbs that were springing up around Toronto in the late 1940s and early 1950s. The NHA—magical letters standing for National Housing Act—was making it possible for World War II veterans and others to buy their first homes with just 25 percent of the cost down and the rest stretched out over thirty-five years of monthly payments.

Many people like the Prices were excited to own a home of their own, to belong to a community they could feel was theirs, and now to have a church where they could belong. When they walked there arm in arm the next Sunday, Don pushing the baby carriage, it all seemed so right. They were not bothered that the church was only a basement filled with stacking chairs instead of pews, or that the music was provided by a pump organ. It was crowded with wall-to-wall people, many of whom they knew as neighbours, and so many of whom were just about their age. As they were leaving, I recognized Mary and made sure she and Don knew about the session I was going to hold for the parents of children to be baptized the following Sunday. And when I offered to arrange a baby sitter, I knew they could hardly refuse.

During this period, similar ministries were reaching out to thousands of men and women just like these two. These were people who, having grown up in the city of Toronto, were now starting their lives all over again in one of the suburban communities growing in the shape of a horseshoe around the borders of the city.

As children, such folk would often have made their way into the heart of the city on a Sunday to attend church. Now the Anglican Diocese of Toronto was reinventing itself as a dynamic, creative, forward-thrusting agency of "church extension," as its expansion program was called, and reaching out to people in the new suburbs where they were living.

A PLAN FOR CHURCH EXTENSION

The plan was progressive but simple. The diocese had bought land suitable as a site for church buildings long before farm fields and market gardens were turned into streets of family homes. Church administrators showed leadership that was both visionary and practical. They did not wait until the community was already built up, because by that time no good property would be on the market. Neither did they wait for the local faithful to take the initiative. They had a plan that started with the Church Extension

Committee spotting a potential site big enough for a church, a parking lot, and a rectory, and then buying it up.

A clergyman was then appointed and was expected to attract and organize a congregation. The new community would often meet in a public school until the church site had at least the basement of a church building on it. The diocese was also willing to lend some of the money needed to build a church, but the local congregation was expected to take the initiative to start their own building fund of cash and pledges so that bank financing could be realistically arranged.

This progressive but simple plan had another important feature: success. In 1950, the Church Extension Committee reported to the Toronto Diocesan Synod that five new sites had been acquired, making a total of twenty-two, mostly in suburban Toronto, but at least two of them in centres such as nearby Lansing (now Willowdale) and more distant Wasaga. All twenty-two communities could be described not only as "newly settled" but also as "rapidly growing." In the previous year, these new congregations had reported a total of 320 baptisms and 169 confirmations, with 2183 people receiving Holy Communion at Easter.

At synod the following year, members were warned that, although progress had been made, the diocese was not keeping pace with the need, and in order to catch up, it had purchased six new church sites. What Mary and Don had discovered—a new life in the church—was being welcomed by so many others that the number of Easter communicants in church extension congregations had leapt in a single year to 4783, with 5722 children in Sunday schools. The diocese had also arranged a line of credit with a bank amounting to $500 000 (perhaps ten times that amount in today's terms) and appointed a part-time director of church extension, Robert Dann, rector of St. George's-on-the-Hill in Islington, itself changing rapidly from a quiet little village into a thriving suburb.

These financial figures were no sooner made public, however, than they were out-of-date because the need was continuing to soar dramatically, with $600 000 being spent on church extension projects in 1954 alone. As the name implied, church extension was moving.

This kind of progress was not confined to the suburbs around Toronto. In 1955, sites were acquired in more distant parts of the diocese like Orillia, Oak Ridges, Peterborough, and Oshawa. Three years later, no less than one-fifth of the congregations in the diocese were church extension projects. It seemed as though the phrase "church militant" had found a new application. Some predicted that within a short time these church extension congregations would together serve an Anglican population larger than that of any diocese in the country except that of the City of Toronto itself. Synod was told with some justification that church extension had created "a diocese within a diocese."

THE CHALLENGE OF PIONEERING

I was part of one of these new and growing churches for ten years, first as a part-time student minister and then as a full-time ordained cleric. The decade had started modestly enough for the new parish I was to lead, with nothing more prepossessing than a vacant lot and a sign proclaiming, "An Anglican Church Will Be Built Here!" However, the new project had been begun some decades earlier, grounded in lay leadership. In what would eventually become the parish, Albert Mercer, a lay person and an early settler in West Islington, had laid the foundations by organizing a Sunday school. There, many men and women had found Christian faith, and they grew into the next generation of church leaders.

As the new student-minister, I hoped to make a good first impression on potential parishioners as I cycled my way around the community, stopping at people's doors to say "Welcome!"—often the first person to do so. We had dreams of a vaulted, new church, but knew that an entrepreneurial type of ministry would be demanded in order to get it off the ground. We also hoped that the same spirit of innovation and enterprise would shape the character of this new local congregation. It seemed obvious to us that the Anglican Church's historic character was evolving into a new mix that combined traditional substance and contemporary style.

At the new church (St. Matthew's, Islington), my wife Margaret organized the girls into what was then called the "Junior Auxiliary," a program comparable to the Girl Guides and Brownies but with a sizable dollop of church-centred teaching. We also conducted a summer school for those children who were not off to cottage or camp, and we enjoyed mornings of games, singing, and Bible stories, all with volunteer leaders.

Most challenging of all, we had to raise enough money in a building fund to persuade a bank manager that we were a reliable risk—not only to build a church but to pay for it.

Starting new congregations was seen at first simply as a way of meeting a new but temporary need. But within quite a short time, it came to be seen as a successful—and permanent—way of turning challenge into opportunity. As the decade of the 1950s came to a close, synod was told that Metropolitan Toronto could be expected to grow 151 percent by 1980. Could continued Anglican growth become a permanent feature of the future? Church Extension clergy—of whom I was one—thought it could. We expected the future to continue to unfold in just the same way as we had seen in the previous few years.

It is not difficult to understand why so many of us made this assumption. Throughout the nineteenth and twentieth centuries, Anglicans had formed the largest segment of the Toronto population, and our centuries-old patterns of ministry had remained effective. Why should bishops and clergy not think they would remain the wave of the future? We knew what the challenges were and what the solutions were. All that was necessary was for churches to continue raising funds to buy sites, purchase rectories, and subsidize building programs—in short, keep doing what had been so patently effective in this era.

A SHIFTING CULTURE

The bigger question we did not consider, and had little way of answering, was whether men and women of the 1980s and 1990s would keep responding in the same way Mary and Don's generation had. We did not foresee the socio-cultural changes that were just over the horizon, which would raise new roadblocks in front of "Christian soldiers marching as to war." As the twentieth century moved towards the twenty-first, we could not see the coming challenges, which were far harder to meet than bishops and clergy had known in the previous decades, when the biggest resistance to church extension had been merely financial. The old order of life in and around Toronto was giving place to a new one, in which there would be less and less space for the Anglican Church as people had known it.

One of these changes was demographic. The collapse in the Canadian birth rate meant that the church could no longer rely on growth from biological increase coupled with Christian education in Sunday schools and confirmation classes. This demographic challenge was compounded by dramatic decline in immigration from the UK, alongside the escalation of immigration from countries where the word "Anglican" was virtually unknown. Toronto was quickly becoming a city where Christian worship on Sundays was offered in dozens of languages other than English, and by many denominations other than Anglican.

As a result of these and other factors, the membership of the Anglican Church of Canada went into a tailspin after reaching its peak in 1965. Yet this reality never made it to the agenda of General Synod unless someone raised it from the floor. When the world's Anglican bishops gathered for the 1988 Lambeth Conference and called for the 1990s to be a "Decade of Evangelism among Anglicans," the most visible result in Canada was the creation of the Wycliffe College Institute of Evangelism in Toronto.

NEW CHALLENGES FOR A NEW CENTURY

As we move deeper into the second decade of this new century, there are several new opportunities for mission that we need to be considering seriously. One is the open door offered by developments in communications technology. New media can provide people with an opportunity to hear the Gospel message without actually joining physically with other people in a church building. Too often we respond to this kind of suggestion in a kneejerk kind of way, insisting that physical gathering is essential and so failing to see that social media can provide a twenty-first century point of contact—just as the new-fangled printing press helped make a sixteenth-century Reformation possible. Social media can often be the first word in evangelism—even if it is not the last.

A second opportunity for mission is the simple fact, constantly discussed in the media, that our population is rapidly aging. Yet evangelism for the elderly and those with disabilities has not yet appeared on the twenty-first-century church's agenda. No one is likely to challenge the fact that one soul—including an elderly one—is as precious to God as any other, and yet recognition of that fact seldom leads to action.

When most parish churches were established in Toronto, their locations were determined by one common cultural feature: the church had to be within walking distance. Everything else lacked priority—the sermon could be delivered in a monotone, the music could be as mediocre as it was earnest—as long as people could reach the church on foot. Now, however, people will drive up to thirty kilometres to reach a church that provides what they want in preaching, music, fellowship, and theology—as long as they can park when they get there.

Church extension as it was practised in the 1950s was an effective strategy for that period, but it does not suit the culture of Canada half a century later. Five decades ago, the culture had lots of space for church. Today, that same space is far more pluralistic. As a result, people in our day cannot comprehend the idea of a church that assumes people will just show up to hear its message. Secularization demands a ministry that finds new ways to communicate its message to people in their day-to-day lives.

It is easy to see why, as the 1950s came to an end, church leaders were encouraged by their progress in the previous decade. It is harder to understand why, for the second half of the century, we spent more time lamenting the loss of the past than in developing new strategies, equally bold and daring, for a new world. In the 1950s, church leaders grasped the challenge implied in the 1960s hit, "The Times They Are A-Changing." During the second half of the twentieth century, however, we failed to grapple with the need for another really fresh expression of church.

Green Shoots

"Other seed fell into good soil and brought forth grain, growing up and increasing and yielding thirty and sixty and a hundredfold" (Mark 4:8). So ends Jesus' parable of the sower. But are there places in Canada where the seed of the Word is finding "good soil" in which to take root? Sprinkled throughout this book are ten stories of "green shoots," growing out of what sometimes seems like dry ground. They represent many parts of the country, different Christian traditions, and various approaches to mission. Some will bear a family likeness to forms of church we have known elsewhere; others will strike us at first as unfamiliar and perhaps strange. Each is unique, and none can be taken as a precise model for somewhere else. Yet every one has something to teach us in terms of creative fidelity—or perhaps faithful creativity. And every one is encouraging: the Word is indeed growing. These stories have been painstakingly assembled by senior Canadian journalists Kristin Jenkins and Diana Swift.

Green Shoots 1
Brave New Bloom

Little Flowers Community: Winnipeg, Manitoba
Diana Swift

As you tread the cracked sidewalks of a crumbling residential neighbourhood in Winnipeg's west end, you will occasionally see tiny wildflowers pushing through the concrete. Against all odds, they manage to survive in the gritty atmosphere of this old-parish section of the city, just off the main commercial strip.

These blossoms are the namesakes of the Pastoral Ministry of Little Flowers Community, a residential and worship entity that blossomed about three years ago under the tutelage of pastors Jamie and Kim Arpin-Ricci. "Like these flowers, we are seeking to be a beacon of beauty and hope in a broken place," says Jamie.

These brave urban blossoms—as well as the collection of biographical anecdotes and miracle stories about St. Francis known as *The Little Flowers of St. Francis of Assisi*—are part of the impetus and inspiration for this new faith community. It is a community that is also informed by the monastic traditions of the Franciscan Mendicant Friars and the Mennonite Anabaptists.

As a church plant, Little Flowers grew as naturally and organically as its botanical namesakes. It traces its first roots, not to a deliberately planned place of worship, but to a secular space designed for community service: a used-book store called The Dusty Cover.

The store took shape after Jamie and Kim had been working for ten years in downtown Winnipeg as missionaries for Youth With A Mission (YWAM), an interdenominational evangelical organization. "We wanted to connect with and serve our community in a concrete but neutral way," says Jamie.

With support from YWAM and donations from individuals, the couple spent a year assembling a staff, renting space, building shelves, and stocking them with high-quality used books in a broad range of categories. "Just because our clients were poor, we didn't want this to be a place for dumping any old used books," he says.

The Dusty Cover, a welcoming, pressure-free refuge for book lovers, opened in 2007 in an urban setting all too often defined by fear and mistrust. "We provided comfy chairs, low-cost books, free fair-trade coffee, and, most of all, a safe, welcoming, and neutral place for neighbourhood people to meet," says Jamie.

The store's clientele consisted mainly of single mothers, university students, and young singles with poverty and/or mental health issues. Soon, a core group of Dusty Cover patrons began to meet in the Arpin-Riccis' huge rambling house—a former notorious gang den—for mid-week potluck suppers. To accommodate work schedules, these eventually moved to Sunday evenings.

"Somebody would bring a guitar and we'd sing—not necessarily but occasionally hymns," Jamie recalls. There was no deliberate attempt to inject a religious element, since many of the core people were unchurched or de-churched. "They had been alienated from or hurt by the church," says Jamie.

Although many participants were, and continue to be, transients, a core group of twenty to thirty participants formed, and they attended the meetings each Sunday. Some of them began to consult the Arpin-Riccis for advice. "They'd also ask us to attend court with them if they had a legal problem, or to pray for a relative who was sick or in trouble," says Jamie. One Sunday night, several in the group approached Jamie and said, "You know, we're a church. Will you be our pastor?"

Jamie and Kim were excited but daunted at the prospect. "We felt the Holy Spirit was leading us to provide a more formal context for them, specifically a church body, but in order to do this, we needed to partner with an established denomination whose values matched ours," says Jamie. Those values include living life simply and in accordance with Jesus' teachings as articulated in the Sermon on the Mount.

Soon a mentoring partnership was struck with the Mennonite Church of Manitoba. "It's not often the Mennonite Church has the problem of a surplus of young twenty-year-olds in a congregation," says Jamie wryly. He himself attended a Mennonite Christian school, although he worshipped in the Evangelical Covenant Church of Canada, belonged to a Pentecostal youth group, and occasionally attended mass with his Roman Catholic grandmother. Today, in accordance with the Franciscan-Mennonite "new monastic" ideal, about one third of Little Flowers core members live together in intentional communities of faith, occupying several houses around Winnipeg. "Kim and I sometimes have as many as fifteen living at our house," says Jamie.

With a strong commitment to social justice, the community buys its food ethically and in a way that helps its low-income members economically. "We often shop for food collectively. We'll order a large quantity of chicken from the Hutterite colony to save us money, and the community can purchase it at low cost as well," says Jamie.

Beyond that, the Franciscan tradition is reflected in the group's high percentage of animal lovers. "We have a disproportionate number of cats and dogs for our community size!" he says.

As for rules, unlike its medieval predecessor, the new monasticism has no dress code, no flowing habits, no periods of silence, and no set schedules for daily prayer. What binds its adherents is this: "We are seeking to discover together what it means to live in radical obedience to the teachings and example of Jesus Christ around the Mennonite tradition," Jamie says.

Beyond its own needs, as a project of social service, Little Flowers is renovating an old three-story apartment building into low-income rental housing. Called Chiara House, the building will reserve its ground floor for those wishing to live in a community of faith, while its top floors will provide affordable, high-quality, furnished apartments. "You can get low-income housing in this area of Winnipeg—but not if you want to maintain your dignity," says Jamie.

Although Little Flowers has unfurled like a fern according to its own organic impetus, its founders remain steadfast in their missional vision. "We remain a church of peace and a community that lives in simplicity by the teachings of Jesus Christ," says Jamie.

As for the future, the establishment of a large congregation is not on the horizon. "We have no ambition to become a huge church. If that happens, praise God, but, realistically, the members of Little Flowers could not financially sustain a building and a pastor," Jamie says. "What we do see is maybe several other small communities like ours springing up around the city. In the meantime, what we want to be is a sign of beauty and life in the midst of brokenness."[1]

---

1. For more on the story of Little Flowers, see Jamie Arpin-Ricci's *The Cost of Community: Jesus, St. Francis and Life in the Kingdom* (Downers Grove, IL: InterVarsity Press, 2011).

PART 2

Nursery Gardens

THERE IS REALLY NO such thing as "Canadian culture." There are in fact many cultures that make up Canada. In the same way, it is difficult to generalize about the church in Canada and how it understands and carries out its mission. There are many different facets, each with its own distinctive joys and challenges. Different plants grow differently in different environments. "All mission is done in a particular setting—the context. So, although there is a fundamental unity to the good news, it is shaped by the great diversity of places, times and cultures in which we live, proclaim and embody it."[1] This section looks at eight different aspects of the church in Canada—nursery gardens where new plants can grow, and indeed are growing—that illustrate this diversity.

1. http://www.anglicancommunion.org/ministry/mission/fivemarks.cfm.

The majority of Canadians these days live in towns or cities. Yet thousands of churches, most of them small ones, are sprinkled across the vastness of the Canadian countryside. There is a certain irony in this, since the majority of the Bible was written from and to a rural context: all the way from the wilderness wanderings of Moses' time to Jesus' parables of Palestinian agriculture. So what is God doing "out there" in rural Canada? What can the rest of the church learn from the experience and strengths of rural churches? Are there ways urban churches can help them in their struggles—or at least not make their work any more difficult?

4

New Shoots from Old Roots

The Challenge and Potential of Mission in Rural Canada

Cam Harder

RURAL CHURCHES ARE ONE of Canada's great treasures. I was baptized in a rural church in Castor, Alberta, and attended a welcoming country church during the summers I spent on my uncle's farm. But I really fell in love with rural churches the summer of 1972. I was working on a pipeline crew near Viking, Alberta. It was a tough job, twelve to fourteen hours a day, seven days a week—except when it rained. I *prayed* for rain. The first Saturday night rain came down in buckets, so I thought we would have the Sunday off. But the foreman dragged us out to the site anyway. Fortunately, it was too mucky to work. On the way back to camp, I noticed it was close to worship time and asked to be let off at the local Lutheran church. I went in, a young unshaven guy in hard hat, jeans, and muddy work boots. I thought I would get some strange glances—and I did. But after the initial surprise, the congregation treated me like a long-lost son; I was invited for dinner afterward. And, because it rained every Sunday I worked on that pipeline, I was able to worship with that congregation several times. They extended to me a hospitality that I have encountered again and again in rural churches across this country.

The value of these churches to the whole of Canada was brought home to me when, as part of my doctoral research, I did a study of Lutheran congregations in Toronto. I was looking at their growth patterns but incidentally discovered an odd thing: the leadership of these urban churches drew disproportionately from rural exports. Apparently, people who grew up in small places assumed that their congregation would not function unless everyone did their part. So when they moved to a city church, and the pastor asked for volunteers to sit on council or teach Sunday school, they assumed that meant *them:* they stepped up. In my study at least, big city churches depended on the discipleship formation that small rural places provided. I am convinced those rural churches produce a kind of Christian that is essential to the spiritual fabric of our nation.

Churches outside metropolitan catchment areas have been under exceptional pressure in recent years, however, and many have been closed. We will look at a few of the reasons for that pressure, and some of the ways in which rural ministry is being renewed. But I first want to take a brief, appreciative look at some of the gifts that country congregations have historically brought to their communities.

ECONOMY OF SCALE:
SMALL CAN BE MORE EFFECTIVE

The term *economy of scale* is often applied in Canada to justify corporate mergers or the consolidation of rural school divisions. But we sometimes apply it to rural church closures, implying perhaps that a congregation's size and economic efficiency—its ability to raise more money than it spends—rather than its effectiveness in making disciples, is the best measure of its value.

We forget the term *economy of scale* did not originally mean "bigger is better"—but rather that for every activity there is a proper scale, a *right* size. For example, we do not assume that in raising children bigger families are better. My wife and I do not feel inadequate because the family down the street has ten children and we have only three. No one says, "Gee, we might as well shut the Harder family down. There's only two old geezers left at home—three if you count the cat—and they haven't given birth to a new child in more than two decades!"

Yet clergy often suffer greatly from pew, pulpit, and plate envy, wishing we could preach to bigger crowds, longing for larger numbers to swell our programs, more money in the offering plates. We can lose the sense that there is a proper scale for every activity and that for many important things in our society, including making disciples of Christ, smaller structures are better.

Not all town and country churches are small. And those that are do not always make the most of their intimate, face-to-face size. But vital ministry often emerges among those who recognize the discipleship-making possibilities of being small. There are several factors.

Everyone's participation matters. It is easier for the young flute player to stand in front of the congregation and play because the atmosphere is informal. She does not feel that she has to be a professional before she can contribute. In a large congregation one may think, "Well, there's someone else who can do this better." In a small church, people know that there may not be anyone else who can do it at all—so they have to step up to the plate. The intimacy helps elicit hidden gifts. A 2004 study by the Foundation for Rural Living found that rural people donate a higher percentage of their time and income than their urban counterparts. They are also more likely to offer direct help to a neighbour.[2]

It is easier to know and care for others. People find out others' business in small communities. That knowledge can lead to shame and misery if people are judgmental. But it can also lead to personal and compassionate care. It is possible to keep track of who is sick, who has time to visit, and who needs encouragement. Since professional care is not always available in rural centres, it is critical to cultivate relationships of mutual support with one's neighbours. A University of Queensland study notes that healthy, resilient communities are those that have developed strong social networks and support structures. And it identifies churches as key organizations in building resilience.[3] Churches have kitchens and large gathering areas. They know how to recruit volunteers and raise funds. They train leaders in public speaking and committee work. They create spaces for friendship-building. And churches bring a word of hope to small communities that are afflicted by large-scale forces; they insist that God loves their community and is bigger than the powers that are squeezing its life.

2. Cathy Barr, Larry McKeown, Katie Davidman, David McIver, David Lasby, *The Rural Charitable Sector Research Initiative: A Portrait of the Nonprofit and Voluntary Sector in Rural Ontario* (Canadian Centre for Philanthropy, now Imagine Canada, 2004). See http://library.imaginecanada.ca/files/nonprofitscan/en/rural/rural_report.pdf, 11–12.

3. See http://www.uq.edu.au/bluecare/docs/toolkit_v5.pdf for a toolkit that describes the research findings and how to use them in assessing the resilience of your own community.

When Maple Creek, Saskatchewan, was hit by a massive flood, Captain Dean of the Salvation Army noted:

> The church was involved from the beginning. They walked the streets with their neighbours, giving what they could. And their neighbours gave back, coming into pastors' homes, helping to pull out damaged carpet, drywall, and insulation. The blessings were in the helping. Friendship and evangelism blended, as did the spiritual and emotional. Parishioners took bottles of water and knocked on doors to offer help and find out how friends and neighbours were doing. Many were working at demolition in soggy basements. The knock at the door offered a welcoming break and a bottle of water represented a simple expression of the love of Christ. The church rallied to look for the "gaps" and the urgent needs, and then did what they could to fill them. By the time the Red Cross arrived, help in many forms was already in place. Food was served within ten hours of the disaster, and meals continued for two weeks after, offering three sittings a day to anyone who needed it. Ranchers and farmers were offered bundles of replacement fence posts, critical to their livelihoods. A make-shift reception centre was organized to hand out clothing and cleaning supplies (brooms, mops, chemicals, masks, gloves—whatever was needed). From July to October a furniture and appliance bank was set up to accommodate requests, donations and exchanges.[4]

All the churches in the area—Hutterite, Pentecostal, Salvation Army, Roman Catholic, and many more—worked together.

It is natural to connect the generations and pass on the heritage. Smaller churches often find it easier to track their history. Members are interwoven by family connections, and their ancestors often lie just metres from the sanctuary in the church cemetery. So it is easy to remember and retell the exploits of a fabled matriarch, the lightning strike that burned down the first church, or the crazy antics of the youth group. God, in such places, is always "the God of Ole, Morgan, and Lois" or the local equivalent. In fact, the stories and life passages (happy or sad) of all members tend to be better known and are more likely to be announced and shared. And because numbers are too few to warrant age-graded activity, the young, the middle-aged, and the elderly share those passages together.

---

4. Colleen Rickard, "A Watery Crisis in a Dry Land," http://www.circle-m.ca/rural-ministry-stories/stories_web/maple_creek.html.

Lay ministry is essential. Pastors come and go in many rural churches. But it is the people who keep the mission strong, with individuals often filling multiple roles. While having a resident pastor is a matter of local pride, the ministry does not really belong to the clergy. One priest in a small congregation told me that he was phoned one Saturday evening and informed that there would not be church the next day because a few of the council members had stained the pews and they were not yet dry. The message was clear—this ministry is *ours.*

Ephesians 4:11 reminds us: "The gifts [God] gave were that some would be apostles, some prophets, some evangelists, some pastors and teachers, *to equip the saints for the work of ministry, for building up the body of Christ*" (emphasis mine). Many rural churches are small enough to do that well.

In spite of their gifts and potential, however, rural churches in Canada face some significant challenges.

ECONOMIC AND CLIMATIC CHALLENGES TO RURAL MINISTRY

The smaller size of rural communities can create significant vulnerability. Because these communities are often dependent on a single major economic engine, shifts in the market, plant openings or closures, weather events and the like can have a dramatic impact on their well-being. I have heard rural sociologists refer to rural communities as having "boom and bust" economies.

The booms put deep stress on local infrastructure. In 2008 and subsequent years, Waskada, Manitoba, had dozens of oil rigs and crews show up on its doorstep, and health facilities, bars, stores, and local roads came under enormous pressure, with little additional property tax being paid by transient workers to assist in serving what will likely be a temporary population bulge.

The busts can be equally traumatic, stripping hospitals, schools, churches, and key leadership from the town. The stresses that accompany the closure of a mine or fishery, the collapse of a cattle or grain market, floods that wash away fences and cattle, or fires such as the one that destroyed 40 percent of Slave Lake, Alberta, in 2011—all these can result in symptoms of post-traumatic stress disorder in rural communities. They can become exhausted from constantly trying to make adjustments. They may sink into a corporate depression, losing energy for planning and adapting, especially when their key resources for dealing with the changes—professional leadership, government funds, core institutions, and so on—are ripped out along with the economic changes.

On the one hand, these crises in rural communities are key opportunities for ministry and mission. Rural churches grow in their compassion and skills as they respond to the crises. On the other hand, community stress hits the church hard, too. The closure of a school may mean the loss of Sunday school teachers and the chair of the church council. A lost harvest may mean that congregational income is deeply reduced, so that the church can no longer afford a pastor.

DENOMINATIONAL CHALLENGES TO RURAL MINISTRY

Denominations that want to honour and sustain their rural congregations have to deal with a cluster of issues that, to a large degree, are related to the lopsided distribution of Canadian population. Imagine Canada as a garden one hundred metres square, planted with people. According to Atlas of Canada statistics, ninety-four of those square metres are sprinkled with just 1 percent of Canadians, the people planted there virtually invisible to the naked eye. In the southeast corner of the garden, crammed into less than a single square metre are three-quarters of all Canadians, so thickly planted they can barely get enough air or water. In the remaining five square metres, which are mostly spread out along the southern edge of the garden, live the remaining 24 percent of Canadians.[5] These are what we might call "town and country" communities centred on forestry, agriculture, mining, fishing, tourism, market gardening, factories, and the like.

Looking at the garden, one might assume that most ministry in Canada would be urban, concentrated in that one densely-populated corner. Historically, however, most denominations planted the bulk of their churches in the town and country squares. And still today a large percentage—in some cases a majority—of members and congregations are there. However, denominational offices and leaders are almost always located in the cities.

The fact that so many of us live in close quarters while the rest are sprinkled thinly (or invisibly) across a vast landscape means that the life experience of rural Canadians can be quite different from that of urbanites.

5. According to the Atlas of Canada, 2006. http://atlas.nrcan.gc.ca/site/english/maps/peopleandsociety/population/population2006/PopDist06/1.

Here is a small sample of the differences and the effects they may have on the ability of rural churches to develop fresh expressions of ministry:

- Decisions in rural settings are made carefully. Efficiency is not the criterion of a good meeting. Rather, it is critical to maintain good relationships in the process, and to consider the impact of decisions on the people who matter most to the decision-makers. Controversial ministry changes are approached very cautiously and (depending on personalities involved) hard-nosed debate is usually avoided.

- Rural communities are often cautious about experimenting because the risks are higher than in the city. In one-industry towns, economic experiments can be hazardous: there is no safety net if the experiment does not work out. Churches, too, may be loath to risk losing membership to failed ventures when numbers are already small. And families that have been in the community for generations do not want to sacrifice hard-earned reputations. So "fresh expressions" of ministry are more likely to be led by relative newcomers to the community who have been there long enough to be trusted, but not so long that they have a lot to lose. If their experiment fails, the community can put it down to the leader's naïveté without too much public embarrassment; if it succeeds, people cautiously get on board. One researcher who looked at turn-around communities in Saskatchewan told me that in most cases it was people "from away"—but trusted— who led the significant changes.[6]

- There is a limited pool of people available for membership in community organizations. While rural population in Canada is stable overall, it is increasingly mobile. Newfoundlanders commute to Alberta oil sands, or a new factory opening in one community attracts workers from another where the factory has closed. City dwellers flock to cottage country in the summer and then leave in the fall. So long-term, committed church members are always leaving, and it is difficult to attract and train new ones. The planting of a new church in a small community already over-served by congregations that are in numerical decline may be seen as a threat to the survival of existing churches. In my experience, the most effective and missional churches in rural settings operate in a strongly co-operative

6. See Al Scholz, *Don't Turn Out the Lights: Entrepreneurship in Rural Saskatchewan* (Saskatoon: University of Saskatchewan, 2000). It was in interviews after the book came out that the author discovered that most of the key leaders were "from away."

and community-connected mode. The focus, however, is not usually on starting new congregations in an official sense, but on starting new forms of *ministry*.

These realities may not be fully appreciated by city-based denominational offices, which naturally view their district or diocese through the lens of the urban experience in which they are immersed. Disconnection from town and country congregations can be expressed in various ways: (1) resources for ministry are directed toward urban congregations, and they do not often draw on rural stories and culture; (2) mission planning is shaped toward urban experience, incorporating techniques (such as distributing pamphlets door-to-door) or technologies (multimedia worship) that do not suit rural realities; (3) rural churches are weakly connected to their (distant) denominations' programs and headquarters, and find it easier to relate to local organizations and even other churches that share their community culture; (4) efforts to "rationalize" rural parishes through the closure and merger of churches create feelings of deep ambivalence toward the denomination: "The main things we depend on the denomination to do," one member told me, "are provide us a pastor, and not shut us down—and most of the time we're able to do without a pastor!"

Ironically, this tenacious independence lends staying power to rural churches. They develop a self-reliant capacity for surviving long pastoral vacancies, the loss of key leadership to out-migration, and the financial booms and busts of resource-based industry, and remain in their communities long after other local institutions have closed their doors. Resilient endurance may be one of their greatest gifts to the community. The church, no matter how many members it has, is an icon of hope, simply through its continuing existence—a statement that, no matter what happens, God is planted in this community and has not abandoned it.

CONDITIONS FOR GENERATING NEW FORMS OF MINISTRY IN RURAL CONTEXTS

How then do we support the development of fresh expressions of ministry in town and country settings? First needed is a change in perspective. This has to happen at both denominational and local levels. Denominations must see rural churches not as a problem to be solved, but as a resource for effective discipleship. That means putting the culture and missional needs of rural churches front and centre in staffing, programming, seminary training, clergy and lay leadership education. Toward this end, the

Edmonton Diocese of the Anglican Church of Canada has appointed a "canon pastor" for rural ministry. The Christian and Missionary Alliance Church has dedicated staff to stimulating new life in its rural ministries. The seminaries of the Saskatoon Theological Union created "CiRCLe M"—the Centre for Rural Community Leadership and Ministry.

A change in perspective also needs to happen at the congregational level. Churches do not always recognize the gifts they bring to their communities. For example, they tell of a God who brings new creation out of tragedy, who uses the small and forgotten as yeast and seed to change the world. They celebrate a God who *is* community (Trinity), *loves* communities, and *works* on their behalf against the powers that threaten them. They have resources for reconciling ancient feuds, and rituals for grieving, celebrating, remembering, and beginning again, *together*. Rural churches create a safety net of hope that helps a community to take risks, live experimentally, and adapt to boom and bust conditions more effectively. And, of course, individual congregations have a host of more particular gifts that emerge from their own history, habits, and personalities.[7]

Second, the processes used in developing new ministry should be positive and story-shaped rather than problem-focused. Rural churches know the problems all too well. So, instead of analyzing the causes behind failures (and assigning blame), ask for stories of what has worked in the past, and why. Help congregations take the best from the past into their future. Ask first, "What has God been up to?" rather than, "What are sin, death, and the devil doing in our community?" And identify and mobilize resources for ministry that actually exist in the congregation and community rather than depending on external sources or ideal models.

We can also ask, "What gifts do we have besides money, clergy, and buildings out of which to create ministry?" Too often we judge a church's viability according to its accumulation of those three resources. I often invite rural church leaders to imagine that overnight, across denominations, God killed all the clergy, struck every church with lightning, and burned  them all to the ground, then evaporated the bank accounts of every congregation. They are left with a smoking pile of ash in the centre of their town and a funeral to attend.

After giving the participants a moment to mourn, we do a ministry-building exercise. I ask them to name what they would have left to do ministry with. We list on the board people's skills, things they are willing

---

7. For more on this, see Gary Gunderson, *Deeply Woven Roots: Improving the Quality of Life in Your Community* (Minneapolis: Fortress Press, 1997).

to give or lend, natural resources (parks, rivers, and so on) to which they have access, spiritual experience and biblical knowledge, access to programs (such as wood carving), businesses, and local institutions (such as hospitals and schools). I ask them to name personality characteristics, community members with leadership ability, people who owe them a favour and might be willing to contribute ("Tom runs the hockey arena and might let us use it for a youth skating party"), and more. Then in small groups I ask them to connect some of these disparate resources in a way that will allow them to do effective mission in their local context.

Once they get past trying to rebuild the church or resurrect the pastor, some wonderfully creative ministry ideas always emerge. They tend to be community-connected, outward-facing, and people-intensive. One group developed a partnership with the local hospital, offering a ministry of music, healing touch, prayer, and conversation. Another drafted a plan for a community pig roast, advertised in hair salons and coffee shops, to draw the whole community into a discussion about its spiritual well-being. A third imagined partnering with a local coffee shop and bookstore to offer a community kitchen, Eucharist, and weekly explorations of such topics as the spirituality of hairdressing, home care, and other community-building roles, treating them as ministries. A fourth designed a "Care Farm" in which troubled urban teens could be taken out of group facilities and placed on ranches in the area to work with horses, hoping that isolation from drugs and friends in the city and the positive affection of animals might help in their healing. None of these options is pie-in-the-sky because they have been constructed from resources that the participants actually have. And nobody has to sell these groups on the ideas because they created them and committed their own resources in the process.

Seeing that they have many options for ministry, participants say that they feel much less anxiety about their future and more energized for mission. They see that ministry can take many effective forms, no matter what the size of their congregation or community. Without a single new dollar in the offering plate, without one new seat in the pew—in fact, having experienced a catastrophic *loss* of buildings, money, and clergy—they move in their own minds from being poor to being rich.

FRESH EXPRESSIONS OF RURAL MINISTRY

What have rural churches been doing to deepen and renew their ministries? For all of the caution that rural churches may feel about experimentation,

I have encountered some marvellously creative new rural ministries. Not surprisingly, the best of them are community-focused.

Night in Bethlehem: Recently, at Christmas, the churches in Oyen, Alberta, host a "Night in Bethlehem" that helps church and community experience together what it might have been like in Bethlehem when Jesus was born. The agriculture building in Oyen is donated for the event. The Knights of Columbus lay interlocking mats on the dirt floor. The Lion's Club donates booths. An electrician hangs the big star, and young and old contribute decorations to create the Bethlehem street and skyscape. Others in first-century costumes take on roles as minstrels and vendors, offering perfumes, "period" farm produce, tie-dyed textiles, small bread loaves, weaving, and the like. The first year was so successful that people travelled long distances in a harsh winter storm to take it in the following Christmas. Best of all, it gave the whole community and people of all generations a chance to create and talk about the story at the heart of the Christian faith.

Blessing of the Beasts: In a town that one of our interns served, significant anger and a growing rift developed between pet owners and others after a dog-inflicted injury. The intern helped to pull the community together in a public "blessing of the beasts" liturgy that helped to honour the town's animals on the one hand and to emphasize the importance of caring for them responsibly on the other.

A service of lament and hope: Armena, Alberta, suffered a debilitating drought that threatened the region's agricultural livelihood. A local pastor organized a service of lament and hope for the community. The service was developed out of conversation with local people and moved through three stages: a period of lament, when the complaints and struggles of the people were voiced; an expression of hope in which the community was reminded that God loves their town and had not abandoned its producers; and a time of blessing in which participants were given a gracious touch of God. Each stage included a reading, prayer, brief reflection, and a song. But perhaps the most powerful element in each stage was the gathering of participants in small groups where they voiced their complaints, expressed their hopes, shared the blessing with each other.

Young people beloved and protected: On a Saskatchewan First Nation reserve, an unusual youth ministry developed when a local pastor was injured in an accident and off work for several months. It gave him time to refocus his ministry. He decided to spend his time meeting with the teens on the reserve and supporting his youth minister. Though he had lived on that land his whole life, he felt he did not know the young people as well as he could. So he invited all the community's teens for a visit. Over the hundred days of his convalescence they came, singly and in groups, to talk about their hopes and struggles. Many wrestle with addictions and painful memories. Some have life dreams they do not know how to reach; too many had no dreams. The pastor told each of them, "You are God's beloved child. You are precious in his sight and that will never change." And then, when he had recovered, he drew them together and began a ministry of music, travel, Bible camp, and disciplined care for each other that has helped them deal with their "stuff" together. In a wonderful exercise of gospel and law, he is helping them stay safe and discover an open future. Most do not go to church, though many have begun to attend, and it has changed the character of Sunday morning worship.

A *"photovoice" experiment*: Another pastor in a small community on the outskirts of Edmonton noticed that while there were a considerable number of young adults in the area, even neighbours did not really know each other. Clubs and events that once drew them together had gradually died out as the city expanded and young adults turned their focus there, away from each other. So the pastor invited a number of the region's young adults to gather for a "photovoice" experiment. With some training from a semi-professional photographer and a bunch of disposable cameras, he sent them out to capture images of what they felt was important about the place where they live. Afterward, they came together and shared their pictures and the stories attached to them. And then they hosted an event at the local school for the whole community. It was deeply touching. Some cried, others said their hair stood on end—the photographs and explanations were such powerful expressions of their life together, including their spiritual life. In the process, the young adults found each other, and the community came to a deeper sense of its own identity through the eyes of their young adults.

"They're used to coming to my house": House churches, too, hold promise for connecting with those who do not normally attend Sunday services. The vast Cariboo-Chilcotin region of the Presbyterian church is home to a dozen or so house churches developed initially by Dave and Linda Webber.[8] They range in size from six members to forty-five, most led by elders who together make up the broader presbytery's governance team. Dave and Linda and other ordained staff serve as "apostles" to the region, stimulating the development of new house churches and training elders.

8. The story of the Cariboo house churches has been written up at http://www. circle-m.ca/rural-ministry-stories/stories_web/house_church.html.

The churches gather in homes on whatever day suits the rhythm of their work lives, using liturgies (including the sacraments) as varied as Roman Catholic and Plymouth Brethren in style. This flexibility has made them attractive to the ethnic groups of the region, including First Nations. There is a tight focus on Bible study and discipleship training. And they reach out into their communities, tutoring children with reading difficulties, working with teens, gathering groups of women, visiting the sick, and assisting in fundraising for special needs.

The value of meeting in homes was illustrated for me by a pastor who described his experience of a multi-point parish in central Saskatchewan. In one country church, ten to fifteen people met each Sunday. At one point, the matriarch of the congregation became housebound and a member suggested that maybe they could hold worship at her place one Sunday, which they did. To the pastor's surprise, the house was filled with people. When he asked the matriarch where they all came from, she said, "Well, they're my friends; they're used to coming to my house." For a while after that, they had Bible study at her house and regularly drew twenty or more, until one member said, "It's getting kind of crowded here, maybe we should move back to the church." They did, and the numbers immediately dropped to half a dozen.

This story illustrates the fact that rural church buildings are, like prairie grain elevators, icons of a community's identity. They are also a sign that God is planted in that place. But the threshold at the church doorway can be very high. Families that have not traditionally belonged to a church are not likely to enter except for public events like weddings and funerals. Fresh expressions of rural church may need to happen in non-traditional spaces.

Connecting spirituality and Christ: I am presently involved in a study that reveals that rural people respond spiritually to a variety of stimuli: meaningful time with family and friends; exercise and sports; meditation; contemplation of the stunning night sky and the seasonal beauty of rural landscapes; community dances, dinners, and celebrations; art, crafts, and music; learning; taking care of people, land, and animals; creative intergenerational events; discovering one's calling in life; meaningful work; silence; adventure; serving others together, and much more. The challenge for rural ministry is to tap into these realities in ways that connect people to the heritage we have in Christ and help them move toward Christian discipleship.

CONCLUSION

Fresh expressions of rural ministry in Canada are being supported by new or renovated structures for ministry. For example, the rapid growth of ecumenical, shared ministries has helped rural churches think outside denominational walls and opened them to more community-focused ministry. There are 104 of these ministries in Canada at the time of writing, and only 16 percent are in metropolitan centres (the largest number in Winnipeg), so this is an area in which rural churches are experimentally far ahead of their urban counterparts.[9] "Wagon wheel" clusters of smaller congregations around a large town centre are also becoming more common and make the gifts of several well-trained leaders available to villages and hamlets.[10]

In all the above, rural Christians continue to pursue out-of-the-box ways to connect spiritually with people who do not go to traditional churches. Looking at the broad picture, I am hopeful for the future of rural ministry in Canada. Rural population may begin to increase, as it has in Saskatchewan, as modern transportation and communication makes it easier to do business there. In some places more attention is being given to rural development: Alberta's hundred million dollar Rural Alberta Development Fund is an example. Denominations are beginning to see their rural churches as a resource to be celebrated rather than a problem to be solved.[11]

And the God who chose to take on human flesh in the tiny village of Bethlehem clearly loves these smaller places and holds their future open with love and encouragement. That is a good thing for all of Canada.

good reminder

9. Shared Ministries bureau statistics, April 2012.

10. See, for example, the Southwest Lutheran parish, led by Rev. Greg Kiel, centred in Swift Current, SK.

11. See, for example, the State of the Synod address by Bishop Sauer at the Manitoba Northern Ontario Synod convention, April 2012, online at http://www.mnosynod.org/convention%20state%20of%20the%20synod%20address.html.

Green Shoots 2
A Christian Community for the Broken

Uptown Church
Saint John, New Brunswick

In 2000, Reed Fleming, a veteran retreat director for Threshold Ministries, left the rigours of inland Manitoba for the rigours of coastal New Brunswick. He exchanged his position as an evangelism specialist with the Diocese of Brandon for a new role in the evangelism studies department at Taylor College, the Saint John training facility for Threshold Ministries (then called the Church Army).

Taylor's principal at that time was the Rev. David Edwards, who was also rector of St. John's Stone Church, an imposing Gothic Revival edifice in the city centre of Saint John, whose building blocks (legend has it) came over as ballast in nineteenth-century ships. Edwards wanted to build relationships with the largely poor, rooming-house residents of the neighbourhood.

So Reed began to work with the rector as a volunteer, to reach out to the city's broken people, many of them single, middle-aged welfare recipients with histories of addiction, mental illness, or criminal offences.

"A lot of the church's congregation drove in on Sunday from the residential suburbs, but the church is located in an inner-city neighbourhood that has mostly rooming houses," says Reed, now lay pastor of the Stone-based Uptown Church. "We were determined to build friendships with people actually living nearby."

Reed and a team of volunteers from Stone decided to start out modestly—an approach he recommends to any church planter. One Friday a month, just before the welfare cheques were due and people's supplies were at their nadir, the group held a free supper in Stone's parish hall. "There'd be music, and volunteers would bring in things like soup, stew, chili, or mac and cheese," he recalls. "Some people would serve and another group would sit with people and just listen and talk with them." It was a safe place for people whose Friday night choices were pretty much limited to being room-bound or hanging out on the street.

The next relationship-building project Reed's team launched was the Stone-Washed Laundry. "We realized that a lot of people in rooming houses have nowhere to wash their clothes. Often they just wear the same clothes until they can't any more, and then they get new ones from a clothing bank," he says.

The church set up two washers and two dryers in the church's old downstairs kitchen and charged a dollar per green garbage bag of clothes, soap included. But the laundering was only the background noise. Over coffee and tea, people became really candid. "They'd stay for a couple of hours and talk about their lives," says Reed. "We found that the people here really do want to tell their stories, unlike in the suburban church, where it can be a long time before people open up."

What was more, the local residents were genuinely curious about the volunteers' faith and their activities within the church. As friendships deepened, thoughts turned to worship, but the Stone team realized that the social distance from the parish hall to the 11 a.m. Sunday service upstairs was just too great for most of the locals to travel. "There was little likelihood they would cross that threshold," he says. "So what we needed to do was to plant a completely new church."

With a Pentecost blessing from Edwards in the late spring of 2003, Reed began to train a core group of twelve volunteers from Stone with the objective of starting Uptown Church, a church-within-in-a-church, whose venue would be the same comfortable parish hall in which congregants ate Friday suppers, did their laundry, and laid bare their concerns about their lives.

"After a lot of praying, meeting, and training, we held our first Sunday service in mid-October," says Reed. It was, and still is, a 6:30 p.m. gathering. "We didn't want to be in competition with other churches—no sheep stealing from morning services. We wanted to fill a new niche," says Reed.

Uptown gathers coffeehouse-style, with as many as thirty-five people relaxing at tables and enjoying beverages and cookies. Although it takes place in the evening to avoid conflicts, the service is actually based loosely on a traditional Morning Prayer model. Music is provided by CDs and occasionally live musicians. "Sometimes we sing a capella, sometimes not at all," says Reed. One of the highlights of the interactive service is "popcorn prayers," which allow people to pop up and offer the prayers of their choice from a laminated sheet.

Uptown also runs a well-attended Bible study class on Wednesday nights and a monthly drop-in night. Some of the congregants have progressed to leading prayers and serving in the kitchen.

Over the years, a few Uptown congregants have even joined Stone's main congregation, and about seven have been baptized. "We borrow a tank from the Vineyard Church, and this witness is very important for some of our people," says Reed. Over the past four months, one Uptown congregant, who was baptized at Pentecost, has undergone a notable transformation, recovering from drug addiction and regaining her lost weight and health.

Uptown has also incorporated a few special rituals into its service—for example, lighting a candle to mark the presence of Christ. "I've come to appreciate how much ceremony means to people," says Reed, who comes from a very low-church background. "If I forget to light the candle, they protest. It's very interactive, and that's one of the best parts."

A cornerstone principle of Uptown is that every Christian should be a minister. "The language of ministry doesn't always resonate with our congregants, so I prefer to phrase it as performing acts of kindness," he says. "That's an important ideal, and we place a high value on it."

While he finds it deeply gratifying to see other people embracing Jesus, Reed admits that the person most changed by Uptown is himself. "Being in the company of broken people helps us to accept our own brokenness and to minister out of that," he says. "I've got more out of this than a lot of the people who come."

Reed has this advice for would-be church planters: "Just begin, but begin small and don't be discouraged. Be persistent and keep plugging away."

D.S.

Cities in scripture are generally negative places: think of Sodom and Gomorrah, Babylon, Nineveh, Rome, even Jerusalem (notorious, after all, for "killing the prophets"). Yet the world that God loves includes cities—and the growing proportion of our population who live there. Cam Roxburgh is a long-time reflective practitioner of mission in the city, and a great storyteller into the bargain. As the church's flight to the suburbs, which happened in the 1960s, continues to be reversed, more and more Christians are trying to figure out what God's mission to the cities looks like. Cam's stories are heartening and at the same time challenging, and he gives us hope for the cities—hope that, as he points out, is ultimately confirmed by Scripture.

5

Discovering God's Heart for the City

Cam Roxburgh

THE GREATEST STORY OF all begins in a beautiful garden. As we move through this story of God and God's mission in the world, however, there is a clear progression from the garden, where there was a close relationship between God and God's people, to the city. Eugene Peterson speaks for many of us when he says, "The surprise in St. John's rendition of heaven is that it comes in the form of a city. . . . Our sin resulted in expulsion from a garden; shouldn't salvation be a restoration to it?"[1] But no: when the final chapters of the Bible describe a restored relationship between God and God's people, it takes place in the greatest city of all—the New Jerusalem.

Today, we are still in the midst of the story, and it involves God's calling to the cities of our world. "At his conversion, Saul was instructed to 'get up and enter the city, and you will be told what to do' (Acts 9:6 RSV). A spirituality adequate to the challenge of urban discipleship today will make a similar metaphorical journey of conversion."[2] As God's people, we have been invited to join with God in God's mission. In Canada's past, our story was at one time more rural, but today the vast majority of us live in cities. Our task now is to reflect on how we might partner with God in

---

1. Eugene Peterson, *Reversed Thunder: The Revelation of John and the Praying Imagination* (New York: Harper Collins, 1998), 173.

2. Ken Luscombe, "City," in *The Complete Book of Everyday Christianity: An A-to-Z Guide to Following Christ in Every Aspect of Life*, ed. Robert Banks and R. Paul Stevens (Downers Grove, IL: InterVarsity Press, 1997), 151.

reaching Canadian cities with the Gospel through understanding God's heart, recognizing God's presence and participating in God's work.

My own entry into God's story and participating in this mission began in the city of Vancouver. After formal preparation at seminary, I began a different kind of training, one that was less formal but at the same time more difficult: I planted a church called Southside Community Church. I found myself in the midst of a neighbourhood where prostitutes offered their services, drug dealers marked street corners, and homeless people slept under the church steps. We were determined not to "steal sheep" from other churches, but to reach people who had no church connections. As we did so, I fell in love with God and the city, as God began to shape my heart to resemble his own by showing us where he was present and at work among these people. I began to see God at work in the city on a regular basis.

My family moved into the neighbourhood. I walked the streets trying to determine local needs. We tried to join in with what God was doing through such things as food banks, after-school programs, job creation, refugee aid, and thrift stores. As a result, like the early church in Acts, we came to enjoy "the goodwill of all the people" (Acts 2:47). We saw many people from a wide range of backgrounds introduced to Christ. Today, twenty years on, we are still in and for this neighbourhood—even though it has now transitioned into a more diverse and multi-ethnic place than it used to be, and God is teaching us afresh what it means to be Jesus' hands and feet and voice here.

The Southside story, however, is only one example of how God is at work in cities across Canada, among both poor and rich. All across the country, there are growing numbers of stories of followers of Jesus forming themselves into communities in order to make a difference in their neighbourhoods. Many of these wonderful stories have to do with an increased passion for the church in the city—and some of them are told in this book.

Suburban churches continue to see modest growth, often by being program based and attractional, but most of their success is among those who already know something of the Christian story. This approach is less effective, however, in the heart of our cities, where the number of people who have never been involved in church, and do not know the story, is growing rapidly.

In order to join God on this important endeavour of reaching our cities, we must be filled with the heart of God, recognize God's presence in diverse neighbourhoods, and receive his invitation to join in the work God is already doing. We begin by discovering the heart of God.

GOD'S HEART

You will not often find me sitting on a park bench at 10:30 on a Sunday morning. But, on a particular Sunday in August 1992, there I was. We had left our previous church and moved into the neighbourhood where we would be starting a new church plant. At twenty-seven, I was naïve enough to think I could pull this off yet aware that I needed help. I just did not know how much help.

As my dog and I sat on the bench, I could see a man making his way across the field towards me. While I did not feel particularly social, my dog certainly did. After petting her, the man assumed he was invited to sit on the bench with us. "How do I get out of this?" I wondered.

After exchanging names, he offered me a beer. In fact, he had twenty-four of them under his arm. It looked like it might be a long conversation. Drinking beer has never been my favourite pastime, particularly at 10:30 on a Sunday morning. So I declined but asked him where he lived. I discovered that Ed had been kicked out of his house by his wife only four days before on account of his drinking.

"Where are you staying now, Ed?"

"I have been sleeping in the dumpster behind the Shell station two blocks away," he replied.

I remember the next sentence out of my mouth as clearly as if I had uttered it less than five minutes ago: "Well, Ed, I am the pastor of a church that will be meeting at the building right down the street from the Shell station. Why don't you come by the office one morning and let me buy you breakfast?"

With that, I left. I had wanted to be quiet on this morning, and it seemed a good opportunity to leave. I got to the corner of the park and then it happened. I have seen movies where lightning strikes someone who has just done something to upset God. I actually wish that had happened. It might have been less painful. Instead, God stopped me in my tracks and spoke to my heart with a laser-like clarity I had never before experienced: "If you think that you are going to plant a church in this neighbourhood with an attitude and a lack of love like that, you are sorely mistaken. You had better learn to love those that I love."

I did not go back and share my faith with Ed. I was crushed—and rightly so. That kind of attitude was, and is, and evermore will be, inappropriate for any believer, let alone one who thinks he is going to plant a church. But one thing did happen that day. I committed to the Lord that I would change and that our church—whatever it would be called—would learn to love those whom God loves so deeply, including the Eds of this world. That event has shaped me and my approach to ministry perhaps more than any other in my whole life. No longer was the task at hand to grow a big church but rather to grow compassionate disciples of Jesus who shared his heart and would become his hands and feet in the midst of the mission field where he had placed them.

That experience also gave me a new appreciation for a story of Jesus that I had known for many years, a parable we often call the story of the lost sheep—although it is really more a story that reveals the heart of God. The scene is painted in the first two verses of the chapter: "Now all the tax collectors and sinners were coming near to listen to him. And the Pharisees and the scribes were grumbling and saying, 'This fellow welcomes sinners and eats with them'" (Luke 15:1–2). Teachers usually sat on a stone in the corner of a courtyard as their listeners squatted in the front row, with others standing behind. On that day, those in the front row were the tax collectors and prostitutes—the outcasts of that society. Behind them stood the Pharisees and teachers of the law. They held that Jesus could not be the Messiah because Yahweh was holy and could not possibly be associated with anything unclean, as these people were.

Seeing this scenario, Jesus became upset and told three stories that were passionate pleas for these leaders to see the heart of God—and to participate in God's mission. "Suppose one of you is a shepherd," he began. The prostitutes and tax collectors would have howled with laughter. Jesus was calling these leaders shepherds, who in that society were considered the lowest on the ladder of social success. And then he told them they were not even good shepherds because they had lost one of their sheep. Then the tone changed as Jesus zeroed in on his point: "Which one of you . . . does not leave the ninety-nine in the wilderness and go after the one that is lost until he finds it?" (Luke 15:4). To us, the phrase to "go after" lacks much of the punch it would have carried to those listening to Jesus.

I learned the meaning of this phrase in personal experience many years ago now, when all four of my kids were under the age of eight, and we went with two other families to the Pacific National Exhibition. All eleven children were under the age of eight. A day at the PNE with eleven under-eights? This is called . . . stupid. Every ten minutes we would count them to make sure we had them all. One, two, three . . . eleven. Great! One, two, three . . . eleven. Fantastic! One, two, three . . . ten? Oops. Nobody would ever say that the loss of one child was unimportant because, after all, we still had ten. No: nothing else mattered in the entire world except searching until the lost one was found, and nothing was allowed to stand in the way of achieving that goal.

This is the force of the phrase "goes after" that Jesus uses to describe how the shepherd would search. And the point was clear to all who had ears to hear: the heart of the Father towards the lost was one of not resting, not being distracted, and not giving a half-effort. God was willing to put everything else on hold until the lost one was found. As we began our church plant, we tried to take seriously the fact that all sheep, every sheep—every person—demanded our all in our efforts to find them if we were to have the same heart as our Father in heaven.

When we planted Southside, we began by emphasizing the importance of having a strategy for church planting. Now, it is true that we need to be organized and intentional, but too often we have planted churches in the city that have reflected our own cleverness, without bringing transformation to people and places. We must move from "strategies" to being shaped by the Spirit of God and directed by hearts of compassion like that of the Creator.

Many churches across Canada are seeking to bring transformation to the neighbourhoods where God has called them with compassion. This approach seeks to join God, not just in attracting numbers to weekend gatherings but in caring for the people God cares for.

I could give many examples, but let me mention one in my own city of Vancouver that I am particularly familiar with: Grandview Calvary Baptist Church. Tim Dickau, the long-term pastor there, continues to coach the people of this great church to have the heart of the Father towards those God loves in that place. And it has brought about great transformation.

This church, in a multi-racial neighbourhood, has a history of embracing refugees, creating housing projects, developing businesses for the unemployed, caring for single moms in the neighbourhood, being involved in local social justice projects, and developing a prayer house for the whole community.

One of their projects that particularly points to the heart of the Father began years ago as a traditional soup kitchen, where many were fed soup and a sandwich, which met their need for an evening. More recently, however, this act of compassion has taken a new course. A smaller number are now invited in off the street to prepare a meal together and then eat it as a community. Supplies are provided and organization given, but what is different now is that people who once suffered the humiliation of asking for a hand-out, and being on the receiving end of charity, now find dignity and empowerment in being part of a team that produces a good meal. That experience offers sustenance that lasts beyond the meal itself. They are encountering the reality of the Gospel in the presence of Christ through people with the heart of God. I believe Jesus would eat at this table any time.

This kind of movement of love for the city flows from the realization that God is already present there. As Ken Luscombe, himself a city-centre pastor, puts it, "To enter [the city] is to become aware and more keenly discerning of the movement of God in and through the city."[3] Let me give you an example.

GOD'S PRESENCE

Recently, my mission group was serving food and giving clothes to the homeless at a ministry called Nightshift. Through many conversations with the homeless, my past generalizations about them have been deeply challenged. Among other things, I have discovered that there is great in-genuity in the ways they fend for themselves but also a greater sense of joy and community than I could have imagined. They welcomed this hour the group spent together.

On this occasion, the effect of the warm soup would only last a brief time. I asked several of them how they planned to survive what promised to be the coldest night of the year on the streets of Vancouver—minus seventeen Celsius. One man assured me he was not as badly off as others. His friend let him sleep on the couch instead of out in the cold. I asked why he came to this gathering of the homeless. He replied that he liked coming because he knew there was something different here. He pointed to a woman across the parking lot and shared how, several weeks previously, he had seen her give her coat to a woman without one. There was something about that woman and her kindness, he told me, that he saw often in that place. I was deeply touched because that woman was my wife.

Then the story got even more interesting. He had been so taken by her actions that he felt compelled to respond. He knew that she was a

3. Luscombe, 151.

tennis coach, so he began to scrape together a little money to buy her a tennis racquet. He told me excitedly that he had managed to afford a racquet, which he had presented to her as a gift. Because of her stature in the tennis world, my wife gets free $300 racquets from companies as advertising. In fact, I am not sure she has ever paid for a racquet her whole life. And on one level, this "new" racquet that she had just been given was the worst one she had ever owned. But she has never had one more valuable. Tears came to my eyes as I heard the joy in this man's voice as he talked about what was happening to him as a result of being together with others in that place.

I learned a valuable lesson that night. I had lived under the assumption that it was up to me to take Jesus with me into that kind of situation. But Jesus was, and is, already present there. When we go into neighbourhoods of all kinds in the city, we need to look for signs of God at work already and then join God in what he is doing. As Luscombe says, "The voice of God . . . addresses us in the very act of paying attention."[4]

This event reminded me of the story of the two disciples walking the road to Emmaus after the resurrection (Luke 24). They had been witnesses to the events in Jerusalem over the previous week, but now these "witnesses" of Jesus could no longer recognize him. Then he began to reveal himself. Firstly, he retold the story of God and explained how he could be found in the scriptures. Then he accepted their offer of hospitality that evening. Thirdly, as he broke bread with them, their eyes were opened and they recognized who he was. And only then were they able to reflect on that deep inner sense (their "hearts . . . strangely warmed") that they had while speaking with him on their walk. When they came to "see" Jesus, they immediately high-tailed it back to Jerusalem to tell the others what they had seen and experienced.

One difficulty we have today is that we, too, fail to recognize the presence of Jesus. Nobody can be called a witness unless he or she has actually seen the event or person in question. Many Christians today have little or no idea of what it means to be a witness to the reality of Jesus Christ in their lives, in the lives of others, or in an entire neighbourhood. If we are the sent ones, we must stop much of our current approach of seeking God's blessing on our clever strategies and instead learn to recognize the presence of Christ in the midst of our neighbourhoods. We must no longer trust in our strategic plans to help the church be "successful." Instead, like those disciples on the road, we must learn to pay attention—through the

4. Luscombe, 151–152.

text of scripture, through hospitality, through participating at the Lord's Table, and through listening to the deep inner voice of the Spirit—in order to recognize God already at work in our midst.

Jesus is not dependent on us to take him anywhere. Instead he works in multiple ways to accomplish his work—and working through the lives of believers is certainly not the only one. We must look for how and where he is already present and then join him in his mission. Ray Bakke, a pioneer of urban ministry in the twentieth century, reinforces this idea: "We can look at any place in London or Chicago as sacred because God is present and at work there."[5]

When we begin to develop the heart of God towards those who do not know him, and we begin to recognize God's presence in the midst of our neighbourhoods, we can receive his invitation to join him where he is already at work.

GOD AT WORK

The practice of hospitality is crucial in joining God at work in the city. When we planted Southside Community Church in the early 1990s, our core team adopted a strategy of making friends in the neighbourhood and inviting them to a well-crafted service on Sundays. Our idea of practicing hospitality was to make sure we had developed relationships with three people whom we might invite. In those days, it seemed as if half of the people with spiritual questions in the neighbourhood would attend church in order to try and find answers; today that number seems to be less than 10 percent. It would never occur to most people today that church might be a good place to go if you are exploring your spirituality. As a result, over the years, we have developed a different definition of hospitality.

The story of Jesus sending out the seventy-two in Luke 10 has provided some much needed insight for us in the practice of hospitality. At the start of the chapter, Jesus tells us that the task will be difficult ("lambs into the midst of wolves"), that we must pray fervently ("ask the Lord of the harvest"), and that we are not to be distracted ("greet no one on the road").

Then Jesus states a principle that has made a big difference to our mission. He advises, "Whatever house you enter, first say, 'Peace to this house!' And if anyone is there who shares in peace, your peace will rest

5. Ray Bakke, *The Urban Christian* (Downers Grove, IL: InterVarsity Press, 1987), 63.

on that person; but if not, it will return to you" (Luke 10:5). Hospitality, in this instance, seems to have less to do with inviting others into our space and more to do with being invited to the home of another—the "person of peace." I suspect the explanation is this: in my space, I control all of the events—the food, the conversation, and the customs. But when I am invited into the space of the other, I take up the posture of powerlessness and of being served. And somehow this makes space for God to work.

Jesus instructed the seventy-two to find the person of peace and say, "Peace to this house." This was not a cool expression from the 1970s. It was more like that piece of spaghetti you throw against the wall to see if it sticks, and is therefore ready to eat. In the same way, Jesus invited his witnesses to throw out this line to see if they would be received—an indication that he was already at work in these people and that they were ready to receive his message. That was the key. The goal was not to force a conversation on spiritual matters but rather to see by blessing them whether Jesus was at work. If the hosts' circumstances in life had been negative, the offer of a prayer would serve as a blessing, and they might respond with eagerness. If, on the other hand, their experience had been positive, then the suggestion that God had been good acted as a simple test of whether they recognized God at work in their lives.

Too often, we look for the one great program that will be the key to seeing lots of people come to Christ. Alan Roxburgh is correct, however, when he suggests that we would do better to put less emphasis on programs and to focus instead on the practice of hospitality.[6] After all, hospitality, when rightly understood, is more than a barbecue, but includes what Jesus stated to the seventy-two: we are to heal the sick (however our tradition may interpret that) and proclaim that the kingdom of God is near. We need to see where God is working and then join God's work by acts of kindness, which include feeding the hungry, housing the homeless, standing up for those who need an advocate, and healing those who need healing. But these acts of kindness and social justice must be joined to the proclamation of the Gospel—the joyful announcement that the kingdom of God is present.

I can think of no place where this is more evident in Canada at the moment than in Edmonton. Back in 1907, God worked through the city council to zone the whole city into Community Leagues. Life in these neighbourhoods was formed around networks of geographically based clusters of neighbours. Still today, community is being created in these

---

6. Unpublished lecture.

neighbourhoods with the help of the Community Leagues. Social and economic relationships are being established. People are looking out for one another and are seeking the wellbeing of the whole neighbourhood.

In one such Community League, Christians have recognized both God's presence and God's work in their midst. From a grassroots perspective, they invest more heavily in the neighbourhood than in their own "church." Many had for years been driving out of their neighbourhood in order to attend a church service somewhere else. But increasingly they are seeing that life for them is to be lived in their local area. People of this neighbourhood, some of them professing Christians and some of them not, have engaged together in many life events. On one occasion, sixty of them went on a mission trip together to an area of Mexico in order to serve the poor. Last year, they invited three hundred people to attend a summer camp that had a Christian emphasis. None of this has happened because of a clever strategy or a well thought-out program but rather because God is present and at work in these people.

The foundation for the church's mission in the city is therefore simple. God has a heart for those who do not know the Gospel in the cities across our land. God longs for us to have the same heart and to become missionaries in the places where God has put us. God does not send us into areas where he is not already present and at work. Our task is simply to recognize God's presence and to join with him in that work.

There are many churches today that are joining with God in reaching the cities across Canada. Those who are exploring the heart of God, recognizing his presence and participating in the work that God is already doing, are the ones who will be most effective in reaching those across our land who are least familiar with God's story and the new life it offers.

Heaven, says Peterson, "is the invasion of the city by the City."[7] Churches who share God's heart for the city can be agents of that City in the here and now.

---

7. Peterson, 174.

Canadian Christians of European descent are sometimes oblivious of what is going on in churches of other ethnicities than their own. Sometimes it is merely a matter of the limited circles they move in; at other times it is (frankly) a kind of churchy snobbery, perhaps with an undercurrent of racism: "They're hardly real churches. They're pretty conservative, you know. And, of course, their leaders are not properly trained." And as a result, the remarkable things that are springing up all over the country can be invisible, even though, at the present rate of growth, they could in a few short years become the majority of churches in Canada. We all need the humility to acknowledge that the wind of God's Spirit blows where it wills, and to glean whatever wisdom we can from wherever we can. In these "immigrant churches," there is passion, there is vision, there is a willingness to sacrifice, and there is a nimbleness to change strategies in light of new circumstances. Perhaps above all there is the conviction that the Gospel is actually good news that is worthy of our best efforts—a pearl of great price.

6

Church Planting by Immigrant Christians— And What the Rest of Us Can Learn

Connie denBok

THE SEASON HAS TURNED in Canada, and the suburbs are changing their colours. The great multicultural experiment launched in the 1970s is now in full bloom. In the early 2000s, Toronto passed the 55 percent mark for residents born outside the country. A new generation of immigrants has moved into urban centres across the country, their numbers surpassed only in the surrounding suburbs, where Canadians of European descent have become a visible minority.

What is more surprising is that, according to a report from the Pew Research Center, of the 7,200,000 immigrants to Canada, 59 percent describe themselves as Christians. (This compares with 9 percent Muslim, 4 percent Hindu, and 4 percent Buddhist.)[1] Thus, while a second- or third-generation Canadian might believe that "no one goes to church anymore," another reality is hidden in plain view. The board chair of a suburban congregation recently told her pastor, "Our church is dying. No one lives in the community around us anymore." But in this prosperous suburb of well-kept houses, many original residents are simply oblivious to their new neighbours.

---

1. "Faith on the Move: The Religious Affiliation of International Migrants," The Pew Forum on Religion and Public Life, 8 March 2012.

THE CHANGING LANDSCAPE

Our friend might notice a new mosque, temple, or gurdwara on one of the city's main arteries, but outside her social networks another church phenomenon is putting down roots in living rooms, strip malls, and industrial properties across her city. There are Christian worship gatherings, congregations, and even new denominations popping up like mushrooms after a rain. There are church headquarters for denominations she and I have never heard of—with large buildings bought and paid for by newly formed churches from developing nations, many of them charismatic in style and some with their own Bible schools. They are growing rapidly and yet, unrecognizable to Canada's traditional Christian population, they are unseen and unrecorded. No one knows their actual numbers, but by some educated estimates 75–80 percent of church attendees on any given Sunday in urban Toronto are recent immigrants, and most are persons of colour.[2]

Columnist Margaret Wente, writing in the *Globe and Mail*, expressed surprise that the fastest growing religion in the world is Christianity. She quoted the Pew Research Center, which found that "while Christianity is on the wane in the global North, it is exploding in the global South. Nigeria now has more than twice as many Protestants (sixty million) as Germany, the birthplace of the Protestant Reformation. Brazil has more than twice as many Catholics (one hundred and thirty million) as Italy. The biggest Christian congregation in London, England, draws twelve thousand people every week. It's mainly West African, and its pastor is Nigerian."[3]

A generation ago, when church and society in Canada were almost synonymous, the decline of churches that had their origin in Europe was hailed or mourned as the end of Christianity in North America. The front cover of *Time* magazine reflected on this decline with its then-trendy question, "Is God Dead?"[4] It may well be that the church Canadians of European descent have known is disappearing, but the faith of the apostles is reappearing in new forms.

The emergence of new strains of church can be traced back to the day of Pentecost, when Jews who had come to Jerusalem from all parts of the

2. Interview with Brian Seim, International Urban Consultant with SIM International, December 2011.

3. Margaret Wente, "God's Far From Dead in the Global South," *Globe and Mail*, 24 December 2011.

4. *Time*, 8 April 1966.

known world to celebrate the festival first heard the apostolic preaching in their own languages. Early persecutions and the fall of Jerusalem in 70 AD might have crippled or annihilated the early church, which used the Temple for public preaching, had it not been for this international gathering of Jews and converts to Judaism from every region of the known world (Acts 2:9–11). Moreover, because the Gospel had been carried to multiple locations by travelling apostles like Paul, who planted churches throughout Asia Minor, indigenous Gentile churches continued to spread across the Roman Empire.

Today, as the memory of almost two millennia of Christian ascendancy appears to be fading in the West, the predictable question, "What is the future of the Church?" ought to be changed to, "What varieties of the kingdom will grow in this new soil and climate?"

Immigrant churches are a positive challenge to traditional churches that have lost their confidence that the Gospel of Jesus will survive them. They are also a challenge to those who expected secular society to prevail. New varieties of church are going viral in the industrial properties of urban Canada, and there are significant changes in grassroots religious culture that are somewhat puzzling to those who thought they knew what religion looked like in this country.

WHO'S AFRAID OF RELIGION?

As a Canadian pastor of European heritage, I would never dream of wearing a robe or collar in public. Very few professional religious workers do so anymore, except during designated ceremonies or functions. One day, however, I was wearing a button-on, halo-around-the-neck style collar after a wedding, and needed to pick up something in a big box store in urban Ontario. The store entrance was crowded with immigrants from the Punjab—also dressed to identify their religion. The neighbourhood is predominantly Sikh. They parted deferentially to let my clergy shirt pass, smiling politely.

I had made it almost all the way to the back of the store when a man behind a specialty counter called out, "Hey! What do you do for a living?" In a moment, I realized he was talking to the collar on my shirt. "I'm a pastor," I said. He stepped into the aisle. "You must get pretty sick of people telling you all their problems all the time." "Actually," I said, surprised at this spontaneous public recognition, "I find people really interesting."

"Well, I'm Jewish and not very religious!" "Jesus was Jewish," I retorted, "and not very religious. You guys have a lot in common."

In the middle of the busy store, with customers milling around, he talked about hurt and alienation and disconnection from his faith heritage. And we talked about reconnecting with his faith.

At the end of the conversation, I asked, "Would you like me to pray with you? I can make it look like you're still at work selling me stuff." We invited a third person into the conversation and prayed with our eyes wide open.

As I turned to leave, he shouted after me, "You're not going to believe this, but I've been thinking I've got to start praying again." "Maybe someone's trying to tell you something," I called over my shoulder, moving on to the next stop. And on the way out of the store, the Sikhs who were waiting in line allowed me to pass to the front of the check-out—in deference to my Christian clergy shirt.

Had it not been for a wardrobe malfunction, I might not have noticed how the balance between secular and religious people has tipped. Religious people are actually a majority—sometimes a significant majority in the densely populated cities of this country. And in this new world, which I had thought secular, de-churched, and irreligious, the collar is visible identification that says, "Open to religion." Evidently there are people waiting to engage in spiritual conversation or relationship. If they catch you in uniform and looking approachable, they approach.

As a vital Christian church emerges in Canada through immigration, other religious groups are also more visible. A Buddhist priest has set up shop down the road from my office. I recognize him by his saffron robes as he pushes a broom on the front walk. The man crossing the road in front of my car is visibly a mullah, and the school down the street offers space for Muslim prayer on Fridays. In a multifaith and multicultural society, the assumption Canadians used to make that religion should be entirely a private matter is no longer a given—except perhaps in long-established churches that have not noticed the changes going on around them. Outside of church I find a fresh expectation that Christians will engage in spiritual conversations.

Howard Olver, who leads the Intercultural Church Network for the Free Methodist Church in Canada, observes that "the collapse of Christendom, coinciding with the rise of multiculturalism as a central Canadian value, is good news for us."[5] In the realm of faith, a Filipina nanny, a

5. Interview with Howard Olver, Adjunct Professor of Missional Leadership, Tyndale Seminary, Toronto, ON, December 2011.

Jamaican personal support worker, or an Ethiopian taxi driver may speak openly of Jesus. Because they are not white, their witness does not trigger the cultural bias that opposes traditional Western Christian privilege. The fact that white Christians are no longer culturally dominant in Canada may actually be an asset, not a liability, when seeking to gain a hearing.

As this implies, one blessing that immigrant believers have brought to Canada is infectious faith. Olver comments, "The traditional Anglo-Canadian church appears to be so comatose that if anything will ignite it, it will have to come from outside." And it has. The Christian and Missionary Alliance Church of Canada, for example, has been revitalized in recent years largely through an influx of immigrants from Asia. Today 25 percent of the Free Methodist Church in Canada consists of new church plants, most of them consisting of first-generation immigrants.

CULTURES OLD AND NEW

It remains to be seen, however, whether immigrant church planters can create fresh expressions of church that are more than just transplanted congregations from the old country. Dan Sheffield, author of *The Multicultural Leader*,[6] observes that the majority of new churches are most effective at reaching out to those of their own ethnicity: this is the case for church planting groups from Syria, Hong Kong, mainland China, Ethiopia, Sri Lanka, the Congo, Rwanda, and Burundi. The members of these communities have often come as refugees, many of them already well-taught Christians who arrive wanting to start a Canadian congregation, a new spiritual home in a new country—but not necessarily in the style of that new country.

Churches made up of immigrant Christians—often called diaspora churches because they have been scattered from their original home countries—can, however, expand beyond their original nucleus. Sheffield cites his experience with Sri Lankan congregations, which began with a Christian nucleus from the old country, but since then have planted growing churches among their compatriots from a nominal Hindu background. Some diaspora churches are particularly good at reaching out to others. One Toronto congregation was planted in the last decade by a young

---

6. Interview with Dan Sheffield, Director of Intercultural and Global Ministries for the Free Methodist Church of Canada, December 2011. See also Dan Sheffield. *The Multicultural Leader: Developing a Catholic Personality* (Vancouver: Clements Publishing, 2005).

businessman from Ethiopia. With a handful of evangelically-minded families from Ethiopia, they have now gathered a congregation of one hundred and fifty Ethiopians with little or no faith background. To someone who has lived in Canada for generations, this may still look like immigrants keeping to themselves, but each instance is actually a significant step beyond the group's comfort zone.

That having been said, immigrants have good reason to stick together. Many experience culture shock as they leave a vibrant Christian environment at home and come to Canada, only to run up against a wall of absolute materialism and anti-God sentiment. An immigrant group will often respond by banding together around their faith in Jesus Christ. The price of cultural isolation from other Canadians is high, but to them it seems a small sacrifice compared with what they see as the alternative: abandoning their faith and letting their children become assimilated into the secularism of Canada.

Many immigrants also experience culture shock as they encounter Canadian churches. Immigrant pastors often experience a particular form of culture shock when they approach Canadian church officials about having their credentials recognized, to ask for meeting space in existing churches, or even for fellowship with colleagues. Some immigrant pastors have been told that they will have to repeat their entire seminary education in order to be recognized as ordained ministers in some denominations. They wonder why their education and outlook are not respected.

As often happens, parachurch organizations are demonstrating a greater capacity for rapid adjustment and are filling the gap. In 2010, the Tyndale Intercultural Ministry (TIM) Centre at Tyndale Seminary in North York launched Foundations in Missional Ministry and Church Leadership as a diploma program for immigrant pastors for whom graduate school was out of the question. The aim was "to provide accessible and affordable training to immigrant church leaders to be certified by the denominations partnering with the TIM Centre." The Canadian Baptists of Ontario and Quebec (CBOQ) have already accepted the validity of this diploma.

The truism for all missional activity is that we must change who we are in order to connect with others. As the Apostle Paul put it, "I have become all things to all people, that I might by all means, save some" (1 Cor 9:22). For centuries, a central part of Eurocentric evangelism was, "How can we make these other people more like us?" One of the blessings of Christendom's collapse is that today it is very clearly not the correct question.[7] The baton of world leadership in the Christian church has already passed to the Global South, and the ramifications are just beginning to be felt in the established churches in Canada and around the world.

CROSS-CULTURAL PARTNERSHIPS?

How cultural groups relate to one another in the church has been an issue ever since Greeks and Hebrews clashed in the early church (Acts 6). In Canada, some immigrant churches share denominational roots with traditional Canadian churches and want to connect with other Christians of their tradition. What often happens, however, is that existing churches may simply see new churches as a source of new members to bolster their dwindling numbers, and conversely, immigrant churches may see only the potential for financial support and the use of real estate. Some newcomers, seeing the sad state of existing churches, also wish to contribute leadership. One Ghanaian pastor told me of his dismay at coming from a country where movie theatres and restaurants are routinely purchased to be turned into churches to a country where church buildings are routinely sold to theatre groups and condominium developers.

However, immigrant church planters have identified some significant obstacles to partnership. In 2002, a group of pastors from the Greater Toronto area brought thirty immigrant pastors together for a spaghetti dinner in return for answering a question: "What do newcomers to Canada desire in the church?"[8]

At the top of the list was a plea to established churches to embrace new immigrants. Just as immigrants are often isolated in high-rise urban towers, so also they can feel alone when they visit established Canadian churches. According to the immigrant planters, new arrivals sometimes feel judged and diminished in established churches. Canadians try to be kind, of course, either pretending there are no significant differences, or focusing on superficialities like food or traditional costume. But for the recipients of these good intentions, it often feels like being marginalized or patronized.

Arriving pastors also found resistance to the idea of ethnic or generational diversity in leadership that went beyond tokenism. Even on a diverse team, cultural differences may create misunderstandings leading

7. Interview with Brian Seim.

8. Interview with Yasir Dildad, Senior Researcher with the Centre for Community Based Research, Kitchener ON, December 2011.

to ill will. For instance, in some cultures, a request for help will often be met with an enthusiastic response just for the sake of politeness, but without any intention of following through. Someone from a different culture, however, interprets the failure to keep the apparent commitment as the breaking of a promise. Or a traditional Canadian denomination might promise "support" to a new pastor who believes that it means a salary and meeting place, whereas the denomination was offering the use of the denominational name. The sponsoring denomination may then be upset by what it perceives as excessive demands and withdraw from the partnership. Cultural miscommunication and divergent expectations are to be expected.

Finally, immigrant church leaders stressed that, for them, full participation in a denomination or congregation would require a break with the present overwhelming homogeneity, and the welcoming of a critical mass of visible minorities and other cultures into active participation. It is difficult to become full partners where there is only a smattering of other colours, languages, and cultures. The implication is that a huge demographic shift is needed in the leadership and visible makeup of churches wishing to evangelize interculturally.

Canadians of European origin might be embarrassed to acknowledge their cultural privileges, so obvious to immigrants. Although difficult to discuss among traditional North Americans, it is broadly understood in immigrant groups that there is a de facto global hierarchy of cultures that asserts itself wherever there are immigrants. Status is perceived in relation to the size of a group's established middle class. That is, the more poor and marginalized a population, the less status it has among other more prosperous groups.

North Europeans, despite discomfort, guilt, and denial about having a place of privilege, find themselves treated with the greatest deference in an unspoken hierarchy followed by East Asians, South Asians, West Africans, North Africans, and Aboriginal Canadians. This hierarchy has significant implications for leadership when multiple ethnicities are present. Refusing to acknowledge the issue merely exacerbates it, as when a well-meaning European Canadian church committee insisted on placing "ethnic ministers" in "ethnic congregations"—regardless of cultural affinity. The hierarchy is slowly changing as second-generation immigrants and First Nations earn graduate degrees in significant numbers, but the change is sometimes glacial, and immigrant church planters are not all willing to wait for existing churches to catch the fire.

On the flip side, immigrant church planters may be disinclined to speed a cultural partnership by simply adopting the theology and practices of host denominations. Immigrants from a vibrant Christianity wonder how a nation's churches have become lethargic, have come to deny portions of the ecumenical creeds and reject a supernatural worldview, and are largely depressed about the future of the kingdom. Canadian denominations, accustomed to forms of Christianity developed in Europe, may express discomfort with or even reject Christianity as it has developed elsewhere. Philip Jenkins, author of *The Next Christendom: The Coming of Global Christianity*, writes, "The types of Christianity that have thrived most successfully in the global South have been very different from what many Europeans and North Americans consider mainstream. These models have been far more enthusiastic, much more centrally concerned with the immediate workings of the supernatural, through prophecy, visions, ecstatic utterances, and healing. In fact, they have differed so widely from the cooler Northern norms as to arouse suspicion that these enthusiastic Africans (for instance) are essentially reviving the pagan practices of traditional society."[9]

Academically trained North American church leaders, for whom raising one's hand during a moving piece of music might be considered excessively emotional, are too readily dismissive of such spiritualities. At a meeting of very liberal church people I attended recently, a new Korean pastor described in glowing terms a church retreat where many had become Christians and had been baptized in the Holy Spirit and spoken in tongues. The audience—who would have considered this anathema among their own—wished to be welcoming to the ethnic pastor and applauded enthusiastically, but clearly expressed among themselves that he didn't know any better yet and that he must learn "proper church" and teach his congregation likewise. It made no difference that the man already has a graduate degree in theology from a recognized seminary in Korea.

TURNING OUTWARD

While some new immigrant churches will turn inward, according to Sheffield, more typically immigrants turn outward, seeing entry into the Canadian mainstream as the better choice and preferring not to worship in churches of their own ethnic group. This presents an opportunity for

9. Philip Jenkins, *The Next Christendom: The Coming of Global Christianity* (Oxford: Oxford University Press, 2003), 134.

dynamic immigrant faith to make a mark on Canadian culture. Most of these churches will be new worshipping communities, including recent arrivals to Canada and those who are invited to join in a different kind of church.[10] Most thriving intercultural and multicultural churches are church plants led by new immigrants.

Other churches sincerely want to reach out, but evangelical passion sometimes encounters cultural barriers. A Congolese church wishing to reach others in the neighbourhood has found, not surprisingly, that worshipping in the Babendi language is a significant obstacle. A similar fate attended the Cantonese church that blitzed their community door to door, inviting their neighbours to church on Easter—unaware that the white neighbourhood was predominantly Jewish and preparing for Passover. Of course, established churches that say, "Our doors are always open. Those people would be here if they wanted to be part of our church" are equally misreading their culture!

Sheffield stresses the difference between multicultural and intercultural churches. "Multicultural" refers to a church of many nationalities where everyone does things the same way, adapting to a single dominant culture (probably the one that is numerically greatest). "Intercultural," on the other hand, refers to a church of many nationalities where such things as the leadership and worship represent most (if not all) the cultures involved.

Multicultural churches are often largely made up of people who grew up Christian in other cultures and wish to be less identified with their culture of origin. The typical multicultural congregation has many ethnic groups led by a white pastor, perhaps with someone of another ethnicity on staff. Worship, structures, and fellowship patterns are the same for everyone, and look very much like other long-established Canadian churches.

There has been an upswing in the number of new, genuinely intercultural churches in the first decade of the twenty-first century, particularly within the Pentecostal Assemblies of Canada and independent charismatic groups. These include house churches, storefront churches, and churches whose size almost qualifies them to be called mega churches, which are often well known within the black and South Asian communities—but invisible to their near neighbours in traditional Anglo-European churches.

For example, Kingdom Covenant Ministries, led by Dr. Pat Francis and founded in 1999, draws more than three thousand people to weekly

10. Interview with Dan Sheffield.

worship on the border between Mississauga and Metro Toronto. Most are from Caribbean and African countries (often seen as a single black identity by European Canadians but actually representing over thirty different countries and cultures), but there are growing numbers of people from other backgrounds, including European Canadian. I quizzed a dozen pastors from nearby traditional churches: not one was aware of Kingdom Covenant Ministries' existence.

Sheffield cautions that the stories of immigrant churches take decades to unfold—like those of Chinese churches initially founded by immigrants from Hong Kong. The immigrants who arrived from Hong Kong in the 1990s worshipped in Cantonese for the five to ten years it took for their children, who spoke English socially, to get to the point of wanting to worship in a different milieu where they could invite non-Chinese friends. By 2010, significant numbers of Mandarin speakers from the Chinese mainland were arriving. Some were already evangelists and church planters. And many others were receptive to invitations from Cantonese speakers to discover Christian faith in a Mandarin-speaking congregation. As a result of these shifts, in places like the lower mainland of British Columbia, and Markham, Thornhill, and Richmond Hill in Ontario, a majority of Chinese churches now offer worship for more than one language group, many worshipping with three congregations on the same site. In one, Cantonese is spoken with "overseas born" Chinese; in another, the environment is English language so that friends and spouses of the second generation can be invited; and, most recently, in a third, Mandarin-speaking congregations attract the most recent wave of Mandarin-speaking immigrants from mainland China. Of these three, often the Mandarin-speaking church is the most dynamically alive, with people who are new to Canada and to Christian faith. The English-speaking church tends to struggle, as overseas-born parents are uneasy about handing over the leadership of the church to Canadian-born children who share a faith but not all the parental values. For the parent generation of most immigrant churches there is a tendency to move into "crusty self-preservation mode" as the children grow up after fifteen or twenty years, and to retreat deeper into their ethnic enclave.

While the second generations who continue in faith most often go to multicultural churches, the immigrant churches of their parents may themselves be reluctant to form relationships with such churches, since they are sometimes perceived as a threat to their own church's future. Denominational leaders of ethnic churches describe an 80 to 96 percent loss of the second generation as that generation distances itself from its parents and strives to integrate into secular Canadian culture, perhaps aided by a universally secular public school system.[11] It is the second generation who remain Christian but who move into the new Canadian culture who will have the greatest impact in the future.

Canada is an immigrant society that has been transformed by each wave of immigration. On the one hand, Canada will continue to have new deposits of spiritually dynamic immigrants whose voices need to become part of an integrated conversation. On the other, Canadian culture often has an entrenched bias against religious faith as a first choice among many lifestyle options.

Church planting by immigrants and fresh expressions of immigrant churches are a global phenomenon. In her *Globe and Mail* article, Wente argues that "Christianity is simply returning to its roots. It was born as the religion of the outcast and the dispossessed. Today, it's embraced by young rural migrants flooding to the giant, impersonal cities. Like Islam, Christianity is a reaction to urbanization, cultural upheaval and displacement. It provides meaning, community, refuge, support networks and an anchor. It also offers blessings and redemption. Christianity, in its original form, preaches that supernatural intervention can help you in the here and now. And it promises the gift of eternal life as a reward for the pain and suffering of this one—surely the greatest selling proposition of all time."[12]

The net result is new faith communities, some entirely immigrant, and some new combinations of several cultures, including Canadians of European descent. Certainly some churches form primarily in order to preserve their culture and their faith, but others actively seek to break free of ethnic enclaves in order to share the good news of the Gospel with their new homeland.

There is no standard protocol for established churches to engage recent arrivals. Some view the most recent immigrant wave as Sunday guests or potential members of existing churches, or perhaps a subset of ethnic congregations to be adopted by a denomination. Others, such as the Free Methodist Church of Canada, are creating new leadership networks of second-generation leaders as they prepare for the next wave of congregations. This may be the single most important development for the next generation of churches, which will have more in common with

11. Interview with Brian Seim.
12. Wente, "God's Far From Dead."

the emerging global youth culture than with the older generation of the countries from which they came.

There is some evidence of a new kind of hybrid church, neither traditional Canadian nor multicultural mix. They are not really intercultural or multicultural but "pancultural," a new hybrid of people who have grown up in one culture and gone to school in another, or have grown up among so many cultures that they have very different sensibilities from those of their parents. These churches are planted by those Soong-Chan Rah calls "the 1.5 generation"—neither what is generally called "first generation" nor "second generation."[13] This is the generation who immigrated as young people. They are fluent in both languages and are trusted by the permission-givers in both cultures. These Christians show the most promise, taking the strength of their parents' churches and reaching beyond their own generation and ethnicity.

Established denominations need to work out how to relate to arriving immigrant Christians who have seen God do great things in their countries of origin, who are eager to merge with a Canadian church, and who hope to add their grace and strength to their new denominational home.[14] Christians in established churches have difficulty recognizing the shifting changes in culture and faith in this country. Again, parachurch organizations are quicker to respond to the new reality. In 2009, an ecumenical report expressed a shared vision of Canadian churches where recent immigrants are fully welcomed and included, with the expectation that others will come to share this vision.[15]

Can the church of the Global South help regenerate the faith of the Global North? According to Seim the answer is no, if we think in terms of immigrants behaving like traditional missionaries. The answer is yes, however, if we look for evidence of new churches being seeded around the world in ways no one seriously planned or anticipated. The new global youth culture, often characterized by hopelessness, lack of jobs and resources, and anger at big business and modernism (with their assumptions of unending resources and progress), has created a new international tribe of humanity. It is distinguishable from other generations by the use of new technology that is central to relationships, communication, and identity.

13. Soong-Chan Rah, *The Next Evangelicalism: Freeing the Church from Western Captivity* (Downers Grove: InterVarsity Press, 2009).

14. Interview with Brian Seim.

15. "Beyond the Welcome: Churches Responding to the Immigrant Reality in Canada," World Vision, The Centre for Community-Based Research, and the TIM Centre, October 2010.

The multiplicity of churches arriving and hybridizing from around the world is bringing new and hardy strains of Christian faith to the changing environment of the Western world.

In North America there is evidence of dynamic strains of Christian faith, ingenuously shared in the workplace and with neighbours. There is a resurgence of belief that Jesus represents life and joy for all, and a compulsion to share with humility and care. I see and hear anecdotal evidence: families who return to church because their Filipina nanny has influenced them; cleaning and maintenance staff from the West Indies singing hymns while they work, and inviting others to worship; hospital and nursing care workers from West Africa who share their faith naturally and easily with clients and patients. These incidents challenge an inherited church to humble itself and to learn from the great-great-grandchildren of those missionized by their great-great-grandparents.

Can existing congregations and denominations be transformed by the vitality of new Christians arriving in Canada? It can happen if the host churches and denominations are willing to lose an old identity and learn a new. And if they are not able to change? Clearly, there are other possibilities emerging from the infinite resources of the Spirit of Jesus. The rise of fresh expressions of church has been a constant theme from the beginning of the Christian church. It appears that something fresh is in our midst.

Green Shoots 3
Artistic Sensibility Meets Christian Spirituality

Artisan Church
Vancouver, British Columbia

Back in 2008, Nelson Boschmann was completing eleven years of teaching at Columbia Bible College in Abbotsford, British Columbia, when he began to feel the stirrings of a new calling. "I don't think I'm meant to be a lifer here," he said to himself.

A licensed and credentialed pastor in the Mennonite Brethren tradition, Nelson is also a jazz pianist and leader of a professional, Duke Ellington–style trio that bears his name and features piano, double bass, and drums. "As a musician, I was interested in the long-standing role of the arts in worship and in the relationship between the artist and the church," says Nelson, who has recorded two volumes of jazz for the seasons of the church year called *Keeping Time, I* and *II.*

Nelson was well acquainted with the guitar-and-singing role of contemporary artists in worship but found himself asking about the whole spectrum of artists: what of the painters, sculptors, dancers, poets, actors, and filmmakers? The centuries-long connection between Christianity and the highest achievements in the visual, verbal, and musical arts was proof that the church and the artistic imagination were not mutually exclusive. "Somehow in this century, though, the two had grown apart. I wanted the church to own up to that, and let the artists back in," he says.

Nelson's thinking was influenced by the theology of the city articulated by Tim Keller, pastor of Redeemer Presbyterian Church in Manhattan, and his premise, "As the city goes, so goes the culture." Another formative influence for him was Andy Crouch's book, *Culture Making: Recovering Our Creative Calling.*[16] "I began to realize

16. Andy Crouch, *Culture Making: Recovering Our Creative Calling* (Downers Grove, IL: InterVarsity Press 2008).

that if the church is serious about shaping and transforming culture, it had better be in the place where culture is being shaped—the urban centres," he says.

Nelson was increasingly convinced that an inner-city church serving largely, though not solely, artists would fill a significant gap in downtown Vancouver. So, in the summer of 2008, he and his wife, Terri, moved to the city to apprentice at Pacific Church, a young plant connected with a Canadian church-planting network called C2C. During the apprenticeship year, the Nelsons began to form their all-important core team, drawing on old acquaintances, Nelson's former students, and actors and administrators from the Pacific Theatre, a Christian dramatic-arts organization. "It is important to journey with people you know and trust," he says.

Nelson also knew that location was paramount. "If we wanted to attract artists and creators, we needed to be downtown, at the intersection of people working in the arts." That location would prove to be a room in the Vancouver Public Library, on Georgia Street.

By October 2009, and with support from C2C, Artisan held its first gathering with about twenty core participants. For the next six months, it held its Sunday evening gatherings just once a month in the library, getting the word out mainly by means of strategically placed sandwich boards that read simply, "Artisan: a Creative Christian Community," followed by the time and place of worship.

Once the 2010 Winter Olympics had cleared out of Vancouver, Artisan gained more frequent access to the library and, in March of that year, began its current schedule of weekly Sunday services, which typically attract a hundred people to their simple, "liturgy-lite," Mennonite format. At first, C2C paid 100 percent of Nelson's salary but currently pays just 25 percent. "Now the church is ready to support a full-time pastor on its own," he says.

As for the congregants, they are principally in their twenties and thirties, and Nelson admits there are a few demographic gaps he would like to fill. "We have a few people in their fifties, and we are hoping and praying for more in that age group," he says. "There is virtually no youth presence, as there are few secondary schools in the downtown and, of course, we don't have their parents either."

Artisan draws its theological vision from the creative wells of Genesis 1 and 2, and the last chapters of Revelation, which focus on the generosity and creativity of God, and the concept of the creation of a new heaven and new earth. "Part of the reason that church tradition has led to alienation is that it often starts with the fall in Genesis 3, the assumption that humankind is depraved and crooked and must be fixed," Nelson says. "We choose to go back to the chapters showing the goodness and creativity of God, and his good intentions for the world."

Although some may not think of themselves as particularly creative, creativity is part of the image of God that resides in each one of us, he says. "We get to participate with God in the work of making all things new. The scope of redemption includes the saving of souls, but beyond that, we are participating with God in the renewal of all things and the creation of the holy city that is coming out of heaven and involves all aspects of art and culture."

Nelson's vision of the new city has solidly held together his original team, and he sees himself staying right where he is. All but one of the founding couples is still with Artisan, and that one couple has gone on mission to India. Nelson's co-pastor is currently looking into starting a new church plant in east Vancouver.

Artisan remains committed to a highly collaborative, highly relational model and to keeping things small. "I see great value in being a small community and not a megachurch," Nelson says. As with most Christian churches, its sense of community entails reaching out in mission and stewardship to those around it. So Artisan has partnered with downtown groups such as the Union Gospel Mission, JustWork, JustPotters, Global Mothers, and More Than a Roof, a British Columbia Mennonite housing program for the poor, the addicted, and the mentally ill.

In support of these organizations, Artisan stages fundraising events such as improv comedy nights and jazz concerts. "We try to instill the notion of being missional in whatever walk of life we find ourselves." And although Artisan's primary target group remains professional artists, its vision does not exclude others. "We want to be an accurate reflection of the diverse nature of the downtown and its surrounding neighbourhoods, and that includes the diversity that lies outside the artistic world," says Nelson.

D.S.

Christians in Canada have traditionally thought of "the mission field" (if they have thought of it at all) as overseas. Until the mid-twentieth century, at least, "the Christian West" sent missionaries to the rest of the world. Of course, over the centuries there has been an evolution in the West's understanding of overseas missions: by the twentieth century, it had moved beyond the imperialistic impulse to export "Christian civilization" and had become much more of a co-operative movement between sister churches. But the traffic was still more in one direction than the other. At some point in the last twenty years, however, the direction of flow began to reverse. The West, instead of being the supposed channel of blessing to the world, became the startled recipient of missionary efforts from overseas—no longer with overtones of cultural imperialism but with a genuine desire to "re-evangelize" the very cultures that had seeded the church overseas in the first place. Instead of feeling insulted and even patronized that anyone might think that Canada needs missionaries, Christians of European descent need to listen to what the Spirit may be saying to us through those once considered "the weak and foolish."

7

What's a Missionary Doing in Canada?

The Story of Greenhills Christian Fellowship

Narry F. Santos

FIVE YEARS AGO, MY church in the Philippines sent me, along with my family, to do church-planting in Canada. This act of sending a missionary to Canada raises unfamiliar questions for Canadians. In particular, Why would a missionary be sent to Canada? Is Canada really a mission field needing evangelizing and the planting of new churches?

PREPARATION FOR A VISION
BEYOND THE PHILIPPINES

IN 1994, I STARTED serving as Christian Education Pastor at the Greenhills Christian Fellowship (GCF), a thirty-three-year-old church founded by a Baptist missionary from the United States, which now has fifteen satellites (or church plants) in the Philippines and six in Canada. Three years into my GCF Christian Education ministry, the senior pastor asked me to begin GCF-South Metro, the first GCF satellite south of Manila. I agreed, and was blessed to see GCF-South Metro grow and help launch three other satellites farther south of Manila.

In light of this experience, in its fifth year, GCF-South Metro leaders sensed that the Philippines was too small a place for our response to the

Great Commission, and that our mission was meant to be nothing less than global, though there was no opportunity for us to bring that conviction to fruition.

However, in the next three years we saw an exodus of five families from GCF-South Metro. They left one after another, in order to migrate to Toronto. At that time, I felt frustrated and discouraged. After investing in the discipleship and leadership development of these families—one leader even served as the chairman of our church board—I saw them leave our spiritual home. It took two years before these frustrating circumstances turned into hope-filled confirmation.

The GCF senior pastor then asked me to start the first GCF satellite outside the Philippines. I agreed, seeing that this was confirmation of our opportunity to minister globally. When we explored where we were to be sent, Toronto became the designated mission field. Why? Toronto was the city that the five families called their new home. These families could then be part of the core leadership team, who would take the lead in launching GCF-Toronto.

In 2005, we challenged these five families to take ownership of the vision to start GCF-Toronto. By faith, they accepted the challenge and owned the vision. We now understood in hindsight that what started as a frustrating experience of an exodus from our church in the Philippines was to be transformed into a fresh experience of church planting in Canada.

Another reason we saw Toronto as a mission field was that this city is a favourite destination for immigrants from the Philippines. Out of the four hundred thousand Filipino-Canadians, about half reside in the Greater Toronto Area. There are more than 102,000 Filipino-Canadians who call Toronto their home. We sensed that God was about to use dispersed Filipino Christians—the diaspora—to reach Filipinos and other ethnic groups in Canada.

Thus my family and I were sent off to Canada by the GCF mother church and the Philippine satellites in April 2007 to help fulfill the GCF vision of reaching people "through satellites in strategic areas worldwide." Toronto was to be the starting point for our new global missions assignment.

GCF-CANADA CHURCH-PLANTING VISION AND ITS UNFOLDING STORY

The GCF-Canada church-planting vision is directly linked to the birth of GCF-Toronto. GCF-Toronto was officially launched as the first international GCF satellite on 6 May 2007, at the Centennial Community Centre in Toronto. A month later, we discussed three affirmations of prime importance at our first prayer, vision-casting, and planning retreat for leaders. The three affirmations may be summarized as follows: (1) We are all placed in Toronto by God's providence; (2) We will not be a Filipino church in Toronto; and (3) GCF-Toronto will be a church-planting church. The leaders agreed with these affirmations and committed to take part in this Canadian church-planting vision. As a result of the GCF-Toronto leaders' commitment to this church-planting vision, the GCF-Canada "Triple Vision" was conceived. This vision is taken from the process implied in Acts 1:8. Mission begins in Jerusalem, then progresses into Judea and Samaria, and peaks at "the ends of the earth." For the first seven-year cycle (2007–2014), we are trusting God to bring about this GCF-Canada Strategic Vision: seven GCF satellites in seven years in four provinces of Canada (Ontario, British Columbia, Alberta, Manitoba). The vision unfolds in three movements:

GCF-Toronto Triple Vision
The vision to launch GCF-Toronto (our "Jerusalem")
+
The vision to birth GCF-Peel (our "Judea and Samaria")
+
The vision to birth GCF-Vancouver (our "Ends of the Earth")

GCF-Peel Triple Vision
The vision to launch GCF-Peel (our "Jerusalem")
+
The vision to birth GCF-York (our "Judea and Samaria")
+
The vision to birth GCF-Winnipeg (our "Ends of the Earth")

GCF-Vancouver Triple Vision
The vision to launch GCF-Vancouver (our "Jerusalem")
+
The vision to birth GCF-Surrey (our "Judea and Samaria")
+
The vision to birth GCF-Calgary (our "Ends of the Earth")

Once this first cycle of the GCF-Canada Triple Vision is fulfilled, GCF-Canada will pause, pray, and plan for a second cycle. God willing, the next GCF-Canada Triple Vision will be by countries: (1) GCF-Canada as our "Jerusalem"; (2) GCF-USA as our "Judea and Samaria"; and (3) GCF-Australia as our "ends of the earth."

As God confirmed the GCF-Canada Triple Vision to us, God gradually opened doors to make the launch of these new satellites possible. Three months into our GCF-Toronto launch, we received a request to start GCF-Peel. In response, we started small "growth groups" for Christians interested in growing spiritually and being involved, in two areas of Peel— Mississauga and Brampton. In September 2007, we held two "preview" worship services, and shortly afterward started weekly services until GCF-Peel was finally launched at Easter in 2008.

In early 2008, we challenged a few former GCF members who now live in Vancouver to consider starting GCF-Vancouver. In response, they formed one growth group in March, another group later in the year. These two groups became the core team, conducting monthly and later biweekly preview services in 2009 and weekly services in January 2010. On 2 May 2010, this satellite was launched officially, with a former GCF satellite pastor from Manila serving as the full-time GCF-Vancouver Pastor.

In 2011, we saw the birth of GCF-York, the "Judea and Samaria" satellite of the GCF-Peel Triple Vision. Four families from GCF-Peel volunteered to be involved in this satellite, along with three families living in Vaughan. God also sent an elder from GCF-Toronto, who sensed a call to serve this satellite, volunteering his time and efforts while studying at Tyndale Seminary. This core team began with two new growth groups, and held worship services, increasing from monthly to biweekly and finally to weekly services, until GCF-York was officially launched on 5 June 2011.

As well as seeing God start new satellites by this process of church "birthing," we also saw God open doors to having new satellites "by adoption." In early 2009, a Winnipeg pastor requested that GCF-Toronto consider adopting the church plant he had initiated the previous year as part of the GCF family of churches. In the spring of that year, a Calgary church planter was referred to us as a possible GCF partner. This pastor asked if the church plant he was planning to start in 2009 could be part of the GCF family.

Because GCF to this point had always started satellites from scratch, we were initially hesitant about these two requests. In the sixteen satellites that had been launched by GCF in the past sixteen years, we had intentionally initiated the work in different strategic areas. However, we sensed that these requests from Winnipeg and Calgary warranted our prayer and discussion, believing that this might be a supplementary way to fulfill God's Triple Vision for us.

GCF-CANADA LEADERSHIP SUMMIT AND GCF-CANADA COVENANT

At the first GCF-Canada Leadership Summit held in the spring of 2009, GCF-Toronto leaders agreed that they were open to the idea of satellite development by "adoption." At that summit, sixty-eight delegates from GCF-Toronto, GCF-Peel, and GCF-Vancouver also agreed on the value of the GCF-Canada Vision in light of our multicultural realities and changing circumstances in Canada.

That summit also saw the signing of a manifesto intended to catalyze the formation of a "GCF-Canada Covenant," to establish a framework of unity and partnership among the different parts of GCF-Canada. This Covenant specifies four points of agreement—mission, vision, statement of faith, and ethos. These are the values intended to shape the unity of all satellites in Canada, and to serve as the framework as we continue to "birth" and "adopt" GCF satellites.

The GCF-Canada Covenant also specifies three governing perspectives: "GCF-Canada shall be missional, metropolitan, and multicultural in its strategies and ministries."

1. *Missional* speaks of churches: the satellites will intentionally seek to multiply themselves, following the Triple Vision, and will incarnationally add value to our communities.

2. *Metropolitan* speaks of communities: the satellites will strategically minister in urban centres, targeting our cities.

3. *Multicultural* speaks of the country: satellites will deliberately be on a mission to the diaspora of "all nations," that is, reaching out to immigrants in countries that are open to receiving different ethnic groups.

Thus, by God's grace, GCF-Canada will continue to multiply and reproduce missional churches in metropolitan communities in the multicultural context of Canada.

Satellite Development Shift: Both Birthing and Adopting

With the ratified GCF-Canada Covenant in hand, we went for an explor-atory visit to Winnipeg in the summer of 2009. We were sent by GCF-Peel because they regarded Winnipeg as the best location for their "ends of the earth" satellite. We met the pastor and the core leaders of the new church plant hoping to be adopted, presented to them the GCF-Canada Covenant, told them the GCF-Canada two-year story of satellite development, and joined in the meetings of their two small groups and their worship service.

On their end, the Winnipeg group agreed to present to their people the option that their new work be adopted as GCF-Winnipeg, to pray about it for one month, and to inform us of their decision at the end of August. In a month, they informed us of the group's decision to be ad-opted as GCF-Winnipeg. We visited Winnipeg again in the fall to sign the official Memorandum of Agreement between GCF-Canada and the new group. This marked a major shift in our GCF-Canada policy: as well as birthing daughter churches, we can now adopt new churches. As a result, GCF-Winnipeg was launched as a satellite on 2 October 2011.

We then explored the possibility of adopting the new Calgary church plant as GCF-Calgary. We presented to the pastor and his leadership group the GCF mission, vision, statement of faith, ethos, and the GCF-Canada Covenant. Two weeks later, they committed to be part of the GCF-Canada family of churches. We returned to Calgary in October to conduct satellite development training, to take part in their small group sessions, to partici-pate in their worship service, and to sign a memorandum of agreement.

When we asked the pastor in Calgary and his leaders why they chose to be part of the GCF-Canada family—knowing that we were just over two years old then, and that we had meagre resources to aid them—they re-plied that they wanted to be identified with a group that has a clear vision of planting churches in Canada and beyond. As a result, GCF-Calgary was officially launched as a satellite in May 2010.

Thus, in its first four years, GCF-Canada has seen the launch of six satellites: GCF-Toronto (May 2007); GCF-Peel (March 2008); GCF-Van-couver (May 2010); GCF-Calgary (May 2010); GCF-York (June 2011); and GCF-Winnipeg (October 2011). God allowed us to see this fruit as part of our intentional effort to plant churches throughout Canada.

WHAT HAVE WE LEARNED THROUGH THIS PROCESS?

Our GCF-Canada story has not only been a journey of planting new churches but a story of learning missional and intercultural lessons in a multicultural ministry context. These lessons came in the form of two encouragements and two challenges facing GCF-Canada.

Encouraging Lesson #1: Strategic Partnership with Like-Minded Groups

Since there are no Baptists of our particular denomination in Canada, we decided to partner with a like-minded family of churches, the Canadian Baptists of Ontario and Quebec (CBOQ) for GCF-Toronto, GCF-Peel, and GCF-York, and the Canadian Baptists of Western Canada (CBWC) for GCF-Vancouver, GCF-Calgary, and GCF-Winnipeg. It is affirming to belong to a bigger family of churches whose mission and vision resonate with ours. In addition, CBOQ committed to support the GCF-York church plant for three years, while CBWC has supported the church plants of GCF-Vancouver, GCF-Calgary, and GCF-Winnipeg for two years. We are blessed to be part of a larger family that comes to our side and assists us in fulfilling God's vision.

We are also blessed to have an ongoing partnership with the Tyndale Intercultural Ministries (TIM) Centre. Since we wanted to learn how to become missional and intentionally intercultural, God provided the TIM Centre as our partner to teach us major lessons about these approaches. This partnership began in the fall of 2008 when the centre's director, Robert Cousins, conducted an eight-week class for fifteen of our GCF-Toronto leaders on "Preparing Leadership for Intercultural Ministry." This class was followed by an ongoing coaching relationship with Robert that began the following September. Through consulting, teaching, and preaching, he has come alongside our leaders to help us to apply missional and intentionally intercultural lessons.

When GCF-Toronto relocated to a ballroom at the Centennial College Residence and Conference Centre (CCRCC) for our worship services in May 2010, we sensed that God had a specific purpose for placing us in the midst of students. We discovered that the residence had four hundred students, one hundred of whom were international students. Since we did not have the experience and expertise to do campus ministry among international students, we saw the need to partner with International Students

Ministries Canada (ISMC) in order to minister to these students. As a result, ISMC's Toronto director, Margery Topalian, now assists and coaches us on how to connect with and care for the international students in an ongoing manner.

Encouraging Lesson #2: Creative Training for Home-Grown Church Leaders

Aside from strategic partnerships with like-minded groups, our other encouraging lesson as a missionary church has been the creation of a training program for our church leaders. Since we cannot keep "importing" GCF-Philippines pastors for GCF-Canada (something we had done for Toronto, Vancouver, and Peel), by 2009 we saw the need to "home-grow" local leaders.

As a result, the TIM Centre sought and received approval from Tyndale Seminary to give our fifteen GCF leaders (and other church leaders from different ethnic groups) an eight-course, non-degree, diploma program called Foundations of Missional Ministry and Church Leadership. The eight courses are divided into two categories, four courses on missional ministry and four on church leadership, with each course requiring forty hours of class time and course work.

CBOQ has generously agreed to credential the graduates of this diploma program as Level Two Part-Time Pastors or Church Workers. CBOQ has also given GCF-Toronto a Barnabas Initiative Grant to support this leadership development program. Discussions are continuing through CBWC, seeking to explore possibilities in Western Canada for a similar program to train the leaders of our Vancouver, Calgary, and Winnipeg churches. These training opportunities are critical in developing healthy satellites that will later be able to reproduce other healthy and multiplying satellites.

Challenging Lesson #1: Learning How to Become Missional

The first challenge is to keep learning how to become missional in our ministry. We desire to add value to our community, realizing the importance of a theology of place: that is, God has a purpose for us to fulfill in the neighbourhood where God has placed us. But we have had to realize that missional ministry takes time and that engaging in this kind of ministry can be difficult. In the past three years of experimenting with how to become missional, we feel that we are just taking baby steps in the long journey of developing relationships of trust with our community, and of seeking to love our neighbour.

Yet even in these baby steps, we have seen God open opportunities to serve and show acts of kindness—for example, to the international students at the CCRCC. After much prayer, we approached the CCRCC Community Life Coordinator in September 2010 to ask her how we could serve the international students. She replied that we could help by carrying the bags of new and returning students on the students' "Move-In Day."

After that, the coordinator allowed us to hold some holiday events: a Canadian Thanksgiving dinner for the one hundred international students; a Christmas lunch for ten international students in the week before Christmas; three Ontario Family Day luncheons for thirty-five international students, hosted by twenty church members at the college-run restaurant; a seminar with an immigration lawyer from our church for forty-two international students in April; and an Easter dinner for eighty international students. As a result, I was able to conduct weekly Bible studies with three international students (two from mainland China and one from India) during the spring semester.

Then, toward the end of the school year, the coordinator phoned to tell me that of all their residence activities for the school year, including the events sponsored by the church, those related to international students had received much commendation. Apparently, that year had seen the highest number of international students ever to be involved in community events. She requested a meeting with me to personally thank the church, and to ask us to be involved in planning the next school year's student events since CCRCC now considers us part of their community. In addition, she gave us permission to have a Thursday evening "Chips and Chow," an informal get-together to play games, eat chips, and practise English conversation with the international students.

Challenging Lesson #2:
Learning How to Become Intentionally Intercultural

The second challenging lesson that we are faced with is to keep learning how to become intentionally intercultural. Since I am a pastor of Filipino ethnic background and our church leaders are of the same background, many of the people who have been coming to church are Filipino Canadians. Therefore, we need to be intentional if we are to become intercultural.

[handwritten margin notes: Gradual building of trust b/w communities. One can't parachute into the mission field?]

In 2008, GCF-Toronto hired a part-time Youth Ministry Worker who was born and raised in Toronto, but whose parents originally came from Trinidad and Tobago. Three years ago, the TIM Centre director began to coach our leaders on how to take practical steps to move toward an intentionally intercultural ministry. Then, two years ago, a Karen leader from Myanmar was elected as a member of our satellite council.

Though these baby steps have yielded baby results, we are challenged not to give up on this journey. In fact, since mid-2011, GCF-Toronto has seen some open doors of communication and service to the residents of Tuxedo Court, a high-need area in Scarborough, Ontario, housing over five thousand people in five buildings, one of which is part of Toronto Community Housing Corporation (TCHC). In Tuxedo Court, 81 percent of residents are considered visible minorities, many of them South Asians, and, in the 2006 census, the unemployment rate was 14.8 percent, compared to the 6.7 percent average for the rest of Toronto.

As a result of prayer and a visit to Tuxedo Court in the summer of 2011, a couple from the church started a weekly Bible study there with three elderly Filipino women. This has now grown to eleven residents, from a variety of ethnic backgrounds. The church was also able to host a Canada Day celebration in the party room of the building. We brought South Asian delicacies, performed a traditional dance, sang special songs, and gave a message of hope in both Tamil and English. Forty-three residents came, half of them South Asians, and thirty-nine church members helped in the food and program preparation.

This relationship-building event was followed by a summer barbeque in the backyard of the TCHC housing at the end of the summer, and by a Christmas party for the residents in December. These events have led to two worship services, one in March and the other in April 2012, in Tuxedo Court, attended by twenty-three residents and led by those who attend the Tuesday Bible studies. These residents were also visited during the week and prayed for in their homes.

In these ways, we are able to see more fruit coming out of our intentional intercultural ministry. But I look forward to the time when different ethnic groups will not only be present in GCF but will be partners in serving, leading, and guiding GCF's ministries.

MY PERCEPTION OF THE CHURCH IN CANADA

I would like to share my limited understanding of the church in Canada during my five-year residence in Toronto, and my church-planting experience in the GTA and some cities in Western Canada. This limited understanding is nuanced by my exposure to and involvement with the ministry of the Canadian Baptists for the past four years. In this light, I present two areas of strength and two areas for growth.

Two Areas of Strength

The first area of strength that I see in the Canadian church is the presence of long-term established churches, along with parachurch groups, seminaries, and mission agencies, which provide a legacy of valuable lessons in ministry. The Canadian church has had a wide range of opportunities during past decades to serve in different contexts—rural, urban, church planting, First Nations, and international students. The Canadian Baptists, with whom we are now linked, for example, began in 1889, and have engaged Canadian culture through multifaceted ministries such as church plants, contextual outreach, mission catalysts, social justice, and ministry to refugees.

The second area of strength I observe is the rich array of church and mission resources. These resources are available for pastoral training and for the development of emerging church leaders. Resources also come in the form of finances, facilities, and systems that can make church ministry more effective. Our denomination, for example, has created clear guidelines for ministry placement (through a manual on the topic) and for human resources (through the personnel handbook), offers ongoing means of communication (through the Canadian Baptist magazine and several e-news services for church, pastors, and youth), provides annual grants for new ministry endeavours, and has given upgrades in ministry and leadership skills for emerging and established pastoral leaders (through new pastors' orientation and Reignite conferences).

Two Areas for Growth

In addition to these two areas of strength, I observe two areas for potential growth for the church in Canada. First, it seems to me that, given the changing times and circumstances in the nation, there is a need for more willingness on the part of the Canadian church to make needed changes in how to minister—for example, providing more training for church planters and evangelists.

One observable change in the Canadian church landscape has been the decline in attendance over recent decades. While there is admittedly some variation in the statistics, the clear trend over the last fifty years is a considerable decline in weekly church attendance.

Another major change in Canada over the last few decades has been the steady replacement of Christian values with secular ones. Bruce Clemenger, president of the Evangelical Fellowship of Canada, observed that Canada is in transition: "In the aftermath of a period of rapid secularization, Canada is searching for a clearer sense of its identity amidst the diversity of culture, race, religion, lifestyle, social, and political visions."[1]

In light of this trend, the church in Canada could benefit from a greater willingness to make major adjustments in ministry. One such adjustment is the move toward becoming more incarnational, integral, or missional in our approach to ministry. As GCF-Canada has learned the importance of adding value to our community and of loving our neighbour, the church in Canada can also be more intentional in doing this kind of missional ministry to those in our community.

I also observe the need for traditional churches to be more open to recognizing the role and contribution of diaspora Christians, and of missionary churches, to the cause of Christ in Canada. According to the United Nations Development Program, there are now 214 million international migrants. All nations have been affected by this international mass migration.

By the end of 2008, Canada had a total of 302,303 foreign workers as temporary migrant workers, had granted initial entry to 233,971 foreign students, had welcomed 27,956 refugees, and had given 236,758 people permission to make Canada their home as permanent immigrants. Of these, the top ten source countries for permanent immigrants were (in descending order) China, India, the Philippines, the United States, Pakistan, the United Kingdom, Iran, South Korea, France, and Colombia. According to Canada's migration experts, visible minorities or non-Caucasian Canadians are predicted to dominate Canada's three megacities (Toronto, Montreal, and Vancouver) by 2017.

1. Jim Coggins, "The State of the Canadian Church," *Canadian Christianity* (21 December 2007), www.canadianchristianity.com/ faith/state-canadian-church-part-iii -christians-danger-persecuted-minority.

In other words, the immigrants who come to Canada are a huge mission field. They can be reached for Jesus while they are here among us. Immigrant Christians can also be mobilized to partner with missionary and established churches to serve other immigrants as well as Canadian-born residents. The sooner established churches can see the potential of the diaspora, and the value of missionary churches, the better prepared the church of Canada will be to have an intentionally intercultural ministry and to develop a fresh or renewed passion for church-planting.

THE FUTURE: WHAT MISSIONARY CHURCHES AND ESTABLISHED CHURCHES CAN LEARN FROM EACH OTHER

Finally, I would like to offer two lessons that can be learned from missionary churches, and two lessons that can be learned from established churches. These two sets of lessons can help us see our shared value and unique contribution in building the body of Christ in Canada.

Two Lessons that Established Churches Can Learn from Missionary Churches

The first lesson that can be learned from missionary churches is their zeal in starting church plants and new ministries. These churches and leaders bring with them the passion and determination to plant churches and to pioneer new work in Canada as their host country, coming as they do from thriving, dynamic ministries in their home countries. The leaders of these missionary churches have either been officially sent to Canada to do ministry (as is my case and that of GCF ministry), or have arrived as new immigrants, later sensing the call of God to be part of church ministry in Canada. Either way, missionary churches thrive with a sense of destiny, eagerness, and passion for Jesus.

The second major lesson that can be contributed by missionary churches is a flexibility of approach and creativity of method in order to fulfill the mission in any area. Being relatively new in Canada, missionary churches are teachable and eager to learn how to become effective in ministry, given the different set of contexts, cultures, and circumstances. They are quick to make changes, open to experiment, and keen on flexing whenever there is a need to adjust. They are committed to becoming students of culture and people in their area of assignment.

Two Lessons that Missionary Churches Can Learn from Established Churches

I also see two lessons that missionary churches can learn from established churches. The first is the importance of stable structures and support systems for the church's ministry. The stability that these resources offer comes out of a wealth of experience in doing faithful ministry, and surfaces from a reservoir of programs and projects that worked in their time and context. From these sets of effective practices have arisen principles and perspectives that missionary churches need to consider in their new work.

The second crucial lesson to be gleaned from established churches is the depth of their understanding of different cultures and varying contexts for ministry in Canada. The established churches have been faithful ministers over the past decades. They have been witnesses to changes in Canadian culture and in their communities in relation to different aspects of life. Brian Stiller, former president of Tyndale University College and Seminary, observed that the established Canadian church has a better sense of how the Gospel touches the intellectual, social, physical, and spiritual dimensions of life.[2] Missionary churches and leaders must learn this lesson, especially those of us who are simply content to proclaim the good news of Jesus without being sensitive to the social needs of the poor and dispossessed.

My prayer for the church in Canada is that our missionary and established churches can learn how much we need each other and that we are partners in building God's kingdom in Canada and beyond.

2. Ibid.

Green Shoots 4
Transforming Communities

Neighbourhood Life Ministry
Edmonton, Alberta

For Karen Wilk, the new way of doing church started the day she and her husband, Steve, decided to shoot themselves out of the "attractional vacuum cleaner" church and connect with their neighbours.

"We were acquainted with a few of them, primarily through our kids' activities, but there was little more to our relationships," says Karen, a Christian Reformed pastor at Edmonton's The River Community Church—itself a thriving church plant, established in 2003. Truth be told, she admits, the Wilk family was so busy, not least with church, that its members were more likely to avoid stopping to talk to neighbours. "But after a while, you have to pay attention to the angst in your soul, and something was definitely missing," says Karen.

Convening in a school gymnasium, the Sunday service at Karen's home church typically attracts 350 worshippers but, as gratifying as the attractional success of The River's weekly gatherings were, Karen came to a hard realization. "People in our neighbourhoods—people who needed to know how much God loved them and how good is his kingdom—weren't coming," she says. "And if God is a sending God, and we are his sent ones, surely that must mean more than inviting people to church, to participating in our events, programs, and services—no matter how good they are."

Lingering in Karen's inner ear was the second great commandment: "Love your neighbour as yourself." So, in 2007, she embarked on a journey of discovering what God might be up to in her neighbourhood—of loving her neighbours and serving with them, in order to make their shared community a better place to live, a place that emulated the *shalom* of God's kingdom.

"The question was, what would happen if we moved from being a come-and-see church to a go-and-be church?" she says. And she knew the answer had to begin with her. For starters, she and her family decided to host a neighbourhood Christmas open house. "We made colourful invites and put them in the mailboxes of everyone on our street—we were too chicken to knock on their doors." The first responders rang her doorbell before she had her coat off. "We just had to come and see who would do such a thing, inviting strangers into their home!" they said.

Once she had become intentionally present in her neighbourhood, sharing the stories of "what God was up to out there," Karen began to discover others, throughout Edmonton and beyond, who were also seeking to serve as the presence of Jesus where they lived. She saw the huge potential for engaging God's people in his mission, simply by sending them to love their neighbours. Her colleagues at The River, as well as at Home Missions of the Christian Reformed Churches of North America, encouraged and supported her in this new direction, which is called Neighbourhood Life Ministry.

The next step was to find likeminded people in her west-end residential neighbourhood who were willing to collaborate in the new missional venture. "It took at least another year, and a lot of creativity, before we found other Christians living in the vicinity," she recalls. Now, however, the inter-denominational group has swelled to a dozen people, who meet every other Monday evening for supper, prayer, Scripture, and "responding to what God is up to in the neighbourhood," she says.

Since then, other Christian groups have sprung up in her neighbouhood, and a number of congregations in Alberta and British Columbia have been "casting the vision, and equipping, encouraging, and empowering their members to 'go and do likewise' in their neighbourhoods," says Karen.

The mandate of these groups is to live intentionally as disciples of Jesus in close connection with their neighbours, to learn their concerns and needs, and basically to do whatever needs doing. They inhabit their home streets by engaging in practices shaped by three postures summarized by the words *among*, *in*, and *with*: living *among* neighbours, abiding *in* Christ, and serving *with* others. "We practise hospitality, pray for our neighbours, and come alongside their needs and concerns, which could be anything from helping senior citizens to supporting a neighbourhood soccer team," says Karen. She recalls how, after the suicide of their alcoholic father, two local teenage boys found refuge for a time with some caring local residents, thanks to one of the groups in the vicinity.

In her home district, Karen and her Christian colleagues have helped create a "neighbourhood engagement team." Its most ambitious project has been the conversion of a forbidding vacant lot, formerly a gas station, into a community park. After a few setbacks, the owners, a large oil company, agreed to lease the 70,000-square-foot parcel of land to the community for one dollar a year.

The group is now gathering volunteers and seeking donations from individuals and local businesses. Its hope is to transform this bleak, formerly petrochemical-contaminated space into a meeting place with grass, trees, rocks, benches, and a gazebo. "It has a great location, next door to a coffee shop, and it shares the intersection with the local school and a senior citizens' housing complex, so it will be well used," she says. "Parents can gather there as they wait to pick up their children from school, and people can drink their coffee in the gazebo."

Not too far away, in an inner-city neighbourhood, other followers of Jesus with a similar vision are participating in a block-to-block initiative to create a safer community, as well as a people's garden, which will help provide food for needy residents.

Local congregations are facilitating the movement by freeing up their members to get involved in their neighbourhoods. One church has set aside $5,000 for neighbourhood initiatives. Another has purchased two large barbecues, canopies, folding tables, and an inflatable bouncy castle for block parties.

As a member of the national team of Forge Canada, a church training network, Karen remains passionate about multiplying missional communities in neighbourhoods across the country. "God is at work in and through all kinds of people, from many different tribes, in all kinds of neighbourhoods—from rural farms to urban apartment buildings, from young families to empty nesters, from young singles on their own to senior citizens in housing complexes," says Karen. "It's an organic, subversive movement and I am so thankful and excited to be a part of it."[3]

D.S.

---

3. For more on Karen's mission, see her guidebook, *Don't Invite Them to Church: Moving from a Come and See to a Go and Be Church* (Grand Rapids, MI: Faith Alive Christian Resources, 2010).

Many churches begin among a specific sociological grouping: Chinese immigrants, suburban middle-class families, those who love medieval liturgy, or young urban professionals. Yet the vision of the New Testament is much wider than any of these: it is of a church where the barrier between Jew and Gentile has gone, where slave and master worship side by side, where "all tribes and tongues and nations" belong to the same family. Yet the movement from a "niche church" to all-inclusive church is difficult to make—even when it is seen as an ideal—and many churches do not even try. Sam Owusu, inspired by the biblical vision, has made that journey from monocultural church to multicultural church to intercultural church. That vision, and the story of Calvary Worship Centre in Vancouver, can guide others of us to attempt the same journey to a church that is, in a unique sense, a taste of the world to come.

8

"To All Nations"

The Distinctive Witness
of the Intercultural Church

Sam Owusu

IF YOU TAKE A bus in Vancouver, Toronto, or Calgary—or in any number of other cities in Canada—you will be impressed by the vast array of languages, skin colours, and cultures around you. Our world, our nation, and our local communities are rapidly changing. Immigration has had a profound effect on the complexion of our nation. It has shaped our past, and it is setting the course for the future.

Canada is becoming the most diverse country in the world. Very few Canadian communities are free from the touch of immigration, especially in the urban centres. This is our world. This is our new society. We are not of one kind, we are of many. According to Statistics Canada, by the year 2025 all of Canada's population growth will be due to immigration.[1]

In one sense, Canada has always been a country of cultural diversity. Even before the first landing of European settlers on Canadian soil in the sixteenth century, the First Nations were already diverse in culture and in language.

1. "Canada's Ethnocultural Mosaic, 2006 Census: National Picture: Visible Minority Population Surpasses 5-Million Mark." See http://www12.statcan.ca/census-recensement/2006/as-sa/97-562/p5-eng.cfm.

Today, Canada's rapid growth in cultural diversity poses a unique challenge to Canadians and to the church. How will we welcome others who are different from us into our communities and our churches? How will we create safe environments, so that those who are different from us will feel comfortable in our churches?[2] Dr. Martin Luther King said of the United States in the 1950s, "It is appalling that the most segregated hour of Christian America is eleven o'clock on Sunday morning."[3] Unfortunately, this is also often true of Canada, even today. How is it possible that different races can work together and go to school together, but so seldom worship together?

Canada will not be won to Christ by establishing more churches like the majority of those we now have. In an increasingly multicultural and urban society, several types of people do not fit into traditional homogeneous churches: interracial couples and families; people of ethnic minorities who prefer speaking English to their native language; urbanites who appreciate living, working, and ministering in the midst of ethnic diversity; and Generation-Xers who often despise racial separatism. To these we may add many second-, third-, and fourth-generation immigrants, and those living in ethnically changing urban neighbourhoods.[4]

In the past, homogeneous churches serving discrete cultural groups have been seen as the most productive in terms of growth. There are certainly contexts where a monocultural church is still culturally appropriate or perhaps the only option. However, in the present social milieu, the church urgently needs to consider other models. It will take multicultural and intercultural churches—interethnic and heterogeneous—to reach these growing groups.

Having said that, there are not only strategic reasons for thinking about this kind of church but, more fundamentally, biblical and theological reasons.

2. One Canadian agency addressing this issue is the Centre for Community Based Research in Kitchener, ON. See http://www.communitybasedresearch.ca, and particularly their "Welcoming Church" project.

3. Martin Luther King, Jr., *Stride toward Freedom: The Montgomery Story* (Boston: Beacon Press, 1958), 202.

4. North American Mission Board of the Southern Baptist Convention (NAMB), *A Guide for Planting Multicultural Churches* (Alpharetta, GA: NAMB, 1999), 6.

THE BIBLICAL MANDATE

God's intention for creation has always been multicultural. God is not colour blind, but colourful. Take a look at the beautiful flowers and the diverse colours of the animal kingdom. The human race is the only species that does not celebrate colour, but rather allows it to divide us.

The theme of cultural diversity runs through the whole of the Bible like a scarlet thread. As early as Genesis 10, just before the story of the Tower of Babel, the writer tells us about the descendants of Noah through his three sons, Shem, Ham, and Japheth. The writer makes an interesting comment about Japheth's descendants: "from these the coastland peoples spread. These are the descendants of Japheth in their lands, with their own language, by their families, in their nations" (Gen 10:5). In other words, as Walter Brueggemann expresses it, Genesis 10 gives us "a verbal 'map' of the world."[5] The nations are certainly united in their origins, but they are also diverse in the places they live, the languages they speak, and their nationhood. At the beginning of the story of Noah's descendants, the writer had already repeated God's earlier command to humankind to be "fruitful and multiply and fill the earth" (Gen 9:1 cf. 1:28). This serves to underscore that the spreading of these descendants into new lands is actually obedience to God.

Seen in this way, then, diversity is one way that God's intention for creation is fulfilled. A diverse humanity was God's intention all along. Yet if diversity is God's intention, what should we make of the story of Babel, where the scattering of peoples appears to be a punishment? In its context, it is sandwiched between the emergence of different nations in chapter 10 and the calling of Abraham to bless the nations in chapter 12. Scholars have suggested that the key to understanding Babel lies in knowing why the builders built. The writer describes the people as saying to one another, "Come, let us build ourselves a city, and a tower with its top in the heavens, and let us make a name for ourselves; otherwise we shall be scattered abroad upon the face of the whole earth" (Gen 11:4). Although some readers have focused on the pride implied in the phrase of "making a name" for themselves, the greater motivation behind the tower is the fear of being "scattered" across the earth. They wanted "to stay in their own safe mode of homogeneity," as Brueggemann puts it. They were afraid of being separated and differentiated from one another, since this would undermine their desire to form a united front against God. Brueggemann

5. Walter Brueggemann, *Genesis* (Atlanta: John Knox Press, 1982), 91.

explains it like this: "There are two kinds of unity. On one hand, God wills a unity which permits and encourages scattering. The unity willed by God is that all humankind shall be in covenant with him (9:8–11) and with him only, responding to his purposes, relying on his life-giving power. Then there is a different kind of unity, sought by a fearful humanity organized against the purposes of God. This unity attempts to establish a cultural, human oneness without reference to the threats, promises, or mandates of God. This is a self-made unity in which humanity has a 'fortress mentality.' It seeks to survive by its own resources."[6]

God judges Babel by doing the very thing humankind hoped to avoid: scattering them. Yet even that was a blessing in disguise. As Stanley Hauerwas explains, "God's confusing the people's language as well as his scattering of them was meant as a gift. For by being so divided, by having to face the otherness created by separateness of language and place, people were given resources necessary to recognize their status as creatures."[7]

In the chapter immediately following this one, the call of Abraham takes centre stage. This is crucial for understanding the church in our multicultural world. The story of Abraham is, I believe, first and foremost a story about God's mission in the world. God's words are these: "Go from your country and your kindred and your father's house to the land that I will show you. I will make of you a great nation, and I will bless you, and make your name great, so that you will be a blessing. . . . and in you all the families of the earth shall be blessed" (Gen 12:1–3). Abraham's call involves being a blessing to many nations—and this is to happen through one particular clan with its roots in the city of Ur of the Chaldeans. They are to be the instruments of God's mission, chosen with the intention that they would be a blessing to many peoples, to express God's universal love for all peoples.

This is why Israel is to be distinct from its neighbours ("a holy people"), as the covenants with Moses and then David would later emphasize. This uniqueness is not for the benefit of Israel alone. Rather, God's purpose is to reach out through Israel to all nations, peoples, and cultures in order to bless them. Missiologist Charles Van Engen states that "Israel had no special merit or significance in and of itself. Its uniqueness did not stem from its ancestry, nor its history, race, culture, or language. It stemmed from Yahweh's unique call. Yet precisely because of Yahweh's

6. Ibid, 99–100.

7. Stanley Hauerwas, "The Church as God's New Language," in *A Hauerwas Reader*, ed. John Berkman and Michael Cartwright (Durham, NC: Duke University Press, 2001), 145.

unique purposes, Israel considered itself different, having a special destiny, a unique mission which set it apart from all other races, cultures, tribes, families, and nations."[8] Lesslie Newbigin summarizes the point like this: God's "love and commitment are to Israel as the instrument of God's love for all nations."[9]

As the Bible unfolds, God reminds the people of Israel that this is their call: "I am the LORD. . . . I have given you as a covenant to the people, *a light to the nations*, to open the eyes that are blind, to bring out the prisoners from the dungeon" (Isa 42:6–7).

Finally, in Jesus of Nazareth, a descendant of Abraham and the Son of God, this mission reaches its fulfillment. Hence his so-called "Great Commission": "All authority in heaven and on earth has been given to me. Go therefore and make disciples of all nations, baptizing them in the name of the Father and of the Son and of the Holy Spirit, and teaching them to obey everything that I have commanded you. And remember, I am with you always, to the end of the age." (Matt 28:18–19) The mission is inclusive of all: "Go to *all* nations, teach them *all* things, and I will be with you *always*." The church has been chosen and set apart, not to segregate itself from the world, but to engage the world on behalf of God's command to bring blessing. So what happened next?

CROSS-CULTURAL MISSION IN ACTS

On the Day of Pentecost, the Holy Spirit descended upon the disciples in the upper room (Acts 2). People who had been separated by geography, culture, and language suddenly found themselves speaking, hearing, and understanding others with whom they had little in common. This is Babel in reverse!

Not that all was plain sailing for the church in Acts. Chapter 6 introduces us to the first intercultural church conflict. The Christians in Jerusalem were all Jews, yet made up of two language groups, Greek-speakers (the "Hellenists") and Hebrew-speakers. The Hellenists complained that their widows were being discriminated against (Acts 6:1). This story offers us a clear illustration of the way in which the apostles dealt with the problem of cultural division in the church. According to Rene Padilla, "A

8. Charles Van Engen, *God's Missionary People: Rethinking the Purpose of the Local Church* (Grand Rapids: Baker House, 1987), 16.

9. Lesslie Newbigin, *The Gospel in a Pluralist Society* (Grand Rapids: WCC/Eerdmans, 1989), 84.

so true!

modern Church Growth expert might have suggested the creation of two distinct denominations, one for Palestinian Jews and another for Greek Jews. That would certainly have been a practical solution to the tensions existing between the two conflicting homogenous units. We are told, however, that the apostles called the community together and asked them to choose seven men who would be responsible for the daily distribution. The unity of the church across cultural barriers was thus preserved."[10]

The lesson still had to be repeated and reinforced in many ways, however. The struggle of the early church to reach "all nations" is particularly evident in Acts, chapter 10, where Peter had to be shown a vision three times before he accepted that he was to enter the house of a Gentile. He finally came to the realization that "God shows no partiality, but *in every nation* anyone who fears him and does what is right is acceptable to him" (Acts 10:34–35). When Peter told the leaders of the church in Jerusalem of this experience, Luke tells us, "When they heard this, they were silenced. And they praised God, saying, 'Then God has given even to the Gentiles the repentance that leads to life'" (Acts 11:18). Like Peter, they had come to understand that the Gospel is not just for Jews but for Gentiles also.

Paul was also convinced of this, insisting that "There is no longer Jew or Greek, there is no longer slave or free, there is no longer male and female; for all of you are one in Christ Jesus" (Gal 3:28). Not that those distinctives are erased, of course. The particularities of ethnicity, sexuality, and socio-economics remain. Yet there is now a universal oneness in Jesus Christ: "Christ is all, and in all" (Col 3:11). Similarly, in Ephesians, Paul recognizes that Gentiles and Jews are distinctive, and yet that they are brought together into one new family in Jesus Christ (Eph 3:6, 3:15).

In spite of this emphasis on unity, there is no insistence that the culture of Christians must be uniform. The Gospel does not mean that Jews must live like Gentiles, or that Gentiles have to live like Jews. Paul follows the ruling of the Jerusalem Council in Acts 15 in affirming cultural differences, yet creating a new oneness in Jesus Christ.

Even now, however, the issue has not been settled for everyone, as the next verse shows: "Now those who were scattered because of the persecution that took place over Stephen traveled as far as Phoenicia, Cyprus, and Antioch, and they spoke the word to no one except Jews" (Acts 11:19). This is as if I, as an African, came to Vancouver and insisted on sharing the Gospel only with Africans. As ridiculous as this may sound, this is

---

10. René Padilla, *Mission between the Times: Essays on the Kingdom* (Grand Rapids: W.B. Eerdmans, 1985), 89.

exactly what we are perpetuating in most of our churches today. Perhaps it is another example of people wanting "to stay in their own safe mode of homogeneity."

As the story unfolds, however, Luke tells us that "some men of Cyprus and Cyrene, . . . on coming to Antioch, spoke to the Hellenists also, proclaiming the Lord Jesus" (Acts 11:20). This was truly a significant step. This was the origin of the intercultural church that grew up in the city of Antioch. Acts 13 describes the diverse leadership of this church. Is it any wonder that the believers were first called Christians in Antioch? Or that the first missionary movement with Paul and Barnabas began out of this intercultural church? It is no surprise to know that "the hand of the Lord was with them" (Acts 11:21), or that when Barnabas arrived in Antioch he "saw the grace of God" and "he rejoiced" (Acts 11:23). Almost certainly one thing he rejoiced at was the intercultural nature of this congregation. Perhaps it is not surprising that three times in the description of this church we read the phrase "large numbers." There was apparently something very attractive about this community.

The New Testament offers us one more vision of an intercultural church, and it comes in the Book of Revelation.

A NEW INTERCULTURAL WORLD

Throughout Revelation, John emphasizes the fact that Christ is bringing together people "from every tribe and language and people and nation" (Rev 5:9, 7:9). In the vision of the New Jerusalem, a picture of the perfected Church, illuminated by "the glory of God," there is a plurality of "nations" that will "walk by its light, and the kings of the earth will bring their glory into it. . . . People will bring into it the glory and the honor of the nations" (Rev 21:24–26). Earl Palmer understands this phrase, "the glory and honour of the nations," to indicate that diverse human cultures will be welcomed into God's new world: "The old distinctions are no longer barriers between people. But the uniqueness of each person and tribe is preserved as part of their glory . . . In this vision, [we have] the fulfilment of the ways in which we have been originally created . . ."[11]

Every Christian can look forward to that day when "every nation, tribe, people and language" will stand before the throne of God. In fact, it is not until the Gospel has gone "throughout the world, as a testimony to

11. Earl F. Palmer, *Mastering the New Testament: 1, 2, 3 John and Revelation* (Vancouver: Word Publishing, 1982), 246.

all the nations" (Matt 24:14) that the end will come and the multicultural feast will begin. The church is incomplete until it reflects all the cultures and peoples Christ came to save.

From the New Testament perspective, then, the church is a new community, a new race composed of people of all ethnicities, tribes, and cultures. Therefore, people of all races, traditions, and cultures can learn to live, work, and worship together in harmony in Christ. John Stott, in his commentary on Ephesians, puts it this way: "Through Jesus Christ, who died for sinners and was raised from the dead, God is creating something entirely new, not just a new life for individuals but for a new society. Paul sees an alienated humanity being reconciled, a fractured humanity being united, even a new humanity being created. It is a magnificent vision."[12]

Anyone who has been part of an intercultural church would agree that such a church is truly a magnificent sight to behold. The richness of its diversity, particularly as expressed in worship, is awesome.

How the Church of Jesus Christ deals with the complexity of this multicultural, postmodern ethos will tell the world whether or not it has any reason to listen to the message we proclaim. If it is morally and spiritually imperative to integrate our schools, workplaces, and neighbourhoods, how can we simultaneously preserve the segregation that we practise every Sunday morning? What, then, can we do?

As new students from Ghana arriving at Regent College, Vancouver, in 1991, my wife Rosemond and I soon realized that there were four kinds of churches in Vancouver: white, black, yellow, and brown. After much prayer and fasting, we felt that God was calling us to begin a church that would embrace all nations. We held our first service on 7 June 1992, with four people in the congregation. The church grew slowly, but for the first three years the church was made up almost entirely of Africans. This was not what we had been aiming at. We were Christians claiming the promise of Pentecost that the Gospel has broken down ethnic and cultural barriers. We were also parents of three, longing for our children to grow up in a society where the colour of their skin did not matter. Not surprisingly, we found ourselves asking, how can the church of Jesus Christ become a witness in a multicultural world?

We realized that if we were to become truly international, we would need to take deliberate steps to incorporate other nations into our worship, leadership, staffing, and ministry teams. Since then the church has

12. John Stott, *The Message of Ephesians* (Downers Grove: InterVarsity Press, 1986), 146.

grown to become a ministry representing over seventy-five nations from all continents, gathering weekly to worship in many tongues but with one heart. We meet in three campuses and run three services on our main campus in New Westminster with an average attendance of a thousand people each week.

What steps does it take, then, to move a congregation from being a monocultural (or even a multicultural) church to being an intercultural one?

SOME PRACTICAL STEPS

First, we must *pray*. There are no simple solutions or shortcuts. Jesus said, "Apart from me you can nothing" (John 15:5). The leadership of the church must soak themselves in prayer for direction and vision. When our leadership made the decision to move from being an all-black congregation to being an intentionally intercultural church, we spent almost a year seeking and asking God for the right direction and timing.

Second, we need to *prepare the church*. We need to be intentional in teaching the biblical and theological foundations of the intercultural church. We need to take the necessary time to instill these biblical convictions into the leaders. This step cannot be rushed. Leaders need time to engage in Bible study, to grasp biblical principles of diversity, and to own them before there can be any forward movement.

Healthy diversity will need at some point to be reflected in the building blocks of the church's organizational structure. But a biblical mindset is the foundation upon which such a structure is built. This foundation is the belief system, the core values a visionary pastor must infuse into his or her leadership and congregation.

Furthermore, we need to make sure that the church understands both sides of the intercultural coin. There are pros and cons to the change, and we must be careful to share the whole picture—especially what we will have to give up. This is important because even the most kindly intentioned among us takes it for granted at a subconscious level that, as our relationship with people of other cultures develops, it will do so on our terms. That is, these other folk will become like us—not that we will become like them. They will learn English, the rules of baseball, how to drive a car, and how to eat hamburgers! Yet we have to guard against these assumptions.

Third, we will need to take *intentional steps*. I have spoken to a few pastors who say they would welcome people of various cultures to be part of their church. I suspect that what they really mean is that they are welcome as <u>long they become like their hosts</u>. <u>We need to make our goal not assimilation but accommodation</u>. Assimilation means "to integrate somebody into a larger group so that differences are minimized or eliminated," whereas accommodation means "to adjust actions in response to somebody's needs."[13] Thus it is the responsibility of those in the dominant culture <u>to adjust their own attitudes and actions in order to include others</u>. At Calvary Worship Center, for example, in order to become intercultural, we had to forego singing a lot of our much-loved Swahili African songs in our worship services. Our intention was that those who did not come from Africa would not feel excluded, and we wanted to add the music of other cultures.

Fourth, we need to empower *diverse leaders*. <u>This is where credibility begins.</u> In Acts 13:1, Luke lists the prophets and teachers at Antioch not only by name but also by saying something of their cultural origins: Barnabas was from Cyprus, Simeon (a Hebrew name) was "called Niger" (black), Lucius of Cyrene was from North Africa, Manaen was related to the court of Herod, and Saul was from Tarsus in Cilicia—representative of the diversity of this intercultural church.[14] In like manner, we must seek to represent each culture we hope to welcome, at every level of organization and leadership, whenever possible. The Lord will honour our intentions by bringing the right people. Our pastoral team at Calvary Worship Center now comprises two Caucasians, one African, and one East Indian. Our board, deacons, and ministry leaders are as diverse as our church community.

Fif<u>th, we must pursue *cross-cultural competence*.</u> To build a healthy intercultural church, we must commit ourselves to understand what seem to us the idiosyncrasies of cultures different from ours, and why people do things the way they do. This will move us beyond ourselves, toward <u>a deeper understanding of another person's perspectiv</u>e. Some of the perspectives that at first seem strange and alien may then find their way into the life of the congregation. This may include, for example, expressive worship such as dancing and the clapping of hands.

13. Anne Soukhanov, ed., *Encarta World English Dictionary* (New York: St. Martin's Press, 1999).

14. John R. W.Stott, *The Spirit, the Church and the World: The Message of Acts* (Downers Grove: InterVarsity Press, 1990), 216.

Sixth, we need to study *our community*. We need to familiarize ourselves with the demographics of our community and its needs.[15] Ministering to a person's felt needs opens the door for us at some point to minister to the real need of forgiveness. Community-service type ministries not only meet the needs of the community, but they also build a bridge across which the Gospel can be shared. For example, at Calvary Worship Center we provide English as a Second Language courses and immigrant services for our community. Many people have decided to follow Christ as a result of the relationships and the caring they have found there.

We need, seventh, to broaden our *worship styles* and allow more variety of expression in worship. Believers need to be taught that there is no one right style of music or way of worship. These are usually based on no more than personal preferences acquired within a particular church culture. We need to emphasize not the *how* of worship but the *heart* of worship. People must be given the freedom to express their heartfelt worship with music styles that engage them. And those will be different for every culture.

And finally, we need to *keep at it.* Don't give up. Major changes like this can take a year and often more. Trust is built on time and a good track record. We need to accept the challenge of mission, rather than seeking to withdraw or escape from it. The Gospel is our comfort and our strength; at the same time, it is radical, and will demonstrate that it is "the power of God for salvation to everyone who has faith" (Rom 1:16).

There are many reasons for Canadian churches to consider transitioning into intercultural churches. In some cases, the impetus will be sociological realities—the need for justice, the question of economic equity, or simply a desire for a unified society to thrive. In other cases, it may spring from a straightforward desire for churches to grow, or for older churches to flourish in neighbourhoods whose ethnic character is changing. I would suggest, however, that the most basic and convincing reason is the universal scope of God's mission as depicted in scripture and explained by Jesus to a man called Nicodemus: that God so loved the world—with all its many peoples, tribes, tongues, and nations—that he gave his Son.

15. Glenn Smith's chapter 14 (page 218) discusses in some detail how to do this.

One of the challenges of mission is that of enculturation. As Jesus entered into a specific culture in the Middle East in a particular point in history, so the Gospel enters into particular cultures and expresses itself in unique ways. So far, so good. But the tension occurs over particular expressions of the Gospel in any given culture: is this authentically Christian, or has it lost something essential in translation? An old joke says, "The translator is always a traitor." The problem, of course, is that in the case of the Gospel every one of us is a translator. None of us has an objective place from which to criticize. In this chapter, Mark MacDonald writes about how the Gospel has been enculturated in First Nations cultures in Canada, and what the rest of us can learn from that experience. Mark himself has Native ancestry and grew up in an Indigenous environment. Most of his adult life has been spent in ministry in Indigenous contexts, so he speaks with authority born of long and wide experience.

9

The Surprising and Improbable Mission of God among the Indigenous Peoples of Canada

Mark MacDonald

THE DAMAGE DONE BY Western churches to Indigenous Peoples in North America is well known. Although the story as it is told is broadly accurate, however, it does not fully portray what happened. The popular story does nothing to address the ongoing dispossession of Indigenous Peoples. Neither does it seem able to generate insights that might catalyze healing between the church and the People of the Land. Indeed, for most Christians, the story appears to generate little more than defensiveness and missiological inertia.

But there is another, mostly hidden, aspect of this history that should not be missed. The story of the Gospel in Indigenous life is also an account of the trajectory of the living Word of God among Indigenous Peoples. This is the Word that became incarnate in Jesus. But it is also the Word that shaped, and continues to shape, Creation. This Word moves through history towards the end God has planned for all. And this same Word interacts with humanity and its many cultures towards this goal, creating all that forms and sustains life among us.

When one looks at the history of Christianity among Indigenous Peoples through this lens, there are some unexpected lessons to be learned. Not least is an account of how the Gospel is able to rise above the limitations of those who bear it, to "jump ship," institutionally speaking, and to find a home in unlikely places. This insight is turning out to be the launching pad of a spiritual movement that is shaping Indigenous life across North America.

The issue is not that church institutions are so good or so bad (speaking of them as human institutions); rather, what is significant is that God's horizon for the Church (speaking of it as a heavenly initiative) is greater than the consequences of human action, human evil, and human error. Since the Gospel has proven to be much greater than the intent, moral integrity, and spiritual capacity of church institutions and practices,[1] we can point to some surprising—even improbable—positive developments among Indigenous Peoples in Canada and all of North America.[2]

The most meaningful aspect of this story, in terms of both theology and mission, is the affirmation that the Word of God was present and active in Indigenous life, even before Western missionaries arrived. Even though the Word is present in all of Creation and in every People, it has often been unacknowledged in the Western churches' interaction with Indigenous Peoples. This is not to say that this presence in Indigenous life is somehow more important than other peoples' experience and grace. We should acknowledge, however, that the "seeds of the Word"[3] are present in all of life, and in every culture. This very simple and ancient affirmation not only critiques the missionary practice of colonialism: it challenges the Church to enter a more missiologically dynamic understanding of God's presence in Creation and culture. Tracing the path of the Word of God from its historical manifestations to its living connection with the contemporary life of Indigenous People will inform and shape the work of the whole Church.

COLONIALISM

It is unnecessary to recount in any detail the failings of the missions of the colonial churches in North America. As I have said, everyone knows this story—in broad strokes, at least. If we understand the mission of God as

1. Cf. Phil 1:15–25.

2. I acknowledge that for many Indigenous Peoples in North America, the Land is known as Turtle Island.

3. Justin Martyr, *Second Apology*, chapter 8. See www.earlychristianwritings.com/text/justinmartyr-secondapology.html. The phrase is also found in "Ad Gentes," *Documents of Vatican II*, ed. Austin P. Flannery (Grand Rapids, MI: Eerdmans, 1974), 825.

being the Incarnation of the Word of God in the culture of a people, any mission strategy that advocates the destruction of any culture looks about as appropriate as promoting death in order to cure sickness. There are, however, a number of aspects of this misadventure that still impinge on the churches' relationship with Indigenous Peoples today.

The approach of colonial missions to Indigenous Peoples emerged from a number of theological and political sources. It was animated by some very rugged cultural assumptions and had many detrimental effects. It may be helpful to consider these assumptions as systemically rooted and worked out in law and governance, using the lens of what has been called the Doctrine of Discovery.[4]

The right of discovery assumes that discovered land is uninhabited, and gives the right of ownership, exploitation, and governance to the discoverers. In order for the concept of discovery to be applied to Indigenous Peoples, it was necessary to contend that their way of life was so primitive that it gave the Western nations the right—and perhaps the duty—to "civilize" them according to Western norms—an argument that has appeared in Canadian courts as recently as the early 1990s. In ecclesiastical form, the Doctrine described Indigenous Peoples as being a pre-civilized and non-Christian (or non-Western) form of life. Generally, it was thought that they were unable to become Christian until they abandoned their former primitive way of life and developed a capacity to mimic Western cultural forms.

The series of assumptions centered in the Doctrine were active in church and in the broader society, and have been used over the years to justify dispossessing Indigenous People of their land and rights. In regard to the life of the church, the Doctrine of Discovery can be said to have been a part of the cover that helped to justify the growing idolatrous subservience of the Western churches to Western society, a relationship that had severe consequences for those who were beyond its cultural borders or who found themselves getting "in the way" of Western political or economic expansion. Though the Doctrine was never used as a direct argument for genocide, it was part of an openly acknowledged program to make Indigenous Peoples disappear, melting into the larger Western culture like ice in a desert.

Most would agree that the Western churches' failure to implement fully the goals of the civilizing mission was a good thing. The horrific

4. Mark MacDonald, "The Doctrine of Discovery," *First Peoples Theology Journal*, Special Edition (2010): 1–11.

outworking of policies that aimed to make people disappear were realized only in part—though it is easy to show that what happened was deadly. The ambiguous goal of proselytization has failed, at least in the sense that it sought to assimilate Indigenous Christians into a Western cultural regime. Though many Indigenous People have adopted Christianity, the institutional affiliation of the majority has never been more than nominal. To Western eyes, Indigenous People have shown only lukewarm interest in many aspects of church programming. Indigenous Peoples have shown resistance, for example, to emphasizing Sunday morning worship and have preferred, instead, to stress a regular life of prayer. Very few have shown interest in the material and administrative aspects of church membership.

Despite the challenges of church membership, an extraordinarily large number of Indigenous Peoples consider themselves Christians and at the same time continue to incorporate aspects of Indigenous values and culture into their Christian practice. Though most church agencies have applauded genuine Indigenous interest in the central doctrines of Christian faith, they have also taken a dim view of the ongoing inclination to express that faith in an Indigenous framework. It is often assumed that Indigenous practices will interfere with full integration into the churches' larger program. Further, the fact that they persistently seem uninterested and apparently unable to adapt to Western protocols has often been attributed to an underlying syncretism and a general incapacity for "advanced" forms of culture.

The assumption that Western churches' ways of doing things are self-evidently right has made it difficult to recognize what is a legitimate, creative Indigenous response to the Christian message. To Christians in the West, Western modes of worship, styles of assembly, and the Western intellectual tradition in Church teaching, are often considered non-negotiable for Christian faith. When Indigenous alternatives have developed— the hymn-singing tradition, Indigenous forms of spiritual leadership, and the adaptation of Indigenous spiritual traditions to Christian faith, for example—they have been largely ignored or suppressed.[5]

With institutional successes few and far between, it can be said that the Western churches, influenced by the system associated with the Doctrine of Discovery, have had some spectacular failures, both moral and practical. The reasons for these failures (and even the ability to see that they are failures) have often been difficult for the churches. This is, at least

5. Michael McNally, *Ojibwe Singers* (St. Paul: Minnesota Historical Society Press, 2009), 96–101.

in part, due to the assumption that any failure was caused by the supposed primitive insufficiency of the Indigenous Peoples themselves.

Only recently has there been any serious scholarly interest in those Indigenous Christian traditions that have emerged over the last few centuries. At a missiological level, the proposal that this chapter be included in a general volume on mission is a significant sign that things are changing. There is still plenty of evidence, however, that cross-cultural difficulties remain. It is still hard, for example, for Western churches to recognize progress in the life of the Indigenous church. Distinctively Indigenous Christian traditions have been widely known for over a hundred and fifty years, but they have never been well received, and only rarely encouraged, by Western church leadership.

INDIGENOUS CHRISTIAN PRACTICE

The cultural, geographical, and linguistic diversity of Indigenous Peoples makes it impossible in a chapter of this length to offer anything more than a very limited survey of distinctively Indigenous Christian practice. But perhaps the brief sample here will serve as illustrations of how seeds of the Word are present in Indigenous life and in the development of uniquely Indigenous Christian practice. At the very least, we need to understand that truly Indigenous and truly Christian practice are possible. Up till now, there has been very little work done in this area but, hopefully, increasing interest will encourage others to pick up the task of examining this vital part of the Church in North America. For the curious, those with eyes, ears, and hearts ready to receive, a simple visit to a Gospel Jamboree or an Indigenous Christian community can be very rewarding.

There are many aspects of traditional Indigenous life that have a strong positive correlation with Christian faith—many of which are sometimes less robust in the traditional Western churches. These include an emphasis on loving extended families, including practicing advanced forms of communal charity; an intense focus on the life of the Spirit as an essential aspect of a full life; an approach to the material world that has great sympathy for the Christian sacramental understanding of reality; and, perhaps most important, an understanding of the sacrificial element in life that foreshadows the gift of God in Christ. These correlations between Christian faith and Indigenous life seem to confirm that "the seed of the Word" has already been at work preparing the way for distinctively Indigenous expressions of faith. If this is so, it would seem that it is simply cultural bias that has often made it difficult for Western church leaders to appreciate the mystery of grace at work among Indigenous Peoples.[6]

When the first Episcopal bishop of Alaska reached the Yukon in the late 1890s, he discovered thousands of Gwich'in, literate in their language, familiar with Scripture, and praying the Daily Office in their caribou skin huts. Though they had little or no clergy leadership, they were deeply committed to Christian faith, developing their own traditions and teachings in a way that was compatible with and supportive to their cultural life and nomadic existence. This was the result of the work of native missionaries, Ojibwe Archdeacon Robert MacDonald and Alaska Gwich'in deacon William Loola, who had laid the groundwork for a sustainable and expanding network of Christian communities in the late 1800s. The Gwich'in churches of the Diocese of Alaska, the Diocese of the Arctic, and the Diocese of the Yukon have lived off the fat of this amazingly innovative work for over a hundred years, yet it has only rarely received notice beyond the churches of the North.

As we speculate on the reasons why this story and other examples of Indigenous faith have not been more interesting to the broader Church, a number of possibilities might be suggested. Perhaps it was thought that the work did not contribute enough to Westernization; perhaps the work was considered too unique to have any application in other situations. Whatever the answer, we have in these examples a vivid reminder of the difficulties in seeing across the persistent cross-cultural divide between Indigenous and Western churches.

The most prominent example of this cultural divide is surely the traditions of hymn singing already mentioned that have developed across North America. Known by a number of names—Prayer Meeting, Singspiration, and Gospel Jamboree, to give a few examples—they have been around since the early 1800s and have developed in First Nations, Inuit, and Metis communities. The basic outline is similar: usually a potluck meal is shared, featuring Native foods; opening prayers and hymns are followed by more hymns, interspersed with more prayer, personal testimony, stories, and Scripture readings. In some cases, there is a sermon and time for healing prayer. Especially in the Arctic, groups that attend from neighbouring communities are often sung to and, later, asked to sing to the assembly. Songs shared by family groups are often a valued part of the mix.

---

6 By contrast, Eastern Orthodoxy has demonstrated a comparatively large amount of interest in these "seeds of the Word" in Indigenous life. See Michael Oleksa, *Orthodox Alaska: A Theology of Mission* (Crestwood, NY: St. Vladimir's, 1992) and *Alaskan Missionary Spirituality* (Crestwood, NY: St. Vladimir's, 2010).

In recent years, electrified musical instruments have been added by many communities, though some, like the Ojibwe of Northern Minnesota, have resisted these innovations.

We find these same basic patterns from the East Coast First Nations, who may be the Jamboree's originators, all the way to the peoples of the West Coast, and up to the Arctic. Western church leaders were often unsupportive of the hymn-singing, as it appeared to interfere with regular Sunday attendance. Even so, these hymn singing ceremonies have persisted in popularity. I have been in attendance at hundreds of these events across North America, and it would appear that they are growing in popularity. In Manitoba and Northern Ontario, Jamborees are broadcast to surrounding communities and, in some cases, shared via the Internet.

The uniformity of the basic pattern of these practices is striking. They have developed and thrived across a stunning number of cultural, linguistic, and political boundaries. The hymn singing ceremonies of Native North America seem to resonate with traditional Indigenous culture in a way that the usual pattern of Western Sunday morning services have failed to do. The hymn singing traditions seem to provide a more adequate home to the traditional communal spirituality of Indigenous Peoples, with its base in the home and the extended family, as opposed to the church-building base of traditional Western communal spirituality. The communal meal; the songs and interaction in circular, non-hierarchical format; and the opportunity for the personal expression of spiritual experience, are all done in traditional ceremonial time, a glimpse into the time of the Spirit world to come. This is perceived by many Indigenous people to be in contrast to the cultural norms of the Western churches, even when those are informal and non-liturgical.

The hymn singing tradition is an important example of the way Indigenous traditions have spread, giving us hints of what makes things work. They show the way Indigenous values can shape Christian worship and practice, and the Word of God can shape Indigenous life—the Word becoming flesh in Indigenous communities. Hymn singing is one way that Indigenous communities can link the seeds of the Word in their pre-Christian traditions with the needs of a growing, contemporary Christian community.

Another example of a unique Indigenous emphasis in ministry is the widespread use, up until recently, of recognized lay ministers. Under a number of different names—catechist, deacon, lay reader, and lay pastor, to name a prominent few—these easily trainable, easily deployed ministers were the unsung agents of much of the stable expansion of church life among Indigenous Peoples. Today, these ministers are in decline, largely due to a focus—laudable in itself—on providing Indigenous People with just and equal access to ordained ministry. Though these lay ministries were, at least in part, the bi-product of Indigenous Peoples' lack of access to ordained ministries, the unintended consequence was an expansion of the work of the Gospel and an indigenization of the ministry of the Church.

Indigenous lay ministers were highly mobile. In places like Northern Canada, Alaska, and the Indigenous areas of the US, these workers spread out, visiting fish-camps and accompanying families as they migrated across the Land, following food. Ordained ministers, even the few who were Indigenous, focused on the development of organization and on ministries in a building or institutionalized situation. The lay ministers, on the other hand, were focused on bringing the Gospel and its way of life into people's homes and into their extended families. They were quite effective and, even though they have been a declining presence for decades, they are still well remembered in the oral history of the elders.[7]

These ministries were, perhaps by human accident and divine design, a Christian extension of the values, style, and service of similar workers in pre-Christian settings. Traditional pre- and post-Christian practice seems to have a number of parallels. People who are now known by titles like pipe-carrier—lay ministers, if you will—still today carry the meaning, message, and power of the medicine people and their ceremonies into the practical needs and circumstances of the extended Indigenous family.[8]

THE WORD OF GOD IN CONTEMPORARY INDIGENOUS LIFE

In these ways, we see that there is, and always has been, a capacity for Indigenous inculturation of the Gospel. This capacity has operated, despite considerable obstacles, in a way that has connected the cultural traditions and worldview of Indigenous Peoples from the pre-Christian period to the development of a uniquely Indigenous faith community in the present.

7. See Steven C. Dinero, "'The Lord Will Provide:' The History and Role of Episcopalian Christianity in Nets'aii Gwich'in Social Development—Arctic Village, Alaska," *Indigenous Nations Studies Journal* 1 (Spring 2003): 3–28.

8. It has been my experience that, in today's more welcoming environment, some Indigenous lay ministers function both as church-based and traditionally-based workers at the same time.

It is worth adding here that the doctrinal formulations of Indigenous faith have shown a strong preference for staying within the framework of the traditional Christian consensus. This tendency deserves further study, as it has been accomplished in its own unique way—expressing the basics of Christian theology within an Indigenous worldview—and perhaps this story will contribute new insights to the larger Church, as it seeks to inculturate Christian faith in a society that is less and less interested in the values and assumptions of Christendom. That, however, would be outside the scope of this chapter.

How then is Christian faith expanding among Indigenous communities in Canada? And what key missional ideas might be gleaned that would be of interest to the larger Church?

THE DEVELOPMENT OF GOSPEL-BASED VISION IN A COMMUNITY OF DISCIPLES

Today, Indigenous people are gathering in a number of venues to reflect on issues of inculturation in Indigenous ministry. There are a number of examples from various faith traditions. The annual Roman Catholic Tekakwitha Conference is one such. Another, the North American Indigenous Institute for Theological Studies, is largely evangelical, but includes a number of theological streams, and its annual conference attracts members who come from many organizations and ministries. The vitality of these and other discussions indicates a lively growth in Indigenous missiology.

One of the issues at these gatherings is to consider ways to extend the ministry of the Gospel and the Indigenous Christian community beyond the confines of their established churches, which are mostly found on rural Reserves. This means bringing the ministry of the Church to "remote" communities which, for Indigenous Peoples, would include prisons, distant northern communities without established churches, and urban areas, as well as the many "new" places young people are found, like universities and trade schools.

In the Anglican Church of Canada, various consultations have been held over the past few decades, picking up in frequency over the last ten years. These consultations have been geared towards Indigenous self-determination, not so much in a political or governmental sense, but more directly in a pastoral and missional sense. Some have actually defined self-determination as "becoming what God meant us to be."

Every three years, a national Sacred Circle is held for the spiritual discernment of the path ahead. These gatherings serve as the general, guiding assembly for the network of Indigenous ministry. The Sacred Circle provides the vision for the Anglican Council of Indigenous Peoples and the Office of Indigenous Ministries of the Anglican Church of Canada. As an example of what can be achieved, it is worth noting that the development of the position of National Indigenous Anglican Bishop grew out of the Sacred Circle in 2005. Arising from a subsequent Sacred Circle, the Northern Ontario Region of the Diocese of Keewatin was moved to become its own "Mission Area"; it became its own diocese in 2010, selecting Lydia Mamakwa as the first Indigenous Bishop. Then, in the summer of 2012, by a similar process, the Diocese of Saskatchewan chose Adam Halkett as their first Indigenous Bishop. Indigenous protocols were followed to make the selection, as an appropriate beginning to what they hope will be an Indigenous style of ministry. Conversations about similar developments are going on in Manitoba and British Columbia.

As these various Indigenous entities have acted, each has shown a capacity to innovate within the wider community of self-determining Indigenous Christian faith. Though there are quite a few family resemblances among the Indigenous communities across the Land, each location has something of its own approach to matters of values, faith, and practice. It has thus been necessary to allow quite a bit of room for local communities to develop their own practices. So far, there has been no instance where a practice has developed in a way that would be completely foreign to other Indigenous groups. There has therefore been quite a bit of sharing between groups. A process of transculturation—the merging and converging of cultures—has developed that will profit all of the groups involved.[9]

GOSPEL BASED DISCIPLESHIP

For the past decade, the practice of what is called Gospel Based Discipleship, a type of "dwelling in the Word," developed by North American Indigenous Peoples, has been a central element of Indigenous consultations and gatherings.[10] The Gospel reading of the day, usually taken from

9. Mark MacDonald, ed., *The Chant of Life: Inculturation and the People of the Land* (New York: Church Publishing, 2003), xxi.

10. See Craig Van Gelder and Dwight J. Zscheile, *The Missional Church in Perspective: Mapping Trends and Shaping the Conversation* (Grand Rapids, MI: Baker Academic, 2011), 151.

the Daily Eucharistic Lectionary used by Anglicans, Roman Catholics, and Lutherans, is read three times. The first time, the question is asked: "What stands out for you in this reading?" The second time, the question is, "What is God saying to us in this reading?" The third time: "What is God calling us to do?" The discussion after each reading usually, at the very least, prepares people's hearts and minds for the meeting that follows. More specifically, it is often an entry into the spiritual and theological dimensions of the business at hand. Throughout the time of the gathering, anyone may call for the Gospel to be read again, if they feel it is related to a particular discussion or to refocus the group on the deeper dimensions of the topic being discussed.

The use of Gospel Based Discipleship is now spreading beyond the consultations. Small congregations have found it useful as an alternative to sermons on Sunday or to supplement small group Scripture study. In a number of instances, it has been used to shape the formation and ongoing joint ministry of two or three leaders, as they serve in remote areas where traditional forms of leadership, such as trained ordained leadership, are unavailable. In other instances, small groups of young people, and groups of Indigenous People in urban areas, have found it helpful to use this method in the maintenance of their weekly fellowship.

Gospel Based Discipleship appears to fit well with the traditional cultural patterns of Indigenous Peoples. It removes the barriers between the business of the Church and its faith, barriers that are foreign to Indigenous People. Most important, it locates the authority of the gathered community in the wisdom of the Spirit speaking through the individual. This is more compatible with Indigenous understandings of spiritual authority, and the way that spiritual Truth is authenticated.

ELDERS

The re-emergence of this type of authority coincides with the re-emergence of the voice of the elders in Indigenous communities. Long-stifled by the protocols of Western life in government, education, and church, the elders are beginning to re-enter into the various forms of governance that are arising in what some are calling a present-day Indigenous renaissance. In the selection of area Indigenous bishops, in the ongoing operation of the Anglican Council of Indigenous Peoples, and in the Office of the National Indigenous Anglican Bishop, elders now play a key role of offering advice, counsel, and oversight for the work of the expanding Indigenous ministries network in the Anglican Church of Canada.

RECOGNIZED LAY MINISTRIES

The revival of the role of the elders is happening at the same time that uniquely Indigenous components of preparation for ministry (including ordained ministry) are being recognized. In particular, Indigenous leaders have identified the necessity of receiving instruction "on the Land." Land, in Indigenous understanding, includes the water, air, and all of the various creatures and relationships that sustain life within an area. Words like *biosphere* and *ecosphere* come close to identifying what this means, though the meanings are not identical. Foundational training for particular ministries must happen in an ecological concert of people, natural elements, and the culture of the area in which a person serves. Later training may be, and perhaps should be, in a traditional residential seminary setting, but the initial phase must happen with commitment to the Land and people where one will serve. Training and formation is presently being set up with these factors in mind at various centres across Canada.

INDIGENOUS PATTERNS OF SPIRITUAL LEADERSHIP

Coupled with this development is the identification of the unique cultural patterns of Indigenous spiritual leadership. This includes the role of recognized lay ministries, mentioned earlier. But it would also involve the recognition that effective, authenticated ministry in an Indigenous context has normally involved a circle or council of recognized leaders. Only in times of great stress or crisis would Indigenous communities follow the style of having a single leader that has been characteristic of ordained pastoral leadership in late Christendom. This means that the most effective ministry is done with a group of clergy, lay, and elders working together, making decisions together, and forming a community of ongoing learning. Since this form of leadership has in general been contrary to Western structures, it has developed slowly and gradually. At times, the transition to this kind of team ministry was unnoticed because it was initially thought to be a response to the need for non-stipendiary ministries. Though this may be true at some level, its unintended but happy consequence has been to reveal the importance and effectiveness of this Indigenous cultural pattern.

THE FUTURE

These various elements—Gospel Based Discipleship, a renewal of lay ministries, Indigenous consultations towards self-determination within the Anglican Church of Canada, the growing establishment of Indigenous styles of training for ministry, the revival of the role of elders, and the development of team ministries—are all combining together to form the basis of an authentically Indigenous expression of Anglicanism. More important to those directly involved, it is the basis for the expansion and extension of that ministry to Indigenous communities across the Land.

The hope and plan is that the process of Indigenization, the variety of which is described above, will be extended. Each extension brings more learning, demonstrating to the whole of the Indigenous network new facets of their cultural inheritance. This progressive process of communal self-realization might be called decolonization. As one local group reaches a moment of progress and insight, those in other areas also learn something valuable, something that may have been missed before. When the Northern Ontario region began to consider ways to select a bishop, they were, like others who had considered that possibility, initially inclined to vote for their candidate in the established Western manner. They chose, instead, to follow a traditional way of selecting a bishop: candidates chosen by a council of elders line up in front of the region's general assembly. Members of the assembly then line up behind the candidate they will support, and the longest line indicates the one who has been chosen. This Indigenous protocol was subsequently adapted and used in Saskatchewan which, in turn, has supplied experience and information that will inform the entire network about ways to apply Indigenous protocols to the ongoing governance of a self-determining Indigenous church.

INDIGENOUS URBAN MINISTRY

The cultural patterns of Indigenous Peoples have been amazingly persistent, following them even into the reality of urbanized life. This experience of Western urban environments is not entirely new, but the main difference today is the great numbers who have moved to, and afterwards stayed in, big cities. Beyond the size of this presence—estimated to be somewhere between 60 and 75 percent of the total Indigenous population of Canada—there has been a different quality to this current migration. In the past, Indigenous people were expected to fit into the urban environment.

Green Shoots out of Dry Ground

The process of "civilizing" them was to be completed by their presence in a relatively controlled urban environment. It did not happen, however. Even Indigenous families who have lived in urban communities for two or more generations have maintained their distinctive cultural identity and, in many cases, strengthened it. Before, it was always expected that they would just adapt, assimilate, and fit in. Now it is clear that an Indigenous identity has a valid standing in the family of national identities that is Canada.

Indigenous resistance to Western culture-based patterns of church, so often seen as a failure to adapt to modern conditions, is also a part of the urban experience. Urban ministries that have initially followed non-Western patterns, often similar to the hymn-singing gatherings mentioned before, have done very well, frequently gathering crowds on a regular basis. Unfortunately, whenever the success of these efforts has become apparent to church authorities, there has been pressure to change the program and pattern of the ministry in order to mimic Western-style parish churches. This has, with very few exceptions, been deadly to the work.

As we have seen, the goal of Indigenous ministries, at least as it has often been imagined by governing church bodies, has been to Western-ize Indigenous Peoples. When this goal is applied and the ministries fail, Western church officials only rarely see this as the consequence of a strategy that is hostile to Indigenous Peoples, and indeed hostile to the Incarnational character of God's mission. Urban Indigenous ministries have had a particularly hard time overcoming this administrative bias. Only recently, since non-Indigenous young people have shown an interest in church gatherings that are comparable to those of Indigenous Peoples, has there been sustained interest in allowing Indigenous church communities to develop in a way appropriate to their own cultural style.

Today, the long overdue recognition of the importance of culture to God's mission[11] has created the imaginative space to pray and work for a new way of being an Indigenous Christian community. Based on the experience of the past, and an Indigenous understanding of present-day realities and possibilities, we can imagine Indigenous Christian communities in cities, prisons, schools, and isolated Reserve communities. In Edmonton, Vancouver, Winnipeg, Thunder Bay, Prince Albert, and Ottawa, Indigenous congregations are forming that use many if not all of the elements outlined in the trajectory described above. These and future communities will need to be less building- and program-centered, and

11. Van Gelder and Zscheile, 125.

much more centered in the encounter with the Gospel in a network of Indigenous Christians who are highly reliant on recognized lay ministers. At a recent meeting of the Council of General Synod of the Anglican Church of Canada, Indigenous leaders stated that their goal is to create communities of at least two or three people in every place where Indigenous People are found, communities that can help people receive spiritual birth, the second birth.

FOR THE WHOLE CHURCH

What I have outlined here has specific force for Indigenous Peoples, and the Incarnation of the Living Word of God among Indigenous Peoples certainly has unique elements; but it also has some more general applications that should not be lost.

First and perhaps foremost is the trust and confidence in the action of the Living Word of God in Creation, and in human history and culture. We should not only expect to discover the seeds of the Word in Creation and culture, but we should also have the discipline that will allow us to discern what they are.[12] This is a critical and indispensable act of a truly missional church. Indeed, a missional Indigenous church can provide the Western churches with a surprising reminder of the dialogue it must engage in with its own, Western culture.

At another level, Indigenous Christianity points to a renewed understanding of the cultural shape of Christian community. Many churches today cannot imagine Christian community beyond the unsustainable forms of ministry they enjoy today. As can clearly be seen in their application to Indigenous Peoples, these forms can be detrimental to the work of the Church and hostile to the mission of God when they are reproduced uncritically and without spiritual discernment.

God has a horizon for the whole Church that is unimaginably wonderful. This implies that we should always be aware that our own understanding of God's mission is limited, and we need to maintain an attitude of humility and self-criticism. Unless we begin with this assumption, our own work too easily becomes an idol, and our own hopes become the enemy of God's best plan for us. God has so much more in mind for us than we can predict, plan, or even hope for. We need to hear what the Spirit is saying to the churches, even (and perhaps especially) if that message comes from a source that has traditionally been at the margins.

12. Van Gelder and Zscheille, 165.

Green Shoots 5
Anglican—and Aboriginal

Standing Stones: Edmonton, Alberta
Kristin Jenkins

To understand the ancient and sacred concept of "standing stones" in indigenous culture, you first must divest yourself of Western ways of thinking. Then, you need to open your heart and listen . . . better than you have ever listened before.

It is not a process at which the Anglican Church of Canada has excelled. Travis Enright, who is himself of Plains Cree descent and a member of the James Smith First Nation in Saskatchewan, knows this all too well.

As canon missioner and vicar at All Saint's Anglican Cathedral in Edmonton, Travis is working to bring together two very different worlds in a fresh expression of church, one aimed at healing ancient wounds and the other aimed at "enlightening the next generation of Canadians," he says.

Travis grew up on the James Smith Reserve with a "reserve spirituality" that included Aboriginal history as well as the Book of Common Prayer. Today, he is combining ancient indigenous symbols with Anglicanism in a rite called "Standing Stones," to help the Aboriginal community in central Alberta reclaim its identity as a spiritual people in a Christian context.

As he explains it, Standing Stones has many meanings: it refers to the inlaid stones that the ancients used to mark their ceremonial grounds. It also refers to the notion of standing upright, of becoming whole, and at one with the Creator. It applies to a service that brings together Aboriginal and non-Aboriginal people, using a Christian ceremony infused with Cree symbols. And it means a teaching tool that enlightens and ultimately heals.

"The stones allow you to enter into a deeper relationship with the Creator," says Travis, pointing out that every culture in the world has some version of sacred stones. "We have places where we know ceremonies took place because of the stones that are laid in the ground. They are markers for sacred places of gathering and ceremony. They represent a spiritual relationship to a sacred concept."

There is a lot of work to be done, and Travis is in the right place: Edmonton is home to 57,000 First Nations, Métis, and Inuit people (the total population of the Northwest Territories is only 43,000). His work was made easier when Jane Alexander took office as bishop of Edmonton in 2008. She told Travis that she wanted All Saints to be a "working" cathedral—a functioning model of excellence that spoke to people's needs, both in its liturgies and in its social programs.

As part of that vision of functionality, Alexander acknowledged the largely unmet spiritual needs of the diverse Aboriginal population. That was "probably the most important shift in mentality in the diocese," says Travis, who soon began to talk to elders in the church and in the Aboriginal community at large.

He then called a gathering so that people could participate in a ceremony he calls "Canada/Kanata." In Cree, *kanata* means *village*, and it incorporates the concept of engagement as well as the mythology of encountering. Encountering, or *wicihitowin* in Cree, means sharing together and helping each other; it is a key component in Aboriginal spiritual and political beliefs. Canada/Kanata acknowledges the different ways that immigrant and Aboriginal Canadians perceive and encounter the land.

Here is how the process went: "It started with a meal that was like our version of speed dating," he says of the two-day gathering. The opening prayer invited each person to "come just as you are" and to receive the meal simply as a person, without titles or fancy dress. Travis integrated traditional Cree smudging—cleansing and healing by the burning of sheaves of sacred leaves such as sage, tobacco, and sweetgrass—and pipe ceremonies with aspects of a traditional Anglican Eucharist, so that, for example, the smoke from the smudge and the smoke from the incense were intermingled.

When it was all over, he sat down with Bishop Alexander to debrief. "We decided that it had been quite successful but that we needed to listen further," he says. The challenge was "to develop a service or a place or a gathering prototype where Aboriginal people would feel comfortable speaking," says Travis, adding, "It also needed to be a place where participants would be comfortable hearing and listening."

In the end, Travis constructed a four-component service that included the four rounds of a traditional Cree sweat lodge and the four components of the Anglican Eucharist: four circles woven together to make one strong circle. The circles are centred on the Creator and activities of reconciliation with the Creator and the family.

Travis explains that the smudging ceremony prepares congregants for worship: "When you are smudging, you are also remembering the ancestors who came before you, and also the people who will come after you," he says. "You smudge and you enter into God's holy space in a good way." Then there are readings of Cree stories and a traditional talking circle, followed by prayers and thanksgiving.

There is also a water ceremony, which gives congregants the opportunity to cool their own water with the healing water of God. "Traditionally, Cree healers knew that not only did physical wounds need to be healed but also the deep spiritual wounds that people walk around with," says Travis. "The water ceremony reconnects the person with the Creator. And at the same time, there is reflection on the renewal of one's baptismal vows."

Standing Stones gathers in the All Saints' Chapel at the cathedral. Its circular sanctuary, rounded altar, and textured walls meet the rite's unique liturgical requirements. The chapel's former choir loft was reconfigured so that the space could be located on one level, a concept vital to "engaging the Sacred, the Knowing, the Acknowledging, and the Reconciliation," says Travis. New windows were designed. Paintings were commissioned to tell the story of the Trinity in terms of an Aboriginal worldview.

"Everything is focused on developing a common language," he says. "The actual architecture is Cree, but the decorating is Anglican intermingled with Cree." The service is very inclusive, and attendance is split about fifty-fifty between Aboriginal and non-Aboriginal.

The first gathering at the cathedral took place in November 2011, although several non-official gatherings took place in the year leading up to that.

Standing Stones is held on twelve Sundays a year, although the exact time of services is subject to change. "Aboriginal people don't necessarily want to gather at 9:15 a.m. on a particular day," says Travis. "So I ask people when they would like to pray, and we then call a Standing Stones in the chapel." While twenty to twenty-five people usually congregate in the chapel on the third and fifth Sunday of every month, the last gathering had ninety-two people. Travis also performs Standing Stones baptisms, weddings, and funerals.

In a relatively short time, Standing Stones has become a significant healing focal point for Edmonton's indigenous people. Travis Enright is following in the ancient missionary tradition of taking what is universal in Christianity and relating it to a local culture, thereby helping people in that culture see that the Gospel is meant for them.

Canadian culture is changing fast—like many others around the world. In particular, the passing of the Baby Boomer generation, who have dominated life in the West for the past fifty years, is going to change every aspect of Canadian life. So what is the future? There is great hope, vitality, and creativity among the younger generations who are day by day taking the place of Baby Boomers. But where are those people in terms of faith and church? Perhaps the most cutting-edge Canadian research into this topic is being done by James Penner and Associates (JPA) of Lethbridge, Alberta. In this chapter, one of their younger researchers updates us about their most recent work. The results are sobering but also hopeful.

10

Where Have All the Young People Gone?

What Drives Them Away and What Helps Them Stay?[1]

Erika Anderson

You do not have to be a sociologist to know that the church in Canada is mysteriously devoid of young adults, compared to even thirty years ago. Many young people have trouble with Christian churches and even with Christian faith itself, leading them to abandon both.

Not that all churches in Canada lack a young adult presence, however. Some have lively programs and teem with spiritually healthy youth. Take, for example, the experience of Lea, a twenty-eight-year-old Francophone evangelical from Quebec:

> When I get back in my car after [church] I'm on fire, not necessarily because of the messages, even though they are great, but because of seeing other people who love others . . . as though they were their own family members. And what I retain from this is this massive fire that reaffirms my faith. I exit the church utterly encouraged in my faith.[2]

1. This chapter is in part a modified version of James Penner and Associates' *Hemorrhaging Faith: The Prophetic Call of Canada's Young Adults for Self-Emptying Churches in a Self-Serving Age*. The full report may be downloaded from www.hemorrhagingfaith.com.

2. All young adult names are pseudonyms.

Some churches are vibrant, like Lea's. But the majority of Christians in Canada are asking, "Where have all the young people gone?"

Just across the forty-ninth parallel, recent research has been done concerning the religiosity of American teens and young adults. In 2006, data from the Barna Group suggested that as many as six in ten church-going teens discontinue Christian participation after high school.[3] Then in 2007, Lifeway Research found that by the age of twenty-three, seven out of ten Protestants who had been active in Christian faith during high school disengaged from church participation for at least a year.[4] American research of this kind is unnerving for church leaders in Canada. With a culture and history similar to that of America, is it possible that this nation is experiencing a similar decline? Current Canadian youth research sheds some light on the issue. Reginald Bibby's Project Teen Canada research, for instance, confirms decline in Christian identification. Between 1984 and 2008, the percentage of teens identifying themselves as either Roman Catholic or Protestant dropped from 85 to 45 percent, while those claiming identity with other world faiths or no faith at all rose steadily.[5]

As we ask ourselves where all the young people have gone, we need to remember that Canadian teens' growing lack of Christian identity is in part related to larger social, cultural, and institutional issues. Today, children and teens must successfully navigate a busy, technology-based world, while being blinded by a fog of "isms," such as individualism, pluralism, relativism, and materialism. This is not to say that religion is absent. The Canadian reality, more accurately, is one of religious polarization, where some are highly committed, but more and more simply do not participate in organized religion at all.[6] According to Canadian philosopher Charles Taylor, belief in God is an embattled option and this age profoundly secular.[7] As James Davidson Hunter argues, church-goers need to realize there

---

3. Barna Group, "Most Twentysomethings Put Christianity on the Shelf Following Spiritually Active Teen Years," September 11, 2006, http://www.barna.org/teens-next-gen-articles/147-most-twentysomethings-put-christianity-on-the-shelf-following-spiritually-active-teen-years.

4. Cathy Lynn Grossman, "Young Adults Aren't Sticking with Church," *USA Today*, August 6, 2007, http://www.usatoday.com/news/religion/2007-08-06-church-dropouts_N.htm.

5. Kate Lunau, "Teens Lose Faith in Droves: Islam and Atheism Are on the Rise While Christianity Fades," *Maclean's*, April 13, 2009, 43.

6. Reginald Bibby and James Penner, *10 Things We All Need To Know About Canada's Teens* (Lethbridge, AB: Project Canada Books, 2010), 48.

7. Charles Taylor, *A Secular Age* (Cambridge, MA: Harvard University Press, 2007), 3.

are precious few supports—outside of churches—for young people in society who are looking for God:

> While it is possible to believe in God, one has to work much
> harder at it because the framework of belief is no longer present
> to sustain it. The presumption of God and of his active pres-
> ence in the world cannot be easily sustained because the most
> important symbols of social, economic, political, and aesthetic
> life no longer point to him. God is simply less obvious than he
> once was and for most no longer obvious at all.[8]

Not only are young adults constantly engulfed in a culture with few
societal supports for faith, but they are also expected to "get a life" for
themselves—which often means turning themselves into a brand or a
commodity that they have to market to the world around them. "Individuals become simultaneously the promoters of commodities and the commodities they promote…The test [youth] need to pass in order to acquire
the social prizes they covet requires them to recast themselves as products
capable of drawing attention to themselves."[9] They need the right tech toys,
the right Facebook status, the right definition of beauty, the right credentials, and the right volunteering experiences on their résumés. The teen
task of identity formation has all too often become identity manipulation
as cultural voices outside themselves dominate their thinking.[10] The voice
of culture can easily drown out the joyful vocational call of God.[11] "Who
am I?"—to which the Christian Gospel has always answered, "a beloved
child of God"— has become a question far more difficult to answer in
present day culture. "Rather than a gift (let alone a 'free gift' . . .), identity
is a sentence to life-long hard labor."[12]

Canada's complex "ism" culture, then, is a part of young adults' current trend towards non-attendance at church; however, we cannot place
all the responsibility for floundering church attendance on today's society. For a fuller picture, we need to listen to the young adults themselves,
as they describe their experiences of church. As we listen, we must not

8. James Davidson Hunter, *To Change the World: The Irony, Tragedy, & Possibility of Christianity in the Late Modern World* (New York: Oxford University Press, 2010), 203.

9. Zygmunt Bauman, *Consuming Life* (Cambridge, UK: Polity Press, 2007), back cover.

10. See for example, James Cote and Anton Allahar, *Critical Youth Studies* (To-ronto: Prentice Hall, 2006), 72–73.

11. John Berard, James Penner, and Rick Bartlett, *Consuming Youth: Leading Teens Through Consumer Culture* (Grand Rapids, MI: Zondervan, 2010), 66.

12. Zygmunt Bauman, *Consuming Life*, 111.

merely notice their symptoms. We must seek for the sources of the disconnect they experienced as they grew up in the church. In listening to their voices, we will find clues as to why they have either stayed or departed. And as churches respond to those voices, they might find that young adults are actually more willing to belong to churches and to hold a committed Christian faith than they realize.

EFC'S YOUNG ADULTS "RAISED CHRISTIAN" RESEARCH PROJECT

In 2010, the Evangelical Fellowship of Canada's Youth and Young Adult Ministry Roundtable commissioned James Penner and Associates to study young adults who were "raised Christian" in Canada. The study focused on Canadian young adults who had spent time as children inside the walls of Canadian churches in the 1980s and 1990s, to discover their perspectives on church and faith today. Two research questions guided the study:

1. To what degree do young adults in Canada today commit to or reject faith—whether Protestant, Orthodox, or Catholic?

2. What are the toxins pushing them out, and the drivers keeping them in, Christian churches?

The survey was sent to 2,886 members of Angus Reid's online panel who fit the profile of "raised Christian." An astounding 71 percent return rate meant that the researchers were able to glean the insights of 2,049 young adults from across Canada. This chapter summarizes what was found.

During childhood (up to age 12), 69 percent attend regularly (monthly or more), 29 percent attend sporadically (a few times a year, such as Easter and Christmas), and 2 percent do not attend at all until they come to Christian faith in their teen or young adult years.

By the teen years (13–19), the percentage of regular attenders drops as the percentages of "occasional" and "never" attenders goes up. Already, it has become unusual for young adults who were raised Christian to attend church: 41 percent of respondents attend regularly, 42 percent attend sporadically, and the number of non-attenders jumps from 2 to 15 percent. Clearly, church attendance is a problem that happens before children leave home.

The graph on the next page helps to answer the question of how many are still attending churches.

Church Attendance by Canadian Youth

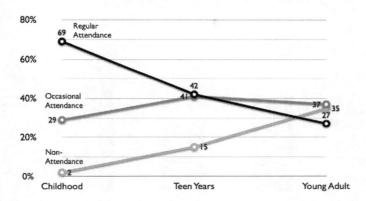

Source: The EFC-Angus Reid Young Adult Why Church 2011 data set

In their young adult years (19–34), only 27 percent continue to attend regularly, while 37 percent now attend sporadically, and 35 percent do not attend at all. Non-attenders now outnumber regular attenders. This means that, for every three Canadian young adults who attended church monthly or more as children, only one maintains that level of commitment into young adulthood.

The bar graph below adds data concerning the shift in religious identification. Regardless of which Christian faith community young adults belonged to as children, significant numbers no longer identify with it. Two out of every three mainline Protestants drop their childhood religious identification by the time they reach young adulthood. For Catholics, the drop is approximately one out of two. For conservative (evangelical) Protestants, the loss is one in three.

What Proportion Of Young Adults Still Relate To Their Childhood Faith?

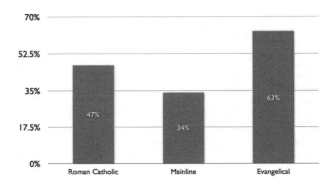

Source: The EFC-Angus Reid Young Adult Why Church 2011 data set

One might wonder whether young adults who give up their childhood faith are turning to other world faiths. Of 2,049 respondents, however, fewer than a dozen converted to other major faiths such as Buddhism or Islam. Rather, when young adults drop their religious identifications, they tend to gravitate toward expressions of faith that are private and non-institutional. They embrace labels such as atheist, agnostic, spiritual, or "no religion." Furthermore, the less they attend church, the more likely they are to drop their denominational label. Sociologist Peter Berger was correct when he stated that people's worldview "hangs on the thin thread of conversation."[13] In a world where there are few social supports for following Jesus when young adults leave church, they tend to leave the conversation of faith. They might even be said to hemorrhage faith as the Christian worldview becomes less plausible to them. The idea of a self-emptying Trinitarian God, who can be experienced as a faithful shepherd, guiding king, and caring parent, simply makes little sense in the broader culture. For those no longer attending church, it becomes easy to peel off the Christian label.

While our study tries to highlight what is happening in the minds of disengaging young adults, we do not wish to overstate this point. Camps, campus ministries, innovative church plants, spiritually focused friendships, and direct encounters with the divine mystery can play a crucial

13. Peter Berger, *The Sacred Canopy: Elements of a Sociological Theory of Religion* (New York: Doubleday, 1967), 17.

role in helping maintain faith into adulthood—not to mention bringing prodigal sons and daughters home.

FOUR DRIVERS OF YOUNG ADULT FAITH

What is it that leads young adults to stay in church in the twenty-first century? This question was posed in various ways to the young adults in the study. Repetition among their stories was evident. The conversations with them, and the survey data, pointed to four experiences which these young adults shared:

1. Parents who had an engaged faith;

2. Congregations that had consistent community;

3. A God who was tangibly loving; and

4. Church teaching that was transformational.

We have called these positive experiences "drivers," since they further convince young adults that God is real and that a faith community is relevant. Of course, these drivers are not a formula that produces young adults with vibrant faith 100 percent of the time. Nonetheless, the research showed that when these drivers were present, youth emerging into adulthood have a greater chance of retaining their faith—and the more drivers, the greater the chance of retention. The experience of these four drivers is a likely indicator of faith, but not a guarantee.

Driver 1: Spiritually Engaged Parents

When it comes to building a vibrant faith, children and youth need their parents, and others who play parenting roles, to model what such a faith might look like. Just as children need to be taught habits such as saying thank you and washing their hands, they also need continuous support for building spiritual habits. Here is the kind of thing respondents say about their parents:

> I got a lot of my faith from my mom. She's always been a great witness to my faith—a quiet witness. She didn't participate in any women's group or Bible study groups, but somehow she just kinda—her faith was—was just such a testament to God's love for us.
> —June, age 29, was raised in a strong Catholic family. Despite temptations through high school, a dynamic

> university Christian group helped her to stick with her
> faith, which continues to be vital.

> My father reads his Bible every day. Sometimes he will read the
> same verse over and over again for a week until he feels it's really
> seeped into his heart. He spends another half hour praying.
> —Don, age 18, was raised Mennonite Brethren. Despite
> struggling with hypocritical and judgemental friends
> at his Christian high school, he has deliberately chosen
> to stay Christian.

Both June and Don belong to the 12 percent in the study who stated they had two parents who regularly attended church, prayed privately, and read the Bible at home. Of those young adult respondents, 81 percent say that they currently engage in personal prayer weekly or more and 55 percent read their Bible weekly or more.

By comparison, of those who had the support of only one Christian parent (or two who were inconsistent in spiritual practice), 33 percent still engage in personal prayer and 8 percent read their Bible weekly or more. Of those for whom neither parent supported them in Christian faith, only 18 percent engage in personal prayer and 6 percent read their Bible weekly or more.

Of course, Bible reading, prayer, and church attendance are not the only tests of authentic Christian faith. In Jesus' time, the Pharisees were also very conscientious in their religious observances, and Jesus was not very impressed with them! The survey could have asked whether parents demonstrated some kind of practical outworking of their faith, such as volunteering in the community, expressing hospitality, or giving generously to social causes. Although this would have been more difficult to measure, it would have tapped into some of those things Jesus was most concerned about. Parents who scored high on the scale of personal piety are certainly not assumed to be Pharisees, of course, but this weakness in the design of the survey needs to be addressed in future research.

The importance of spiritually engaged role models during a child's formative years speaks volumes about the need for mentorship, particularly in situations where only one parent is spiritually supportive. The faith of a child has a much higher chance of surviving if it has more than one adult breathing spiritual life into it. Church leaders need to recognize those children who may be learning the things of God from only one spiritually vibrant adult (or two lukewarm ones) and to stand in the gap, providing additional spiritual support.

Though this is what the latest research has shown, one cannot underestimate what God does in spite of parental circumstances. There are many parents who operate as the sole spiritual example in their homes and are unrecognized heroes of the faith. These parents are to be commended for their faith and diligence in seeing that their children receive spiritual formation. There are also parents who have provided a unified and consistent Christian home, whose children have not chosen to carry faith with them into adulthood, who should not be discouraged. An individual's final choice to accept or deny faith lies beyond the control of parents. And the interviews do contain encouraging stories of prodigals who wandered away. Then, in far off places, these sons and daughters were somehow reminded of what they had learned in home or church and returned to vital expressions of personal faith.[14]

Having two spiritually engaged parent figures is not an absolute guarantee that children will develop a strong faith of their own. However, having a consistent spiritual influence does provide a framework in children's minds that increases the likelihood that they will grow into adult acceptance of faith.

Driver 2: Consistent Community

The community of believers surrounding young people has considerable impact on whether they emerge from their formative years with a faith in which they want to stay engaged. Those who have experienced a consistently self-giving faith community—one that is there for them no matter how messy they are, which builds them up in Christ, and which is active in the world around it—have a higher chance of carrying faith with them into their adult years. Youth need to be surrounded by a strong community that lives out the faith, if their belief in God is to stick beyond the formative stage.

These comments are typical of those who spoke about the impact of strong Christian communities:

> I started to become really, really depressed in university, and addicted to sex, and suicidal, and not really knowing how to get out of this, and really feeling hopeless, and not really wanting to

---

14. For examples of such stories, see John P. Bowen, *Growing Up Christian: Why Young People Stay in Church, Leave Church, and (Sometimes) Come Back to Church* (Vancouver, BC: Regent College Publishing, 2010), 175–183.

live. And, um, I had some good friends that were Christians, and thankfully they were friends with me, and they kept me going.

> —Jeremy, age 28, was raised in an "attendance-only" Catholic family. He is recalling a two-year period of depression that began after his father died when Jeremy was eighteen. At university he had a life-altering conversion experience and emotional support through friends who were part of a campus faith community. He now lives an active Christian life and works as the youth and worship coordinator at his church.

We did a mission trip to the Dominican [Republic], and we did a Bible study school, and helped homeless people. We brought food, so that was actually a very uplifting and life-changing experience—you know, coming out of your comfort zone and being able to help people on the other side of the fence.

> —Tom, age 31, grew up as an Anglican altar boy. He has now stopped going to church, except on holidays, because he moved too far from his dynamic childhood church to continue attending. He still maintains close ties with those from this community and identifies himself as a Christian.

The chances that someone will possess a robust faith into adult years is in part dependent on being involved in a faith community that offers care to its own members (like Jeremy) and makes a difference in the community (as Tom experienced). Of those who have stayed committed to a faith community as adults, 79 percent say they have experienced personal emotional healing through the support of a church; an additional 95 percent believe that church makes a difference in their community. In contrast, of those who have come to self-identify as anti-church and anti-faith, only 19 percent believe church makes a difference in their community, and only 2 percent report having experienced personal emotional healing through a faith community.

In the same way that children and youth tend to hold vibrant faith if they see faith consistently lived out at home, they also need to experience that same spiritual consistency among those within their church. Not only does their faith community need to support them individually and help with personal healing, it also needs to extend spokes into the non-Christian world around them by offering soul care and social justice. Such things as having had personal experience of emotional healing because of a Christian congregation's missional thrust, and seeing the rippling impact of a congregation's self-emptying on the broader world, increase the chances that a young person will maintain a lively personal faith into the future.

In sociological terms, having close group ties (friends, family, and others with whom to live the Christian life) greatly affects the odds that children will stick with faith. This is because serious Christians in Canada today are a "cognitive minority"[15]—a cluster of people who think differently from the majority, believing their priorities are ordered by a loving supernatural referent and not by their own self-directed disposition. Berger says, "The strength of [the possibility of following Christ] . . . will be directly dependent upon the strength of the supporting structure."[16] During childhood and teen years, our youth need a strong structuring community to surround them, to fire their imagination about what following Jesus can look like in our world today. As Sid put it when asked why he stuck with his Christian faith, the biggest thing was "just the other people in our church, like observing how real it was for them." He went on to mention how impressed he was by the older ladies in his church who did prison ministry, were praying for people "all the time" and could have been "retired and coasting" but were "always involved in things, doing things, working with charities, stuff like that."

Once young people lose relationships with other Christians, they also lose the conversation about faith and the observations of its power. This in turn causes faith to lose plausibility, and the individual turns away. Of course, inconsistent faith communities have less influence on youth than consistent ones. Many respondents told stories of being turned off by hypocritical, judgmental, cliquey, or controlling Christians. Most young Christians need to "encounter [dynamic faith] through their ties to other people"[17] in order for them to carry their belief into adulthood.

Driver 3: Experience of God

Young adults today need things that are tangible, felt, and immediate. They like the fact that they can text a friend and immediately receive a text back. They embrace social media because they can know about things as soon as they happen. God, however, does not always readily appear when

15. Peter L. Berger, *A Rumor of Angels: Modern Society and the Rediscovery of the Supernatural* (New York: Doubleday, 1969), 6–7.

16. Ibid., 40.

17. Rodney Stark, *The Rise of Christianity: How the Obscure, Marginal Jesus Movement Became the Dominant Religious Force in the Western World in a Few Centuries* (New York: HarperCollins, 1996), 55–56.

they close their eyes. When they pray, God does not always answer in the way they expect. Elsie is one such young adult, and God's seeming rejection of her in childhood perhaps still influences her lack of participation in church today:

> When Dad died, I was so angry at who I believed God to be that
> I have never been back to my church since.
>> —Elsie, age 23, attended church as a child and a youth
>> group as a teen but now has left church and faith
>> completely.

The research showed that many young adults do not feel that God is impersonal, detached, and uninterested. We cannot say why Elsie did not experience God in her time of deep need. We can, however, share other stories of young adults who claim they have experienced God. Some of these individuals left church and/or faith, at least for a time, but they see a God who is truly concerned about all God's children, whether it be in big things like saving a life or in small things like bringing a car back to life. When listening to these stories of young adults across Canada, it is evident that many are reporting a profound personal sense of God at work.

The next respondent went through such a time and—despite intense darkness, anger, and despair—mysteriously felt God's presence:

> After being dumped by my boyfriend, I attempted suicide and, in
> that dark place, I became profoundly aware of God's presence. . .
> It wasn't any of the things I had expected. . . It was weird because
> intuitively, internally, I knew it was the presence of God, and yet
> it did not fit any of my previous expectations.
>> —Barry, age 34, was raised in an Evangelical church
>> and now identifies himself as "just Christian." He has
>> journeyed into a vital faith with the support of friends
>> who were "Jesus with skin on" amidst excruciating
>> hardships, while reconciling himself to being both gay
>> and Christian.

Here are a few more snippets of the conversations we have had with young adults across Canada about their experiences with God:

> Jim's battery was dead, so I was praying, God start this car. Bam!
> The car started.
>> —Devon, age 18, was raised in a Protestant church
>> while attending a Catholic school. He has stopped at-
>> tending church since moving to a major city because he
>> needs to work on Sundays to pay the expensive rent. He

maintains faith through doing regular devotions and playing worship music at home.

> I woke up one morning at like four in the morning . . . and felt like I was supposed to go in and tell the gas station attendant that God loved him, that he was there for him. I ended up going in and saying that, and he had written his suicide note that night, and was going to go kill himself after shift. The guy became a Christian and turned his life around.
>
> —Sandy, age 28, was raised Protestant. He had a strong relationship with God throughout his childhood and teen years. In young adulthood, church politics and hypocrisy caused him to reject Christianity. After a ten-year journey of experimenting with world faiths and humanism, he again self-identifies as "a Christian" and is part of an innovative church plant.

Answered prayer and experience of God, like the other "drivers," are not guarantees of long-term faith, but they are correlates of church attendance. Of those respondents who have remained engaged Christians, an astonishing 99 percent report having experienced God's love personally, and 100 percent believe that God answers prayer. Conversely, of those who have completely left Christian faith as adults, only 4 percent say they have experienced God's love personally and believe that God answers prayer. These findings are perhaps not entirely good news. Might it be that Canadian churches do not know how to respond to those who say they doubt the love of God because they have not experienced it inside church communities?

Whatever the explanation, the fact remains that a lack of experience of the love of God—or a perceived lack—acts as a deterrent to faith. On the other hand, positive experiences of God keep people in the community—and in the conversation.

Driver 4: Relevant and Engaging Beliefs and Teaching

Many young adults feel that society has outgrown the relevance of the church. Even so, they seem to want to stay in places where the Gospel meets real life. Respondents in our study pleaded for relevant and engaging Christian teaching, alongside the space to ask questions. They want insights, not just on what to believe or how to live, but why. This is a generation that wants to chew! They desire to go deep, to tackle issues in today's society, and to question the things they see or learn. They do not want fluff. What US researcher Ed Stetzer critiques in American youth programming is a key Canadian concern as well: "Too many youth groups are holding tanks with pizza. There's no life transformation taking place. . . . People are looking for a faith that can change them . . . to be a part of changing the world."[18] They do not want to be entertained or to be simply told what is wrong and right or to be asked, "What would Jesus do?" They want to be taught how to discern. Note how Don put it:

> [Churches] get wishy-washy . . . they'll just give [people] this wishy-washy Jesus-loves-you-rainbows-sunshine-puppy-dogs-glitter version of the Gospel to win them over. But it's not about winning people over for popularity points and brownie points with team Jesus. . . . There's no sort of challenge, there's no stretching. . . . It's just trying to make people feel all warm and fuzzy inside and hoping they'll turn out for the best. But what happens when that warm and fuzziness wears out? 'Cause it will. 'Cause it's not real."
> —Don, age 18, quoted earlier.

A strong indicator as to whether youth will have a lasting faith is whether or not they belong to a church whose leadership is able to make teaching relevant and to address tough issues.

Of those who remain committed believers as adults, only 21 percent believe church is out of touch with society, and 90 percent believe church leaders have been able to help them with their toughest questions. Of those who now reject church and faith, 96 percent believe the institution to be irrelevant for today's society, and only 6 percent believe their past leaders have helped them navigate issues well. Young adults want a personally transforming, culturally relevant faith that has surmounted their most difficult philosophical hurdles. Churches they consider worth their time deliver for them at this intellectual level.

A fuzzy, glittery version of the Gospel is not real to Don's generation. They are attracted to leaders who, like Jesus, did not play it safe with what he taught: he relentlessly taught truth, which created controversy. Addressing today's real issues—such as a theology of sexuality, the question of Jesus' uniqueness among world religions, and how to be a Christian in a postmodern world—will get churches traction with young adults. Pat answers are unacceptable. Youth are comfortable with doubt. They can live with unresolved questions, and they are okay with theological disagreements about the answers to complex issues.

18. Quoted in Grossman.

Why should they be eighteen and moving away from home before we take them off the spiritual bottle? Youth get overwhelmed with issues that concern our society today when they are thrust into them without direction. They need to be taught from a young age, not only what to think, but how to approach issues from the perspective of thoughtful faith. They need to learn to chew real spiritual food while still in the relative safety of their families and congregations. Young adults are not asking for concrete, nicely packaged answers—in fact, they are rejecting such things. They are asking instead for leaders to teach them how to problem-solve in order to find the answers for themselves. As Gary puts it:

> I fundamentally believe you can't understand an infinite God
> if you are willing to accept answers and stop questioning. You
> need to be asking questions.
>   —Gary, age 25, is a Baptist pastor's son who became
>   incensed with church politics surrounding his father.
>   He now self-identifies as having "no religion."

Doubts will arise for children and youth when their minority Christian worldview comes into contact with the majority Canadian worldview. Those who have been taught to think discerningly about social issues and spirituality, through regular conversations about faith through their childhood and teen years, will have a greater chance of surviving into their young adult years with a robust faith intact.

CONCLUSION

We need to re-emphasize that these four drivers are not a watertight guarantee of ongoing strong Christian belief. Despite vital faith socialization, some still "fall by the wayside," or have a "prodigal child" experience before returning. Still others, who have experienced very few of the drivers, develop into robust followers of Jesus.

What has been uncovered, however, is a way of life for Jesus' followers. By maintaining a structure that consistently supports faith at home and church and beyond, a relationship with Christ tends to remain relevant for children and youth, even in a society where much is secular.

By listening to the voices of young adults across Canada, we have found that many reasons for their absence lie within the church itself. On the whole, we have not done a good job of fostering spiritual growth in Canada's youth. The symptoms are obvious: young adults have ceased attending church in large numbers and have begun denying their association with Christianity.

Where have all the young people gone? They have gone on a journey. They are searching for something that will fulfill their desire to live a life of significance. These youth want the real deal. The problem that young adults have with churches in Canada is that they can sense what is inauthentic and do not want to be a part of it. Essentially, they want to be part of a faith that is modelled in a community and sustained by an experience of the living God. Like canaries in the coal mine, they are sensitive to toxins in the environment. If they are not singing in our churches, there may be a serious methane gas problem within. Canadian young adults who grew up in church are seeking adults (including their own parents) who are passionate about their own relationship with God, authentic churches that are serious about helping those inside and outside their communities, coaching on how they can personally experience God, and an environment that grapples intelligently and honestly with how to live out a Christ-focused identity in a secular world.

It is true: churches in Canada have lost a significant number of young adults. But the situation in Canada is not new. God has worked with a committed core of believers many times across the ages. And God's heart is always to redeem. On the brink of an earlier exile, God gave Jeremiah this promise for Israel:

> They shall be my people, and I will be their God. I will give them one heart and one way, that they may fear me for all time, for their own good and the good of their children after them. I will make an everlasting covenant with them, never to draw back from doing good to them; and I will put the fear of me in their hearts, so that they may not turn from me. I will rejoice in doing good to them, and I will plant them in this land in faithfulness, with all my heart and all my soul. For thus says the Lord: Just as I have brought all this great disaster upon this people, so I will bring upon them all the good fortune that I now promise them. (Jer 32:38–42)

I believe God wishes to see the church in Canada thrive. Currently, we have a small proportion of those who grew up in church who maintain their faith. Many have lost—if they ever had—a true, living, and transformational faith. But historically, when there has been a remnant, God has promised and delivered restoration. Again and again, throughout the Old Testament prophets—Isaiah, Jeremiah, Micah, and Ezekiel—we read promises of deliverance, of revival, and of shouts of joy. With the help of God, we have the ability to transform our faith communities into dynamic, relational, relevant places to which young adults want to belong.

Green Shoots 6
Being Church, not Going to Church

Emerge
Montreal, Quebec

Nick Brotherwood, pastor of St. Stephen's Anglican Church in West-mount, Quebec, is trying not to view the disbanding of his church plant as a failure.

It is a struggle, he admits, but he is coming to terms with what he has learned. As bishop's missioner to young adults in the Diocese of Montreal, Nick and a team of volunteers set up and ran a new church called Emerge from 2003 until the end of 2010. Emerge sought to attract young, not-yet-Christian adults ages eighteen to thirty-five, living and working in downtown Montreal.

Founded on the values of participation, friendship, belonging, action, and authenticity, Emerge envisioned a growing community of students and young urban professionals, free to follow the Holy Spirit in ways that were diverse but still authentic.

Nick knows young people, and he sees that to a large extent the church does not. "I thought to myself that the church has done a really bad job of connecting with Gen-Xers," he says. (The definition of that group varies, but refers roughly to those born between the early 1960s and the early 1980s.) In the spirit of exploring this group, and planting a church outside the existing church community, the diocese created a position for Nick.

"My expectations were to connect with young people who were not yet Christians," says Nick. Emerge began in early 2003 with a Sunday meeting, at his home, of a group of ten from the Emerge Planning Committee, plus six guests. "They were young adults we already had connections with," says Nick.

The group ate, talked, and prayed together. Calling on his Alpha Course experience, discussions initially included topics, such as music, that people identified as spiritually meaningful to them.

In September 2003, they moved to the Undercroft—a space under Christ Church, the Anglican cathedral in downtown Montreal.

The windowless basement space, which could hold as many as sixty people, was set up coffeehouse-style, and included five round tables, each seating eight. There was a kitchen with a serving hatch, and some extra rooms. Most important, it was "very functional, not churchy," says Nick. It could also be entered through an adjacent shopping mall.

For the first two or three years, there was a meal every Sunday night, which Sue, Nick's wife, "heroically prepared" for as many as thirty-five people. To accommodate any dietary strictures, it was always vegetarian. The meal would be followed by live music and then "some kind of presentation, usually involving Scripture, with conversation and response," he says. Elements of alternative worship, such as prayer stations, were often worked into the service. "We realized that people learn differently, and we wanted to provide something for different learning styles."

Nick recalls, in particular, a display set up for Holy Week. The inspiration was a prayer of the Iona Community in Scotland: "Wield well your tools in this workshop of my life. We who come to you rough-hewn, work on us." The visuals were two juxtaposed pieces of wood—one raw, one carved.

"These objects were non-churchy, but set in a prayerful context," explains Nick, who borrowed heavily from a variety of alternative worship sources. He found that going from the verbal text to the physical object often helped people get beyond abstract concepts.

In addition, the group used the cathedral on Sunday evenings, after it had closed, as a venue to explore seasonal themes. On one occasion just before Christmas, they set up multiple stations that included a large screen with a continuous-loop DVD showing a human cell dividing through the stages toward birth. At one station, an MP3 player very quietly played the words of the Angel Gabriel to Mary. People had to move in close to hear. At another station, participants were invited to light tea candles and use them to spell out a word such as "grace." At yet another, they could craft their own crèche figures out of Play-Doh.

In addition to the Sunday meetings, Nick insisted that the teaching connect with the lives people lived throughout the week. Emerge members would meet together in small groups during the week to talk and pray. And many cooperated on projects. Some played in bands together, others made movies, a few went on out-of-Canada mission trips, and still others collaborated with artists from other churches. "We were really trying to emphasize being disciples and asking what that meant," he explains. "We valued questions more than we valued answers."

Nick himself visited people at their places of work. "The message was that they were worth my visiting, to see how their work was engaging them in God's mission," he explains, adding that "this certainly wasn't a given in the church that I grew up with."

Emerge peaked in 2004 with a membership of between forty-five and fifty. Contrary to plan, however, the plant was connecting with people who were already Christians, but often disaffected because of their previous experience of church. "We had a high proportion of pastors' kids," he says. "This wasn't something we'd expected. What Emerge did not attract was the very group planners had hoped to reach: those with no background in Christian faith or church."

In the late fall of 2007, Nick made a trip to England to attend a Vision Day with the Fresh Expressions people there. There, Nick heard about the "formative journey," which described the typical progression in fresh expressions of church. First comes listening to a community, then serving, then building, then discipleship.

The very last step is worship. Nick realized that by focusing on worship first, rather than on serving the needs of the community, the Emerge team had put the cart before the horse.

"If you start with listening to the community, and asking how you can serve, it's different," says Nick. "We started with the assumption that we needed to meet and gather together on a Sunday. Granted, it was a bit different from other Christian gatherings on Sunday, but we were still worshipping. I think our assumptions were faulty, but I didn't know that at that time. In 2003, I hadn't heard about the formative journey."

By the fall of September 2008, the group began to drift apart. Part of this had to do with the group's demographics: young adults eighteen to thirty-five are highly mobile. "Young people grow up and move away," points out Nick. "We were no longer the new show in town. New churches are cropping up all the time." When Emerge gathered for the last time in December 2010, attendance was down to between sixteen and twenty people.

On the face of it, the whole experiment was looking like a failure. But was it a failure? "I don't think it was," says Nick. "Did those people grow as disciples of Jesus? I certainly hope they did, and I think that is more important than whether Emerge lasted forever and its numbers were big."

K.J.

"Mission" and "environment" are two words that do not often appear side by side, especially in a Christian context. Yet it is utterly appropriate for them to be linked. The work of God to restore all things does not reach out only to individuals and communities, but also to the natural world, and any who care about the mission of God dare not neglect that aspect. Otherwise we would be unfaithful to our Creator's calling. The work of A Rocha (a Portuguese term meaning The Rock) around the world in the past thirty years has given leadership to Christians who are waking up to the environmental crisis and wondering how they can be involved in a distinctively Christian way. Markku and Leah Kostamo are giving leadership to A Rocha in Canada, one of nineteen countries where A Rocha is at work. Their voice is unique and timely.

11

Creation Care as Christian Mission

Leah and Markku Kostamo

IT SOUNDS LIKE A bad joke: what do you get when a Buddhist, a Christian, and a Wiccan sit down for a meal together? Actually, it was one Buddhist, three Christians, one Wiccan, and three agnostics, and what you got was some amazing conversation. This montage of people came to A Rocha, the Christian environmental organization we help lead, as part of a University of British Columbia Earth Sciences class that required participation in a community service project. They had chosen the topic "religion and the environment," which made A Rocha a perfect fit. After spending five days at our Environmental Centre in Surrey renovating a musty Quonset hut into a glorified dorm room, we sat down to a big dinner to thank them for their hard work.

Candles were lit, the table was spread, and we sat down to the feast. The conversation was lively and centred on beliefs. We didn't have an agenda in this regard; we simply asked these students to share a bit of their own stories and, being thoughtful university students, they zeroed in on what motivated them to care about the earth. They shared their genuine grappling with issues of sustainability, the plight of the poor, and their own struggles with the Christian faith in these regards. We sat for hours. The musings were profound, earnest, and articulate, and we both felt like we'd landed in a well-scripted foreign film.

Soon these students were directing their questions toward us. What motivated us? What did we believe? One asked how our Christian faith informed our work in conservation. Another commented on how he saw those working in the environmental field struggle with despair and wondered where we found hope. Last, sweet Janet—an agnostic girl with a church background—asked what we thought was the purpose behind humanity's existence. You know, simple questions. The amazing thing was the openness with which these questions were asked, as if they really expected to find some granule of truth in our response.

While not claiming to have all the answers, we shared a bit of our own stories and how we had personally found hope and purpose. The apex of the conversation came in response to the "What gives you hope?" question. We responded by considering how the incarnation shows God's commitment to creation—the Creator becomes the created in the ultimate act of solidarity. John, the Buddhist, and Christa, the Wiccan, seemed utterly astonished by this idea. Suddenly, Christianity was no longer an unattractive code of ethics but a divine adventure of reckless love. Christa said she would be up all night, her mind whirling with the implications. Ian said believing this would make all the difference in how one treated the world.

Indeed. Belief matters. We work in conservation because we believe certain things about God and the world. In the words of John Wesley, we have found that "faith in Jesus Christ [leads] us beyond an exclusive concern for the well-being of other human beings to the broader concern for the well-being of the birds in our backyard, the fish in our rivers, and every living creature on the face of the earth."[1]

THE BASICS: CREATION AND IMAGE BEARING

Early on, A Rocha adopted Psalm 24:1 as its inspiration: "The earth is the Lord's and all that is in it." Though seemingly benign and simple, the proposition that the earth actually belongs to God and not to us is radical, and often runs counter to popular Christian beliefs. I'm not sure where we got the idea that creation is the possession of people, but it is not the message of the Bible. True, the creation narrative in Genesis sets humans in a unique position among the rest of creation. Even then, however, as Barbara Brown Taylor points out, we do not even get our own day, but must share Day Six with all manner of creeping things and even cows! The specialness bestowed on our species, Genesis says, has to do with our being "created in the image of God." We reflect God's character uniquely, which, rather than giving us divine-size egos, should humble us to no end,

1. Quoted in *The Green Bible* (New York: HarperOne, 2008), I: 105.

and clue us in to the fact that we might have a special role to play in the grand drama of creation.

The notion that we are image-bearers, coupled with the idea that the earth belongs to God, has major implications for how we live and how we respond to God's charge to Adam to "serve the garden and keep it" (a paraphrase of Genesis 2:15). Cal Dewitt, professor of environmental studies at the University of Wisconsin-Madison, helpfully unpacks the Hebrew words for serve (*abad*) and keep (*shamar*). The first, *abad*, is sometimes translated *till, dress,* or *work*—all good gardening words—but it is the second word, *shamar,* that puts a new spin on what it means to be a good gardener for God. *Shamar* is sometimes translated *tend, guard, take care of,* and *look after.* Dewitt contends that *shamar* implies a "loving, caring, sustaining type of keeping."[2] The same word is used in the Aaronic blessing: "The Lord bless you and *keep* you; the Lord make his face to shine upon you, and be gracious to you" (Num 6:24–25).

All this points to our special role in creation, which is one of caretaking or stewarding. In fact, it is our unique position as image-bearers that qualifies us to steward God's creation.

CREATION IS GOOD

"God saw everything that he had made, and indeed, it was very good" (Gen 1:31). The idea that the material world is good makes theological sense. After all, God would not have taken on a human body himself if flesh were inherently evil. Through the incarnation, Jesus both affirms his creation and brings redemption to that creation. Christians believe that Jesus was fully man and fully God. Yes, he came to redeem the world, but he did so eating and drinking, walking and sleeping. And working. Jesus was a carpenter, for goodness' sake—he worked with wood, with callused hands and with sweat in his eyes.

If matter is good and Jesus fully "materialized"—that is, he participated fully in the material life that all humans participate in—then that puts an end to dualistic notions that there is a division between the material and the spiritual, whereby the spiritual always stands over against the physical and is superior to it. It certainly sheds a holy light on woodworking! It also sheds a holy light on all manner of "earthy" jobs, from ditch digging to diaper changing to gardening to fish and frog studying.

---

2. Calvin B. DeWitt, *Earth-Wise: A Biblical Response to Environmental Issues* (Grand Rapids: CRC Publications, 1994), 40.

If the material/spiritual divide is only an intellectual construct, then how does one do one's work Christianly? Does the Christian biologist hum hymns while searching for signs of salamanders? Does she exclaim, "Praise the Lord!" when measuring a fresh water mussel, discovering it's over one hundred years old? Does she preach to the birds as St. Francis was said to have done? Maybe. But more fundamentally, she approaches her vocation and her tasks with a degree of reverence that acknowledges the goodness of creation and the creator who made it.

EVERYTHING IS CONNECTED

The basic premise of ecology is that everything is connected. The very definition of ecology embodies this truth: *eco* from the Greek *oikos*, for "household," and *logia*, for "the study of." Anyone who has grown up in a household understands that it is a complicated web of interrelated relationships. In essence, the word ecology draws attention to the relationships between living things and their environment. It implies that if one tinkers with one bit of the world, the effects are felt in radiating ripples throughout the rest of the world. To paraphrase John Muir, tug at this bit of creation and you find that it is attached to everything else.[3]

The Old Testament prophets were perhaps the first ecologists, drawing a picture for their listeners of the consequences of actions and choices that ripple out into the wider web of relationships. The prophets' genius lay in the way they extended the concept of ecology beyond the natural world to include humankind's broken relationship with God—which then leads to a broken relationship with other people and with creation itself. Consider the words of Hosea:

> Hear the word of the Lord, O people of Israel;
> for the Lord has an indictment against the inhabitants of the land.
> There is no faithfulness or loyalty,
> and no knowledge of God in the land.
> Swearing, lying, and murder, and stealing and adultery break out;
> bloodshed follows bloodshed.
> Therefore the land mourns, and all who live in it languish;
> together with the wild animals and the birds of the air,
> even the fish of the sea are perishing. (Hos 4:1–3)

3. John Muir, *My First Summer in the Sierra* (1911; San Francisco: Sierra Club Books, 1988), 110.

Not exactly a cheery passage. Although it was written thousands of years ago, these words sound startlingly similar to many newspaper headlines today, do they not? Fish, birds, and beasts die. Murder, theft, and adultery abound. People have lost their faith in God. Sounds like the *New York Times*. But whereas the *New York Times* presents such a litany of calamities in standalone articles, Hosea connects them, showing the ripple effect of sin. Creation's suffering is intrinsically linked to humanity's faithlessness, lack of love, and failure to acknowledge God. The trickle-down effect of our brokenness is a land that mourns and all (humans and non-humans) who live in it wasting away. This is certainly what we are seeing around the world today.

The International Union for Conservation of Nature (IUCN) reports species extinction rates that are between one thousand to ten thousand times the natural background rates (the natural rate without human interference). According to their research, we are currently facing the possible extinction of 12 percent of birds, 22 percent of mammals, and 30 percent of amphibians worldwide.[4] These are staggering figures that should raise alarm bells for all who believe that creation is the handiwork of a loving God.

But environmental degradation does not just affect the fish, birds, and beasts, as Hosea so aptly points out. Humans suffer too. The UN recently reported that "environmental refugees" (people who are displaced because of environmental degradation) already outnumber those who are refugees as a result of conflict. Conflicts will, in fact, be increasingly driven by the scarcity of natural resources.

In our experience with A Rocha, it is our brothers and sisters in the developing world who best understand the dire implications of degraded ecosystems and are calling us to change. Our friend Stella Simiyu, a native Kenyan and a Senior Research Scientist in plant conservation at the National Museums of Kenya, writes this about the predicament of the poor. "If you look at Africa, the rural poor depend directly on the natural resource base. This is where their pharmacy, supermarket, power company and water company are. What would happen to you if these things were removed from your local neighbourhood? We must invest in environmental conservation because this is how we enhance the ability of the rural poor to have options and provide for them ways of getting out of the poverty trap."[5]

4. www.iucnredlist.org

5. Stella Simiyu, "The Word, Conversation and a Human Face: An African Perspective," a lecture delivered at *Keeping Earth In Common: A Just Faith for a Whole World* Conference at Regent College, Vancouver, BC, 2006.

Stella and her countrymen and women are calling us to what God has called us all to: "to do justice, and to love kindness, and to walk humbly with [our] God" (Mic 6:8). They are calling us to acknowledge that when we in the industrialized West tug on the thread of our extravagant and selfish consumption, the web quivers all over the planet in the form of species extinction and social injustice.

LIVING HOPEFULLY

Hope is a rare commodity in the environmental world, as our friends at the University of British Columbia pointed out. One of the liabilities of an ecological education, writes Aldo Leopold, one of the foremost nature writers of the twentieth century, is that one "lives alone in a world of wounds."[6] Knowing what conservationists know, it is only logical that they would be tempted to despair. But the Christian way is one of hope—a hope in the very real redemption of all things. Consider Paul's words in Colossians:

> [Jesus] is the image of the invisible God, the firstborn of all creation: for in him all things in heaven and on earth were created, things visible and invisible, whether thrones or dominions or rulers or powers—all things have been created through him and for him. He himself is before all things, and in him all things hold together. He is the head of the body, the church; he is the beginning, the firstborn from the dead, so that he might come to have first place in everything. For in him all the fullness of God was pleased to dwell, and through him God was pleased to reconcile to himself all things, whether on earth or in heaven, by making peace through the blood of his cross. (Col 1:15–20)

This passage roots us in hope—a hope that someday, somehow, someway, redemption is possible for all things. Redemption, as understood by Paul and other biblical writers, has more to do with re-creation than with a whisking away of souls to heaven. N.T. Wright uses the synonyms of "healing" and "transformation" to get at the fullness of this theologically meaty word.[7] Redemption is fulfilled in shalom and the reign of God. In Colossians, Paul links creation and humanity's redemption through the person of Jesus. Through Christ *all things* were created; he sustains (or holds together) *all things* and then through his resurrection he reconciles

6. Aldo Leopold, *Round River* (New York: Oxford University Press, 1993), 165.

7. N.T. Wright, *Surprised by Hope* (New York: HarperOne, 2008), 212.

all things. Where might *all things* stop, do you think? Does it stop with people? That is how Christians often read it. Only people are reconciled. But the radical point this passage seems to be making is that creation itself participates in redemption. It is our anthropocentric view of the world that causes us to read *all things* as *all people*. When reflecting on this passage, Wright contends that "redemption is not simply making creation a bit better, as the optimistic evolutionist would try to suggest. Nor is it rescuing spirits and souls from an evil material world, as the Gnostic would say. It is the remaking of creation."[8]

Paul also hits on this theme of creation's redemption in the book of Romans when he says that "the creation waits . . . in hope that [it] will be set free from its bondage to decay and will obtain the freedom of the glory of the children of God" (Rom 8:20–21). Creation's redemption is part of the warp and woof of his first-century Jewish worldview, and Paul includes it here in a way that assumes his readers already believe it as well. He uses creation's groaning and hoping for release as a metaphor for our own suffering and our own eventual redemption. Creation's "hope" in a future redemption is meant to strengthen our own human hope in the midst of trials.

This understanding has serious implications for our motivation in caring for creation. We do not try to save the world: rather, we join in the saving work God has already begun. We co-operate with the Spirit in making all things new. This hope of all things made new, both present and future, finds its grounding in Jesus' bodily resurrection. And so our ultimate hope is not "disembodied souls in heaven" but flesh and blood resurrection in a new (that is, renewed) creation. While we must remain content to live in the mystery of how this will actually unfold, Christ's resurrected body provides hints of what this transformation will be like, and points to all of creation's future transformation and renewal. Those hints are seen in the physicality of Jesus even after the resurrection. He chews and swallows bread, he is recognizable by friends (though sometimes after some confusion or hesitation), he still bears wounds in his side, and he starts a fire and fries fish for his disciples. He also walks through walls and is teleported through the air and out of sight. Clearly he is still "bodily," but with strange new abilities. He has not only ensured redemption for his creation but has experienced it in his own self.

It is this hope—a hope centred on God's ultimate care for what God has made—that allows us to "be joyful though [we] have considered all

8. Ibid., 97.

the facts," as Wendell Berry says.[9] And hope, if it is true, runs deep, with taproots nourished by a subterranean grace that flows strong and swift despite outer circumstances. It is what keeps us going.

SUMMING UP

The interconnectedness which God has built into the natural world is also apparent in the Gospel and in the church. Biblically understood, the church is one body made up of many parts, and it takes all parts to live out the whole Gospel. Most often the context right in front of us just happens to be the mission field that God is calling us to. Therefore, we applaud the caring community development worker, the humble evangelist, the erudite theologian, the dogged relief worker, the clever novelist, and the compassionate civil rights activist. All these are messengers of God's love and help bring God's kingdom to earth. We need them all (just as we need construction workers, police officers, parents, and artists who see their vocations as "spiritual" callings). But we should not become reductionistic. Just because we all have specific gifts, it does not mean that we can shuffle off our responsibilities in other areas. While creation care *as a vocation* is a specific calling, *as a missional way of life* it is everyone's calling. Just as every Christian is called to witness to God's love and to promote justice for those without a voice, so too, all Christians are called to steward creation. All Christians are called to co-operate with God in his work of redemption of all things.

WORKING IT OUT WITH A ROCHA

Inspired by the biblical mandate to care for creation, A Rocha has taken shape in twenty countries around the world over the past thirty years. In each place, we work to show God's love for all creation through practical, hands-on conservation and education projects. In Canada, A Rocha has restored salmon streams in British Columbia, controlled invasive species on the Prairies, and grown organic vegetables for those living on low incomes across the country. All this has been done in and through community. We two were part of a team that formed A Rocha's first environmental centre on the southern British Columbia coast. To get an idea of what we

9. Wendell Berry, "A Mad Farmer's Manifesto," in *The Collected Poems of Wendell Berry* (New York: North Point Press, 1987), 151–52.

are about at these centres, imagine a youth hostel meets the Sierra Club, and ground the whole thing in Christian hospitality.

That first centre was and is a place where all four of humanity's most fundamental relationships—with God, fellow humans, ourselves, and creation—have a chance to flourish. Interns and volunteers with little or no church background live among people of Christian faith and see what that faith can look like in ordinary, everyday life. People are encouraged to learn to love and forgive those different from themselves as they work, play, share meals, and share common space together. And, of course, everyone who comes rolls up their sleeves and cares for creation in practical ways.

Because A Rocha Canada was born on the Pacific coast, our conservation efforts began with that iconic Pacific creature—the salmon. Few animals on Canada's West Coast symbolize the link between forest and ocean ecosystems better than Pacific salmon. It's the old hip-bone-connected-to-the-thigh-bone song and dance, but with an ecological twist, all done against the backdrop of one of creation's greatest migration cycles.

Hazards abound for the Pacific salmon. Foremost among them are urbanization and resource extraction, both of which lead to the loss of habitat. A Rocha has worked to protect and restore salmon habitat to ensure that this amazing creature continues to thrive. In British Columbia, we have done this primarily in the Little Campbell River watershed in which our Brooksdale Environmental Centre is situated. The Little Campbell is an urban and rural jewel and has recently been named by the Outdoor Recreation Council as one of British Columbia's top twelve endangered rivers.

"But for all this," as Gerard Manley Hopkins says, "nature is never spent."[10] Despite habitat degradation, the Little Campbell River and its watershed continue to host hundreds of species, some of which are recognized as threatened, like the Red-legged Frog (*Rana aurora*) and the Oregon Forestsnail (*Allogona townsendiana*). Another is the critically endangered Salish Sucker (a previously unknown subspecies of *Catostomus catostomus*), recently rediscovered by an A Rocha intern, at a time when it had not been seen in the watershed in more than thirty years. The river is also home to Coho, Chinook, and Chum salmon, as well as Steelhead and Cutthroat trout, all species in various stages of stress.

---

10. Gerard Manley Hopkins, "God's Grandeur," in *The New Oxford Book of English Verse* (Oxford: Oxford University Press, 1972), 786.

We have taken a two-pronged approach to the care for the river and the greater watershed. The first is habitat enhancement and restoration. The second is conservation science research. Habitat enhancement and restoration is basically a fancy way of saying pulling weeds and planting plants. Those who have studied ecology understand that "weed" in this case is code for "invasive species," an issue high on environmental radars. Because they come from afar, some introduced species have no natural predators or competitors in their new ecosystems, and thus reproduce without check, leaving a "desert" for indigenous species whose prey, soil, or forage have been consumed by these newcomers.

Thanks to an endless army of volunteers working under the oversight of our former science director, Glen Carlson, and our new stewardship coordinator, Christy Juteau, we have pulled, cut, and removed literally tons of English Ivy, Himalayan Blackberry, Purple Loosestrife, and Canary Reed Grass from the Little Campbell watershed. We have also planted truckloads of native plants, carved out rearing channels for salmon fry, and laid hundreds of pounds of gravel to guard against erosion. In fact, each year since we moved to the watershed, we have completed three or four restoration projects in partnership with local municipalities, land-owners, and funders like the Pacific Salmon Foundation. All these efforts combine to make the Little Campbell River a more hospitable place not only for young and spawning salmon but for the myriad of species from River Otters to Western Red Cedars that benefit from the salmon's final gift of life's nutrients.

All this, every weed pulled, every truckload of gravel poured, and every species preserved, has been a missional act, for each weed pulled and each stretch of river restored is a participation in God's redemptive work. It is co-operation with God's Spirit working to make all things new.

This commitment to hands-on conservation as mission undergirds everything else we do at A Rocha. While we believe in the importance of advocacy and activism, A Rocha is unique among faith-based conservation groups because of our dedication to on-the-ground conservation and re-search. Yes, we train, educate, inspire, and encourage, but we also pull, plant, study, and restore. This kind of work is not flashy, but it also is not a flash-in-the-pan, since we are committed to specific places over the long term. This kind of commitment requires getting to know our neighbours, both human and non-human, and persistently working for the health of all.

If it is our commitment to hands-on conservation that makes us unique in the faith-based environmental world, then it is doing it well that gives us credibility in the secular conservation world, with whom we partner. In this regard, we are reminded of the Ugly Bug Ball, which we have hosted every second year for the past six years. The ball is not really a ball (though there is a dance in the evening, where everyone comes dressed as their favourite invertebrate), but a full day of encouragement, knowledge sharing, and appreciation put on by the Department of Fisheries and Oceans Canada (DFO) and the Pacific Streamkeepers Federation. The party is a way of thanking volunteers from all over the Greater Vancouver Area for their efforts in stewarding their local salmon-bearing streams. Basically, DFO throws the party and A Rocha provides the setting.

This might seem like an odd partnership—a government entity and a faith-based organization—and, truth be told, the DFO officers initially thought so as well. The scouting delegation they sent to see if our property would make a good site emerged from their big blue diesel trucks looking circumspect. Markku met them in the driveway and grasped the nettle straight away, asking what they thought about us being a Christian group. A couple of delegates admitted that it made them a little nervous. Markku assured them that he was not going to whack them on the sides of their heads with a Bible. A Rocha's conservation work was not a front for proselytizing, he said. They began to breathe a bit more easily. He went on to explain how doing good conservation work was an outworking of our Christian calling to steward creation. They got that. Then Markku rattled off some of our projects, such as our participation in the BC Coastal Shorebirds survey and, of course, our work on the Little Campbell River. By the end of their visit a date was set for the first Ugly Bug Ball and everyone was smiling and slapping backs.

The feelings of goodwill and admiration are mutual and have grown over the six years of partnering. We enjoy the music, games, and presentations when all those ugly bugs descend on the centre and our guests enjoy the property as they stroll down the forest path and wander around the garden. Some even take an interest in who we are and what we are doing.

WORKING IT OUT IN THE CHURCH

Churches are called to be a transforming presence in their communities. Historically, this transformation has happened as Christians have banded together to start hospitals, rally against slavery, and establish schools and orphanages. More recently, the church's potential as a catalyst for transformation is being understood as extending beyond just the societal (vital as that is) and to the creation itself. Therefore, many churches now have "Green Teams" or "Environmental Stewardship Committees." Spurred on by their "green" church mates, more and more churchgoers are getting rid of styrofoam cups during coffee hour in favour of ceramic mugs. They are screwing in higher efficiency LED and compact fluorescent lights bulbs in their sanctuaries. They are listening to sermons on the theology of creation and reading books that inspire them to live out a holistic ethic of steward-ship. These are just some of the myriad of ways a culture of conservation is being fostered in the Christian community, which, when combined, add up to significant acts of creation care. To help equip churches to further their transformational impact, A Rocha has recently launched Good Seed Sunday.[11]

Perhaps the most tangible and effective creation care project a church can embark on is a community garden. Community gardens provide a way for church members to do something incredibly practical—they get to dig, plant, harvest, and help a neighbour through the sweat of their brows and out of the goodness of the hearts.

The members of Saanich Community Church on Vancouver Island certainly found this to be true. In 2006, a small band of green-thumbed congregants joined together to transform half an acre of their church property into a thriving community garden. Their first task was to dig up a portion of a lawn and a tangle of brambles that would serve as their gar-den. Today, the garden enlists up to fifty church volunteers (some regulars, some just for an afternoon) who have built a greenhouse, laid irrigation lines, and grown bushels and bushels of organic vegetables each summer. This produce has been distributed to the Mustard Seed Food Bank where it is made available to hundreds of local families living on low income. Burl Jantzen, a member of Saanich Community Church, has this to say about the garden: "The community building and intergenerational aspect of the project has been fantastic for our church, as seniors work alongside youth on our Saturday volunteer days, in order to help feed our less fortu-nate neighbours."[12]

St. Margaret's Anglican Church in inner-city Winnipeg is another example of a congregation rolling up their sleeves to care for creation, as well as care for those living on the economic margins. They've partnered with A Rocha in our Just Growing project, fostering a connection be-tween food, creation, and community in one the city's most impoverished

11. www.goodseedsunday.com.
12. Interview with authors, April 2011.

neighbourhoods. Because the church property itself is mostly taken up with a building and parking lot, A Rocha community organizer Jen Kornelsen did something creative and adventuresome: she approached people living on the blocks around the church to see if they'd be interested in "donating" their front lawns for this community garden initiative. Amazingly, some were! One woman even offered space in her backyard greenhouse so that the Just Growing gang could start seedlings for later transplant. Residents of several social housing societies have joined in the project, growing and harvesting and canning food. They have participated in regular Friday Feast Days and a fall Harvest Festival where they have enjoyed live music and delicious food grown by their own hands. In all this they have regained a measure of dignity, as they have been empowered to provide themselves with the most basic of necessities.

So, can planting potatoes really be mission? It seems so humble, so simple, so old fashioned—like something our grandmas did. It is so much less dramatic than chaining oneself to a tree to save an endangered forest, or travelling to the Outer Hebrides to band Storm Petrels, or hunkering down in famine-ravaged Africa to start an orphanage. Planting a garden is just so . . . ordinary. But then so are the words of Jeremiah to the Jewish people during the Babylonian exile: "Build houses and live in them; plant gardens and eat what they produce. Take wives and have sons and daughters. . . . But seek the welfare of the city where I have sent you into exile, and pray to the Lord on its behalf, for in its welfare you will find your welfare" (Jer 29:5–7). When we seek the welfare of the city, when we plant gardens, when we care for creation, we join with the first Gardener who walked in the shade of the garden and saw that it was good. We join with the Gardener who walks now through our broken world and who, through our hands and our feet and our trowels, works to make all things new.

PART 3

A Garden that will Last

As EVERY GARDENER KNOWS, it is easy enough to sow some seeds and watch them grow. Any child can do it. But it is quite another to create a garden that will last for years, and perhaps for generations. Lots of new things are springing up in the church in Canada, and it is a delight to watch the creativity of the Spirit of Jesus bringing these things to birth and to first growth. But will these things last? Will they one day celebrate a fifty year anniversary? A five hundred year anniversary? In the ecology of God, it seems likely that some new Christian communities will be like annuals—beautiful in their season, but not meant to last—while others are perennials, and yet others will grow into apple trees, and apple orchards, and even old growth forests. What can be done to encourage healthy growth, so that each new shoot can fulfill its potential? This section looks at the resources needed to grow "a garden that will last."

There is no one-size-fits-all kind of leadership. Every kind of organization, every kind of church, needs a different kind of leader. A small church of fifty requires a different set of leadership gifts from a church of five thousand—and they are not interchangeable. In this day, when the church is learning to make the shift from maintaining the church as we remember it to being a missionary church, yet another kind of leadership is required. This is painful for those who have been leading traditional congregations for years, perhaps decades. We ask, "What did I do wrong?" and equally poignantly, "What future is there for me now?" We may be assured that God will always find a use for the gifts God has given to people, even if they are not in areas we expected. Yet at the same time, the church needs to discover and nurture new kinds of leaders for this new day. Who are they and where are they to be found? And equally important, how can they be prepared and helped to take their place in the leadership of the church for the next generation?

12

What Kind of Leaders Do We Need?

Alan J. Roxburgh

MY HOME IS IN the Pacific Northwest on the North Shore of Vancouver in what was once an old growth forest. Tall trees surround us, a constant reminder of the forest that once stood here. At the top of the driveway stands a straight, tall Douglas fir. At least two hundred years old, its massive bulk towers above all other trees and marks our home. It has withstood a multitude of windstorms, snowfalls, and incessant rains. The reason is simple. Its roots go deep into the ground, into and around the rock. By contrast, there are clusters of hemlock in front of the house. They are much younger trees that grew up quickly over past years, climbing above the canopy toward the sun, providing us with cooling shade in the summer. But there are problems with these young upstarts. Their roots do not go deep. They sprang up quickly by spreading out shallow roots just under the surface, following the puddling rain and taking advantage of the surface soil.

An arborist who has lived in the community for years tells us that he has taken down many hemlocks from our property over the years. Walking around the trees, he shows us the fungus growing on them, hardly noticeable to the untrained eye, and tells us it is a telltale sign that these trees are at risk because their shallow roots produce poor resistance to the fungus. Then he turns to the majestic Douglas, telling us it will last long after our lives are over. Its roots go very deep indeed.

This chapter addresses the question of what kind of leaders we need for the church today. I am addressing the question to those seemingly old

Douglas firs of our church world and the leadership forms they have developed. In the final section, I will return to this image and its implications for churches today.

IT'S NOT MAKING ANY DIFFERENCE

It was one of those in-between days of early spring. Through the windows of our meeting space one could see thick snow screening out the street. An hour later, bright sunshine flooded over the daffodils and the temperature sat in the mid-20s. It is sometimes hard to know what time of year it really is from moment to moment. I was meeting with clergy from a national denomination to talk about leadership in these in-between times. Ann shared why she had come. A graduate of a well-known seminary, with a B.A. and M.Div, and working on a D.Min, she commented, "I'm a well-trained leader. Seminary prepared me well with the skills and competencies of leadership. Without overstating it, I'm good at what I do, at the top of my game, and one of the better preachers in our denomination. But none of it is making any difference!"

Ann's experience is one of trying to be an effective leader, in a context where expectations about church and leadership have shifted. The rules have changed. Leaders find themselves in this new space. Ann is not looking to discard what she has been taught. She knows, however, that it is insufficient and does not know what to do about it. Around the room heads were nodding in agreement. As denominations and churches become de-centered in our culture, leaders are increasingly disoriented and anxious: most of what they are doing is not making any difference. So what kind of leadership do we need for this new place?

CONTEXT: LOSS AND OPPORTUNITY

Churches whose roots go back to Europe and the UK had a long period of success across North America. They are now mostly in decline. Judicatories (whether they be called associations, presbyteries, regions, or dioceses) can no longer underwrite the ongoing life of congregations or clergy. Since the end of the last millennium, an undercurrent of decline has become a tsunami of change threatening to make these systems obsolete. This does not imply the ending of these once dominant European churches but, if they are to thrive, they will need to re-imagine their identity and role. This will require them to re-engage with the stories of their beginnings and understand how these stories were turned into the superficial pragmatics of the modern era.

In this inexorable unravelling, countless proposals have been made to fix, renew, and revitalize existing forms of congregational life and church leadership. These efforts have not changed the trajectory. We cannot address the question about what kind of leaders we need without recognizing that we are at the end of a long period of trying to fix, revitalize, and re-jig. We have arrived at a land where current maps of leadership and ways of practicing church no longer engage the geography.[1]

In this new space, the majority of people under the age of fifty live after the Christian story. They have no memory and no narrative forms of Christian life. Unlike previous generations, there is no established story to which churches can appeal. Inviting people "back to church" is like asking the majority of Canadians to describe the taste of yellow. This has massive implications for the question of what kind of leaders we need. With few exceptions, seminaries are still training managers for the internal ethos of existing churches. Their habits and practices remain directed toward managing existing congregations. They are largely disconnected from, and threatened by, the socio-cultural space in which the majority of Canadians live. We need leaders who are comfortable moving back into their own neighborhoods, becoming missionaries in this strange new place that is now our culture. This requires a re-orientation of focus and energy away from internal management and into the neighborhoods.

This simple movement is actually very complex. It involves addressing the expectations of congregations, who demand that their leaders spend time looking after them and providing religious goods and services. Furthermore, the invitation to re-engage with their community is often cast in the default language of meeting needs. Meeting needs, while important, leaves the church in the place of control, management, and power. We need leaders with the theological frames to understand this dynamic and the skills to assist congregations to make the cultural change implicit in the dynamics of Luke 10:1–12, a story that frames the church as those who need to receive (rather than give) hospitality, and the local context as the primary location of God's activity.

1. See Alan J Roxburgh, *Missional Map Making* (San Francisco: Jossey Bass, 2011).

LEADERS WHO RECOGNIZE
THAT GOD IS THE PRIMARY AGENT

We need leaders who can read our situation from a specific perspective: God is the primary agent in our world. The unravelling of the churches and the transformations of society are not only the result of socio-cultural shifts. First and foremost, they are the actions of God. We need leaders able to perceive the shape of God's activities in the midst of a great unravelling. The "disembedding" of Christian life in our society is the work of God. There is no putting back together the religious consensus that once had the church near the centre.

God's Spirit is up to something massively disruptive across Western societies. Perhaps the Spirit is pushing the churches into spaces they cannot manage or control so that they might rediscover their missional identity. The implication, if accepted, is that we are looking at the re-founding, rather than the renewing, of the church. The socio-cultural milieu in which most of our churches were formed no longer exists. The shapers of the churches in the West were often wise leaders and brilliant missiologists. But in the modern period, churches and their leaders became chaplains to nation states, social contracts, and individualism. We are past the point of renewing church life around these assumptions. Our vocation as leaders is to re-found churches as missionary communities of the kingdom.

LEADERS AS MISSIONARIES

The question of leadership is a missiological question. The primary skills of leadership remain: liturgy, managing programs, preaching, visitation, and presence in life passages. These skills were developed to function in a world of loyalty and memory where the church was an assumed part of the cultural centre. In a missionary context, a much broader tool kit is required. Leaders will need to be comfortable entering and participating in the diverse, mixed communities in which they find themselves. When Lesslie Newbigin went to India as a young missionary, fresh out of seminary, he assumed he was taking "the Gospel" (objective truths to be told). As the result of a bus accident requiring a long convalescence, he discovered that he needed to sit in the village circles, entering their ways of life, in order to understand how the Gospel was communicated in a new space. The result of this experience was his own conversion to the Gospel over and over again. The conversion came through sitting with others, rather than treating them as objects to receive his content.

This shift in the locus and identity of leaders requires a fundamental change in thinking about leadership. It calls for leaders with the confidence and capacities to re-locate their self-understanding in terms of role and energy into the risky spaces outside the walls of the current church. Denominational leaders must model this shift. Their energies must migrate from administration and management in order to become missionaries in their own local contexts, in order to model and form a movement of mission-shaped leaders.

Training schools need to be re-founded. For too long their locus of energy has been directed toward the academy. Roman Catholic missiologist Robert Schreiter describes the critical importance of forming local theologians who, through action-learning, construct local theology in their contexts.[2] These are the kinds of leaders that training schools need to form. Clemens Sedmak, in *Doing Local Theology*, writes about forming artisans who are competent in shaping missional communities "in the local." Such artisans understand that meaning is found more in the local and the ordinary than in the abstract and the universal.[3] And Catholic missiologist Gerald Arbuckle asserts that the crisis facing the churches is now so great that it has to be re-founded.[4] These three writers are naming what is at stake.

When we feel under threat, we retreat to our defaults. Leaders are still searching for techniques that will give them back the capacity to "manage" the churches and turn them around. Energy remains focused on techniques like church health, revitalization, growth, and worship. These powerful defaults for fixing the church are resurgent across North America. This search for models (emergent, missional, fresh expressions, revitalization, planting) is understandable. However, it mostly illustrates the default position of attempting to make the church work again. Like a fight-flight adrenalin rush, these models may give energy for a time, but they will not address the underlying need for a missiological re-founding of the church. Focusing on questions of how to make the church work is a mistake. We cannot address the questions of God's mission by focusing on questions of the church's future. Leaders must ask different questions.

2. Robert J. Schreiter, *Constructing Local Theologies* (Maryknoll, NY: Orbis, 2008).

3. Clemens Sedmak, *Doing Local Theology: A Guide for Artisans of a New Humanity* (Maryknoll, NY: Orbis, 2002).

4. Gerald A. Arbuckle, *Earthing the Gospel* (Collegeville, MN: Liturgical Press, 2002).

The crisis besetting the churches is not one of management, adjustment, or revitalization; neither can it be addressed by local leaders alone. It is systemic. Bishops, denominational executives, teachers, presidents, and boards must lead with the courage to see that the Spirit has pushed us into spaces where the time of fixing is over. All of us—local, regional, national, and school leaders—must become practicing missionaries in the local for the re-founding of the church.

LEADERS WHO ASK QUESTIONS
ABOUT CONTEXT AND TRADITION

The re-founding of the church cannot begin by asking church questions: how do we make the church work in our culture? How do we make the church grow? How do we re-apply the five-fold ministry of Ephesians? How do we develop apostles for the church? Leaders need to ask a fundamentally different question: what is God up to, out ahead of us in the neighbourhoods and communities where we live? We cannot address the refounding of the church without first engaging the missiological questions of what God is doing in our contexts. Church questions are secondary to the missiological question of God's activities in our communities.

One thoughtful commentator on our situation is Walter Brueggemann. An organizing metaphor he proposes for our experience is exile. [5] Not that there is a factual parallel between the Babylonian captivity and our situation. Rather, Brueggemann claims that the North American church in exile is the remnant of a colonial, imperial project. Although the imagery of exile can cause existing churches to avoid asking the hard questions about their situation, Brueggemann helpfully suggests three ways in which the exiles in Babylon responded to their situation—and by analogy, which our churches may do as well:

1. Assimilation, which involves capitulating to the dominant culture by re-ordering our understanding of God and our religious practices around the narratives of the regnant culture. Much of the "attractional church" process is an example of this imagination—as seen in the continuing "worship wars."

2. Despair, which shapes its life around a sense of helplessness, of feeling unable to do anything about the situation. It is stunning, for example,

5. Walter Brueggemann, *Cadences of Home* (Louisville, KY: Westminster John Knox Press, 1997), 115ff.

to hear how many clergy are simply hanging on for retirement (increasingly postponed because the economic dream of the West has failed), or how younger leaders write off existing churches and view church planting as the only viable way forward. In each case, these perspectives are functionally despairing of a God who continually takes that which we give up on and declare useless, in order to call forth the "new thing" of the kingdom.

3. Theological work that births a fresh discernment of what God is doing. We need leaders who can do this theological work. It involves a fresh engagement with both our traditions and our contexts. Bishops, denominational executives, teachers, boards, and local leaders require the courage and competencies to frame the challenges before the churches within a theological imagination of a disruptive God who is unravelling settled practices and has plunged us into uncharted territories. This is what Schreiter, Arbuckle, and Sedmak mean by "local theologians" and "artisans of the local." People like Shane Claiborne on the east coast and Tim Soerens in Seattle, with a host of others, illustrate this new kind of leadership. They are theologically informed and seek to frame the life of their churches in the midst of understanding what God is up to in the local. Schools such as Tyndale Seminary, Toronto (under the guidance of Don Goertz), and the Seattle School of Theology (under the encouragement of Dwight Friesen), are forming leaders shaped by theological work rooted in the local. The "pioneer stream" in the M.Div program at Wycliffe College in Toronto is also developing in this direction.

Brueggemann offers other metaphors that illuminate the theological work needed. In *Tradition for Crisis*,[6] he portrays Hosea as representative of eighth-century B.C. leaders for whom the existing traditions could no longer engage the challenges of their time. These prophets called Israel to re-engage with its more ancient traditions. Babylon, for example, was not primarily an experience of exile but of unmanageable space where God's people painfully re-entered their tradition in order to re-imagine their vocation. We need leaders who understand that this is our situation and have the courage to lead their people into these realities.

Such theological re-imagination, for Brueggemann, involves a twofold engagement—with the ancient tradition and with one's context. There

6. Walter Brueggemann, *Hosea: Tradition for Crisis* (Atlanta: John Knox Press, 1968).

is a dual aspect to Brueggemann's use of the term *crisis*. First, it means that the current ways churches understand themselves as being in crisis, because they cannot address a radically changed situation. The way church life was formed in the post-Reformation, industrializing West is not sustainable in globalizing societies. This is the crisis of a specific historical tradition that, from the sixteenth century to the present, viewed itself as *the* normative way of being the church. The crisis is the unsustainability of this tradition.

But, second, this crisis opens the possibility of rediscovering more deeply rooted but often forgotten traditions that can reconnect the churches with the mission of God. This opening of possibility is theological work, on the ground and in the ordinary, shaped by everyday life.[7] We need local theologians, "artisans of a new humanity,"[8] rooted in the ordinary, local, everyday life of the communities in which they live, who grasp that theology matters—not an abstract theology for the academy, but one that emerges from asking what God is up to in the local.

LEADERS SITUATED IN THE "SPACE BETWEEN"

If leaders ask theological questions in the context of the local, this has a huge amount to say about the primary location of such leadership. Over the past dozen years, the missional conversation has been re-appropriated by the default question of how to make the church work. The word "missional" has become debased coinage, used for everything we do. The language has lost touch with Newbigin's generative missiological question: "My purpose . . . is to consider what would be involved in a genuinely missionary encounter between the Gospel and the culture that is shared by the peoples of Europe and North America, their colonial and cultural off-shoots, and the growing company of educated leaders in the cities of the world—the culture which those of us who share it usually describe as 'modern.'"[9]

Newbigin was focused on the question of how the Gospel engages Western culture. This missiological orientation has been re-colonized,

7. For an important framing of this practice from the perspective of a theologian and anthropologist, see Michel de Certeau, *The Practice of Everyday Life,* trans. Steven Rendall (Berkeley: University of California Press, 1984).

8. Sedmak, *Doing Local Theology.*

9. Lesslie Newbigin, *Foolishness to the Greeks: The Gospel and Western Culture* (Grand Rapids: Eerdmans, 1986), 1.

however, by an ecclesiocentric imagination preoccupied with fixing the churches and reclaiming their central place in culture. But the church was not the subject of his missiological imagination. Newbigin wanted to understand the location of the Gospel in terms of Western culture(s)—a very different perspective.

The reasons for the abandonment of Newbigin's missional perspective go directly to this question of the kind of leaders we need. The churches of European heritage operate out of spatial metaphors that pre-determine how leaders understand their role: this metaphor is inside-outside.[10] It suggests that the primary location of God's activities is inside the church. One has only to reference Reformation ecclesiology to see these metaphors at work. Despite Calvin's brilliant framing of the Spirit's work in the world at the beginning of his *Institutes*, the basic definition of the church in Reformed theology revolves around definitions such as the *place* where the Word is truly taught, the *place* where the sacraments are truly administered, and the *place* where discipline is rightly given. These are spatial metaphors that locate the real, effective work of God inside the church. Beyond that, modernity self-consciously established a *public-private* bifurcation, which carries within it this implicit sense of inside-outside space. It does not take much understanding of history to know where the churches located themselves in order to erect a bulwark against the perceived attacks of modernity.

The primary work of leadership is also inside this space (usually a physical space of bricks and mortar, despite our theological protestations to the contrary). The default understanding of leaders is around that which takes place inside buildings or church activities (liturgy, visitation, programs, and so on). This is why leaders are trained as managers. They are good at doing things when people come into this inside space (hence the interest in things like "Back to Church Sunday"), but uncomfortable navigating a role outside that circumscribed space. Part of the crisis is that people have stopped coming into church space. Leaders then work harder to make the inside space more attractive, hoping that this will bring people into their space of comfort, management, and expertise. An ancillary implication of this default metaphor is that those living in our neighbourhood are viewed as "outside" and objectified as sources of church growth.

This is not an argument against congregations being more attractional or an argument against liturgical practice and worship—that would

10. I explore these metaphors in depth in my forthcoming book, *A Theology of Leadership*.

be a silly argument to make. Indeed, many churches would do well to work on these elements. The point here is to question where the imaginative energies are located. It is to argue that certain spatial defaults predetermine how leaders understand their role and location. All of this was once fine for Christendom contexts, but it makes for a deficient imagination in our present situation.

We therefore need leaders shaped by a different metaphor, whose priestly vocation is to stand continually in the space where they are compelled to ask the question, what is God about among this group of people, in this specific community and neighbourhood, at this particular time? In the Bible, God continually turns up in the in-between spaces. This is how God comes to us in Jesus Christ. In the Incarnation, God chooses to be located in the ambiguous, awkward, continually negotiated spaces of ordinary, everyday life. This is what is going on in the hymn of Christ's self-emptying (Phil 2:5–11). It is about the God who is only known in the space-between. The leaders we need (lay, clergy, bishop, and denominational executives) must relocate their energy and locus in the neighbourhoods and communities where they live. This requires a massive act of will in the midst of centripetal forces. It is in the space-between that leaders learn to be God's missionary people.[11] The space-between has always been the space of generative missional life for the people of God—whether we think of the stories of creation, the desert sojourn, the Babylonian captivity, the Diaspora, the Incarnation, or the way the Spirit continually disrupted and broke apart the settled plans of the young church, so that the Apostles had little idea what was going on. Our disruptive moment suggests the Spirit is once again giving to us the gift of space-between. It is here that God's future breaks forth.

LEADERS: FROM MANAGERS TO MIDWIVES, ENVIRONMENTALISTS, AND POETS

Leaders are still working hard developing vision and mission statements for congregations and denominations. They have values-lists to guide people's attitudes and practices, and strategic plans to guide them into a

---

11. Canadian philosopher John Ralston Saul describes this metaphor of space-between in his book *A Fair Country: Telling Truths about Canada* (Toronto: Penguin Books, 2008) through his depictions of how First Nations peoples engage one another. I apply this to church leadership in more detail in *Missional: Joining God in the Neighborhood* (Grand Rapids: Baker, 2011).

preferred, biblically identified future. Each time I encounter these pro-cesses I ask, "How is this working for you?" The answers tell me that the predictable early adopters support the leader's vision, but that nothing has changed in terms of the broad membership. These activities do not affect a church's underlying DNA. In disruptive spaces, they actually misguide—while providing a certain confidence that the leaders are doing something.

If God is the active agent in this unravelling of church life, then God's Spirit is gestating a different future, and we need leaders with confidence that the Spirit is doing this among the ordinary people of their churches, rather than among experts and professionals. Such leaders are more like midwives and environmentalists than strategists and vision casters. *Midwives* know they do not make babies, but they know how to bring forth a baby. They work with a mother in birthing. *Environmentalists* attend to the rhythms of the local, and work with what is there; they do not impose alien processes, but assemble the elements that cause the local to thrive. Underlying each image is the conviction that in the midst of massive disruption, God is shaping something among ordinary people. Leaders, therefore, lay down their own need for vision and strategies, learning to call forth the unexpected being birthed by the Spirit.

This is not about the heroic leader with a planned future, but rather about *detectives of divinity*, attending to the clues of how the Spirit is forming the kingdom in the midst of the everyday. These are skills for discerning the impish, unsuspected ways the Spirit is pushing up fresh, green shoots among the people. Such shoots are always tentative. They are hardly noticeable to those preoccupied with vision, mission, and value statements. Detectives of divinity lay down their own agendas in order to see what cannot be seen from within assumed narratives. It involves the capacity to create safe spaces where people know they are not being recruited into one more plan. Safe spaces are like tables to which we are invited in dialogue with one another, rather than a spring baseball draft trying to get the A team on the bus.

Poets are listeners and shapers of meaning in the ordinary, not man-agers of programs. They are attentive to people's "off stage" narratives (the stories hidden beneath formal, expected public discourse; the body language that speaks more powerfully than the statements) that intimate the green shoots of the Spirit's nudging into the unexpected. Poets as-sist people to evoke these other narratives. They hardly ever proscribe. They are more focused on connecting off-stage narratives to God's great story than on telling. They do this connecting in ways that invite people to wrestle and discover how God's story is engaging and stretching their worlds. In such encounters, the Spirit calls up shoots from the dry ground in the form of a tentative "perhaps" that needs to be gently invited into experimentation.

LEADERS AS CREATORS OF EXPERIMENTS

The space we are in requires new skills and habits. In Egypt, Israel was good at making bricks and baking bread. In the desert, these were not the skills they needed to thrive. A different way of practicing life had to be discovered. We learn to make such changes through experimentation that invites testing, which implies failure, which engenders new learning and fresh experimenting. This is how congregations and denominations change. We need leaders who can form communities of experimentation.

Several years ago, a young leader in the Seattle area, Paul, moved into a discouraged congregation that had dwindled down to forty people. Most saw themselves as limited, the cast-offs of society. This downtown church had become a haven for hurt people. It was cut off from its community. Paul did not move in with a big plan but spent a lot of time with his people in their rental flats and coffee shops. Like a poet, he attended to their stories, detecting beneath the hurt longings for something more. Most could not give language to these longings, but Paul, in conversations and the weekly liturgy, connected these longings to God's story. Eventually, some tentatively talked about how they might be God's presence in the community. These tender shoots were cut off with comments like, "But I could never do that." At such, Paul gently said something like, "Why don't we try a little experiment?" He was creating a safe space in which people could tentatively risk. Today, walking in the neighborhood of this community, one sees that some of these "ordinary" people have birthed small businesses (a bakery, for example) rooted in the local. Church is becoming parish again; the kingdom is emerging from these tentative, ordinary shoots.

LEADERS AS RE-FRAMERS OF STORY AND TRADITION

The Douglas fir at the top of my driveway reminds me that I am part of an unfolding story about this part of the North Shore that existed long before I arrived and will continue long after I am gone. There are deeply rooted ways of life symbolized in that tree that we ignore to our own loss.

In Tolkien's *Lord of the Rings*, the Hobbits encounter the Ents, ancient tree herders, rooted deep in the rock and soil of ancient forests. They seem immobile, even dead, to the outside, uninformed eye of Hobbits in a hurry to get somewhere. They appear like old appendages, with little relevance to the forces of change swirling about them. But their role in the unfolding of some larger story was not over, despite all appearances. In the story, the Ents now know their lives are being threatened. To stand still, to remain immovable, would mean their death. However, this was not just about survival. They also became aware that they could play a critical role in the unfolding of a life and death drama. They debated for what seemed like (and was!) too long a time, but they finally chose to uproot themselves from cherished places and move. In so doing, they had a part to play in the changing of the times.

This is the moment for existing denominations in Canada. Nothing described above is intended to suggest otherwise. It does, however, suggest the depth of movement required. We need leaders who live into their own ancient traditions, not out of nostalgia, but with the awareness that in their stories are clues to how the disruptive Spirit is calling them out. Anglicans, for example, might rediscover that "parish" in post-Roman England was a secular term, taken up as a profoundly missiological engagement with a disintegrating world. Baptists might rediscover that their founding identity was not rooted in so-called Baptist theological distinctives (theological claims only came later, as a way of legitimating what had occurred), but in courageous people willing to risk and experiment for the sake of the kingdom in a broken society. Baptists have lost this DNA of disruption, dis-ease, and risking in the unknown. Mennonites might rediscover that their founders were Benedictines, writing out of that formative imagination. What might happen if they engaged these founding documents through the eyes of Benedictine spirituality? These churches, and others like them, are far past the renew-and-restructure defaults. The Ents cannot stay rooted in the places they created. For the sake of the world, they have to pull up roots and move. We need leaders who grasp this reality and discover how to join with what the Spirit is already doing in the local, among ordinary people.

Green Shoots 7
A Fellowship of Urbanites

reConnect Community
Toronto, Ontario

Sometimes, the road to life's true purpose does not head in a straight line. Just ask Ryan Sim. He knows all about 180-degree turns. That's what it took for him to leave a career in engineering physics and become an Anglican priest.

In 2009, after his arrival at St. Paul's, Bloor Street, a stone's throw from Toronto's most exclusive shopping district, Ryan helped initiate four fresh expressions of church, all aimed at young urban professionals. Whether they lived in the high-rise condos surrounding St. Paul's or commuted to work from the suburbs, Ryan was determined to find ways to reach out to city dwellers who had no previous connection to church and no knowledge of the Gospel. But he would have to dig deep.

He knew that the only experience of church for many in this group was attending weddings or funerals. And while the immediate needs of this population were not readily apparent—they were not in need of such basics as food or shelter, for instance—Ryan knew they needed the Gospel. But that would come later. First, they just needed to connect. "I'm really committed to that formative period of first impressions," he explains. "It starts with listening, serving needs in a community, and making disciples, and is followed later by worship and a mature church."

With an engineer's efficiency, he methodically set about researching his initial target audience of condo dwellers by starting with the statistics in an Environics poll. He also enlisted friends to do quick on-the-spot street surveys as residents came and went from their buildings. The picture that emerged was that of hardworking, isolated individuals with little or no sense of community beyond exchanging a brief "hi" in the elevator. Most said their friends were scattered across the city and stayed connected via social media.

Sleuth-like, Ryan spent a week walking the neighbourhood, looking for clues. Two of the things that stood out were the number of people coming home late with takeout food and the number of delivery people dropping off prepared meals. He saw a need. "By the time these folks get home, a bag of takeout is as good as it's going to get," Ryan says.

"ReConnect Food" was his answer. Ryan launched the come-and-make-your-own-meals-for-a-week program in April 2010. It ran every second Monday, offering healthy ingredients—cut, cleaned, and prepped—ready to assemble into nutritious meals to take home and eat during the week. The whole thing would take a single hour. The cost? Sixty dollars for four chef-planned entrées, each of which would feed three or four people.

The service was advertised through posters, on Facebook, and by word of mouth. Although people seemed interested, it was difficult to get them to commit. "They loved the idea," says Ryan, "but it was still a lot of money to put down for meals you haven't tasted, involving an organization you didn't know." The program ran from April to August 2010 and then was discontinued. Ryan admits he "learned a lot," but that he also felt "really disappointed personally."

Undaunted, he went back to the drawing board to begin afresh. Using research findings that showed that working types living in condos liked hiking but were having trouble doing it, Ryan launched "ReConnect Nature." The program organized inner-city hikes every other Monday evening. Each hike began at a designated subway station, moved through a wooded ravine, and ended at a pub.

During the first year, the average attendance was about eight people, says Ryan, although one cross-country ski event attracted twenty-five participants. "Almost every time, we had somebody new visiting and a few people made it a regular thing," he says.

Next came "ReConnect Community," again geared to un-churched professionals living an urban lifestyle. This program, which is ongoing, consists of a worshipping fellowship that gathers at 7 p.m. on Sunday evenings at St. Paul's. The welcoming ministry is set up à la Starbucks, with tables, lounge chairs, and café-style drinks.

The service begins with a song from popular culture related to the evening's theme. Then everyone is welcomed and the topic for the evening is introduced, sometimes with the help of a video. The first series focused on controversial perceptions of Christianity, such as whether or not Christians are prudish and judgmental.

"We ask a simple question that anyone would be able to answer," says Ryan, "even those with no previous knowledge of the Bible." A typical question might be, for example, "If you had to name your three greatest weaknesses, what would you say?" Following a five-minute discussion, Scripture is presented, often through on-screen animation; at other times, a single reading is accompanied by music.

Next comes a second question focused on Scripture, paving the way for more in-depth Bible study questions. During the three-minute discussion, people are encouraged to text or tweet their questions, "or just use an old-fashioned piece of paper," says Ryan. Two to four questions are answered each night and anyone who cannot attend can get answers to their questions online.

Although Ryan left ReConnect Community in early 2012 to start a new church plant elsewhere, the fellowship is still going strong. Average Sunday attendance over the course of the first year was between twenty-seven and thirty, all professionals—including lawyers and physicians—living in the condos surrounding St. Paul's. "On any given Sunday, about 40 percent of the people were new to the community," says Ryan. "They wouldn't have been in church otherwise and wouldn't have committed to Christ."

Some people like to call this fresh expression an "internal church plant," he continues, because it is working within the auspices of an established church, using financial resources from St. Paul's and an existing building. Ryan calls ReConnect Community "a great early experiment in church planting."

Now, Ryan is researching a new church plant focused on commuters living in Ajax, Ontario, a community of nearly 100,000 about twenty-five kilometres east of Toronto. Since 80 percent of the town's population commutes to work in the city, Ryan feels the time is ripe for reaching out to a captive, in-transit audience, using smartphone apps to deliver 10-minute Alpha Course sessions on marriage and parenting while they are sitting on the train or bus. The program is aptly called "Redeem the Commute."

"The Gospel doesn't change, but how we present it may," he says. "I want them to encounter Jesus and his teachings as they may apply to their lives, in a way that doesn't demand that they already be Christians."

He hopes to see small clusters of people form, studying the same material—on the train, the bus, in neighbourhoods, or at work. "My vision is that a network of small groups of people will emerge," says Ryan. "They'll be prepared to take the next step, which is something like a Christianity 101 course. When we get a critical mass, we'll have a great big celebration and invite them all to come together and celebrate the community that's forming."

K.J.

Creating new Christian communities is sometimes represented as a matter of entrepreneurial vision, creative planning, and charismatic leadership. It can thus appear to be a thoroughly human enterprise, fuelled by youthful enthusiasm and desperation about a dying church. No wonder some church planters burn out. But mission is not a new invention. The church only exists because of the eternal missionary heart of God. And the reason the church has spread around the world in the past two thousand years is that the Spirit of this missionary God has inspired and enabled it. So it should not surprise us that the sustenance we need for this work is primarily spiritual—and that the church has always known the resources we need. They are ancient, yet ever new. We just need to rediscover them.

13

The Ancient Paths

Spirituality for Mission

Constance Joanna Gefvert

THE CHURCH IS AT a crossroads, and we as disciples of Christ are also at a crossroads. As we seek ways to share the love of God in a culture where people are alienated from their own deepest longings, how can we stay rooted and grounded in our own experience of God?

Listen to these words of the Lord through Jeremiah: "Stand at the crossroads, and look, and ask for the ancient paths, where the good way lies; and walk in it; and find rest for your souls" (Jer 6:16). When Jeremiah wrote these words, he was voicing God's accusation that the people of Israel had rejected the ancient paths—those basic truths and practices of their religion that kept them rooted in their relationship to the Lord. As a result, the mission of God and the strength of the Hebrew people had been weakened.

In Canada, in these early years of the twenty-first century, we find ourselves in the midst of a society that has lost its way. Individualism and consumer greed threaten both our planet and our economic and social well-being. The church of God has been weakened in its ability to proclaim the Gospel. As we rediscover and recommit to God's mission among us, Jeremiah's words offer us consolation, encouragement, and hope. They challenge us to seek the ancient spiritual practices—disciplines that root us in our relationship with the God whom we serve. These practices are grounded in a rhythm of life that includes praying with scripture (*lectio divina*), protected times of silence and solitude to "practice the presence of God," meeting together for mutual support and encouragement, praying together, offering hospitality, making intercession, giving of our substance to others, and fasting (whether from food or from contemporary addictions like shopping and the internet).

Just as the "new" missional emphasis in the church is not really new but only renewed, so with the spiritual practices that give rise to that mission and supports it. The mission of God is as old as Jesus, as old as Abraham and Moses, and it requires the old, tried and true disciplines that root us in the life of Christ, so that our sense of call and our motivation for mission emerge from a relationship of love with the God who is three-in-one—Creator, Jesus, and Spirit—a God of relationship.

WHAT ARE WE TALKING ABOUT ANYWAY?

What exactly are we talking about when we use terms like spirituality, spiritual practice, and mission? Hundreds of books have been written on these subjects and, although it is dangerous to oversimplify, for the purposes of this chapter I use several working definitions:

Spirituality: Spirituality refers to our relationship with the Divine Mystery. For Christians, this translates into relationship with the Trinitarian God: Creator, Jesus, and Holy Spirit. In Jesus' prayer to the Father before his crucifixion, he prays for a relationship of intimacy with the Father that includes us: "As you, Father, are in me and I am in you, may they also be in us, so that the world may believe that you have sent me. The glory that you have given me I have given them, so that they may be one, as we are one, I in them and you in me, that they may become completely one, so that the world may know that you have sent me and have loved them even as you have loved me." (John 17:21–23) All Christian spirituality is grounded in this invitation to unity with God and one another.

Spiritual practices: These are the intentional ways we choose to cultivate our life in relationship with God through various forms of prayer and disciplines of living: teaching and learning, fellowship, breaking bread, prayerful reading and study of scripture, fasting, and sharing resources.

Missio dei: God's purpose for the world is expressed in Jesus' description of his own mission in John's Gospel: "I came that they might have life and have it abundantly" (John 10:10). Or, as the first chapter of this book puts it, the mission of God "is simply a shorthand way of saying that God's love is at work in the world, putting right everything that is wrong–and our invitation to participate in bringing it about."

Mission: Our personal mission is the way we live out our spirituality to help accomplish the *missio dei.* The word *mission* (from the Latin *missio*) literally means "sent." All of us at our baptism receive a commission (*co-missio*) to help bring about the Reign of God, just as Jesus sent out the disciples: "He called the twelve and began to send them out two by two, and gave them authority over the unclean spirits. He ordered them to take nothing for their journey except a staff; no bread, no bag, no money in their belts" (Mark 6:7–8).

GOD'S STORY AND OUR STORY

Missional spirituality (or indeed any kind of spirituality) is grounded in story: God's story, our many and varied stories, and the moment in history where they intersect. The underlying story of our Christian faith is the story of God's work with the people of Israel. Ultimately, that work is a call to covenant relationship. In Deuteronomy, Moses summarizes the law that grounds that relationship in words that have come to be called the *Shema* (from the Hebrew word for "hear"): "Hear, O Israel: The Lord is our God, the Lord alone. You shall love the Lord your God with all your heart, and with all your soul, and with all your might" (Deut 6:4–5).

Very early on in the story of the Hebrew people, that basic priority is established, and the community of Israel is thereby forged: God alone, God is one. Love God first. There is no true community that is not rooted in that reality. And in return, God's covenant with Israel—and by extension with us—is a promise of God's compassionate love for us, as expressed over and over in the prophets and the Psalms: "I have loved you with an everlasting love; therefore I have continued my faithfulness to you" (Jer 31:3); "Do not fear, for I have redeemed you; I have called you by name, you are mine" (Isa 43:1).

The prophet Micah brings together our spirituality and our mission—that is, our way of living out that spirituality: "What does the Lord require of you, but to seek justice, love kindness, and walk humbly with your God?" (Mic 6:8) Mission is inseparable from our relationship with God.

The story of God's mission continues to unfold in the life of Jesus, which is the fulfilment of the first story: God's saving action in the life of the people of God is about relationship. In Matthew's Gospel, the meaning of Jesus' life, death, and resurrection is reflected with the brilliance of a diamond in a famous passage about treasure:

> Do not store up for yourselves treasures on earth, where moth and rust consume and where thieves break in and steal; but store up for yourselves treasures in heaven, where neither moth nor rust consumes and where thieves do not break in and steal. For where your treasure is, there your heart will be also. (Matt 6:19–21)

This is not meant to be a commentary on rich and poor, on tithing or stewardship; nor is it a warning about global economic crises. It is one of the ways in which Jesus conveys the meaning of the *Shema*: love God. God first. Only God. That is the basis of our spiritual practice. It is the ground in which our missional engagement flourishes.

ROOTED IN GOD: THE APOSTLES' TEACHING AND FELLOWSHIP

Shortly before Jesus goes up to Jerusalem for the last time, he is walking with the disciples in a vineyard, preparing them for his death. He uses the organic image of the vineyard to explain the relationship between him, the Father, and his friends: "I am the true vine, and my Father is the vine grower. . . . Just as the branch cannot bear fruit by itself unless it abides in the vine, neither can you unless you abide in me. I am the vine, you are the branches. Those who abide in me and I in them bear much fruit, because apart from me you can do nothing" (John 15:1–5). Unless the disciples stay connected with Jesus and with each other in a companionship of love, they will be ineffective in carrying out Jesus' mission to usher in the Reign of God. The power of this connectedness is dramatically evident in Luke's account of the early Christian community. On the day of Pentecost, the response to Peter's preaching about the resurrection of Jesus was overwhelming:

> So those who welcomed his message were baptized, and that day about three thousand persons were added. They devoted themselves to the apostles' teaching and fellowship, to the breaking of bread and the prayers. . . . All who believed were together and had all things in common. . . . And day by day the Lord added to their number those who were being saved. (Acts 2:41–47)

In the baptismal covenant of the Anglican Church of Canada, the first question asked of the candidates is, "Will you continue in the apostles' teaching and fellowship, the breaking of bread and the prayers?"[1] Without being rooted in those primary disciplines—teaching, fellowship, breaking bread, and prayer—the earliest Christian missionaries, the apostles, would not have been able to spread the message so effectively. The same applies to us today. Without the basic spiritual disciplines, we are in danger of trying to do God's mission without the enabling of God's power. And unless our motivation for mission grows out of our own intimate relationship with God, it will never touch the heart of a people who long to know of God's love.

All the scripture passages quoted so far illustrate that, throughout the history of our faith, the emphasis has always been on the primacy of relationship:

"Love the Lord your God."

"I have loved you with an everlasting love."

"Store up for yourselves treasure in heaven."

"Abide in me as I abide in you."

"Continue in the apostles' teaching and fellowship."

If we are drawn to missional activity just because we think we ought to be, or even because we have a good heart and care about people, rather than out of a deep and abiding love for God, then we will burn out, give up, and become cynical. At the very least, we will lose our passion.

WHAT IS GOD UP TO?

We may know that the *missio dei* is God's plan for the creation, but we cannot know the details of that plan. We do know from Jesus' teaching in scripture some of the broad outlines: God's plan for creation is abundant life—life that brings us more deeply into intimacy with God and, through that, into relationship with each other. We know that the life God desires for all creatures is one in which the potential of all is unleashed, in which all people have enough to eat, in which the earth is sustained through the care of human beings and through careful use of its resources. It is a life in which justice is practiced in such a way that we grow through our mistakes and are reconciled more deeply to each other and to our earth. But we

1 *The Book of Alternative Services of the Anglican Church of Canada* (Toronto: The Anglican Book Centre, 1985), 159.

cannot plan a utopia or guess what God's plan might be. Only God has the whole vision for life on this earth and for life beyond.

Nevertheless, we know that we are called to cooperate with God, to walk into the unknown, trusting that God's purpose in creation will be worked out. And for that reason, missional spirituality must focus on "the ancient paths," the practices that have always kept Christians rooted in a relationship of love with God and the only way we can maintain our stability in a time of such great upheaval.

Phyllis Tickle describes this upheaval as the "Great Emergence," a world-wide cultural shift that is having the same kind of profound impact on the church as the Renaissance did on the Great Reformation. Each time there is a major shift in Christian culture (approximately every five hundred years, according to Tickle), there is a rebirth both of praxis (personal and communal spiritual practice) and of the missional reach of the church. Every time the encrustations of an overly established Christianity have been broken open, the faith has spread, and, "in the course of birthing a brand-new expression of its faith and praxis, the Church also gains a grand refurbishment of the older one."[2]

Alan Roxburgh also writes about this time of transition and upheaval when we are learning that the purpose of the church is not to perpetuate itself as an institution, but to recognize that it exists for the *missio dei*. During this time, Roxburgh warns, "we will not know what God is up to in the world by huddling together in study groups, writing learned papers, or listening to self-appointed gurus."[3] We will know it only by getting outside the walls of the church, among people who have never been inside, or who left it many years ago, but who have a deep longing for connection with the God who has given them life.

And as we venture outside the safety of our church walls, we need to ground ourselves in the ancient but ever-new practices and disciplines of the Christian life. Just as the early church adapted synagogue worship to homes and other places where people gathered, so we forge strong communities by adapting our own spiritual practices—"the apostles' teaching and fellowship, the breaking of bread and the prayers"—but not always in the way we have done it inside our buildings. This is true of all our spiritual practices. As Roxburgh has said, "Practices are the key ways to

---

2. Phyllis Tickle, *The Great Emergence* (Grand Rapids, MI: Baker Books, 2008), 17.

3 Alan Roxburgh, *Missional: Joining God in the Neighbourhood* (New York: Jossey Bass, 2011), 133.

enabling people to discover new maps in the strange, new spaces where they find themselves."[4]

One of the habits of Christian formation undergoing a major revival wherever we find missional church is the daily office, or as it is sometimes called, "fixed-hour prayer"—the round of prayer taken first from synagogue worship and then adapted and developed in the early centuries of Christianity by monastic communities who prayed together at regular times throughout the day, usually seven or eight. According to Roxburgh, "The practice of the daily offices forms a local community of Christians in a radically different set of habits and consequently creates a different imagination."[5] We are able to see the world more clearly through God's eyes, experience deeper intimacy with each other and God, and be energized for mission.

In response to those who would argue that the daily office and other spiritual disciplines are simply naval-gazing, an escape from missional activity, Diana Butler Bass responds that spiritual practices anticipate as well as help bring about the Reign of God:

> Take prayer, for example. Although a deeply personal practice, and in many ways the ultimate in "navel-gazing" spirituality, prayer connects an individual to God. Through it, we enter a conversation with God. But prayer also functions in a more universal and even eschatological way. In God's kingdom, there will be no barriers of space or time between us and God's presence. Intimacy with God, as in the intimacy of prayer, will be the very nature of God's kingdom. In the here and now, prayer creates connection and relationship with God, even as it embodies the sure hope that God is our eternal friend.[6]

Butler Bass points out that, in fact, all Christian practices anticipate the Reign of God in this way: hospitality, forgiveness, charity, stewardship, prayer, and companionship. "Practices shape us to be better, wiser, more gracious people now, even as these very practices anticipate in our lives and communities the reality of God's kingdom that has entered into the world and will one day be experienced in its fullness."[7] Maintaining

---

4 Alan Roxburgh, *Missional Map Making: Skills for Leading in Times of Transition* (New York: Jossey Bass, 2010), 150.

5 Ibid., 152.

6. Diana Butler-Bass, *Christianity after Religion* (New York: HarperOne, 2012), 159.

7. Ibid.

the traditional spiritual practices is the heart of missional spirituality and absolutely essential in a time of radical cultural and ecclesial upheaval. As the church rediscovers the basic Christian mission to share the Gospel of Christ, we must also rediscover and recommit ourselves to the traditional Christian disciplines that root us in the love of God.

THE MODEL OF JESUS

Jesus himself is our model as we try to follow this path. Like him, we first come to know we are God's beloved, and we then test and deepen that relationship of love in the desert experiences of our lives where we come to rely on God alone, and, through those experiences, we are empowered for mission. Everything that Jesus said and did models the critical link between relationship (the heart of spirituality) and mission.

It began with his baptism: "In those days Jesus came from Nazareth of Galilee and was baptized by John in the Jordan. And just as he was coming up out of the water, he saw the heavens torn apart and the Spirit descending like a dove on him. And a voice came from heaven, 'You are my Son, the Beloved; with you I am well pleased'" (Mark 1:9–11). Jesus is God's beloved, and, by extension, so are we. That is how Jesus was able to form an unruly group of disciples into a cohesive community that was able to continue his mission in the world. He did it by living out his own vocation as God's beloved and showing the disciples that they, too, were God's beloved.

In all of Jesus' teaching, in the way he interacted with others, in his treatment of those he healed and welcomed back into the community, he demonstrated the reality of God's love for each individual. And, as we hear that voice from heaven resonate in our own hearts, we know that we too are God's beloved. We cannot spend time with Jesus in the scriptures or in our prayer without coming to know how deeply we are loved.

Following his baptism, Jesus had to confront and overcome all the forces that could draw him away from the love of God: "The Spirit immediately drove him out into the wilderness. He was in the wilderness forty days, tempted by Satan, and he was with the wild beasts, and the angels waited on him" (Mark 1:12–13).

The experience of silence and solitude in the desert, where he was confronted with all the temptations common to human beings—and learned to overcome them—is what grounded him. It confirmed his vocation and enabled his ministry of teaching and preaching and healing:

> Then Jesus went about all the cities and villages, teaching in
> their synagogues, and proclaiming the good news of the king-
> dom, and curing every disease and every sickness. When he saw
> the crowds, he had compassion for them, because they were
> harassed and helpless, like sheep without a shepherd. (Matthew
> 9:35–36)

The same is true for us. We, as the beloved of God, are called, like
Jesus, to confirm and deepen our relationship with God in our own desert
experiences, where we begin to understand just what it means to "love the
Lord your God with all your heart and all your soul and all your might"
(Deut 6:5).

As Jesus continued his public ministry with his disciples, he repeat-
edly sought opportunities to return to places of solitude, balancing his
active ministry of healing and teaching with time for being away and
alone with God. As he travelled with his disciples, he formed them also
in a rhythm of going out and coming in, of active ministry and resting
in prayer, of meeting God on the roads and by the seaside in Galilee, and
of meeting God in the transcendent moments of grace, whether on the
Mount of Transfiguration or in the calming of a storm at sea. And the
ultimate spiritual task of both Jesus and his followers was the self-giving,
humility, and obedience of the cross—the final confrontation of darkness,
for which he was prepared not only by the original desert time, but by
confronting the powers of evil throughout his ministry—the darkness of
physical and mental illness, of exclusion from community, and of secular
power which sought to rule by fear rather than by love.

And so Jesus models for us, too, a rhythm of life that includes times
of prayer (alone and together), of companionship in the body of Christ, of
eating and learning together, of active ministry—all of which include our
own paths of suffering and grace.

THE CHICKEN OR THE EGG?

Which comes first: mission or spirituality? The truth is, both! Knowing
that we are beloved of God motivates us to work for God's mission, and
that work can cause us to long more deeply for an intimate relationship
with the God we serve. Our engagement in mission makes us more aware
of the work of the Spirit in our midst and of our need to nurture that
in a rhythm of life which deepens our spiritual practice, particularly our
personal prayer. In turn, our deepening prayer (personal and communal)

sustains our mission. As we engage more deeply in the *missio dei*, we need also to deepen the stillness, silence, and solitude of personal spiritual practices.

But it is easy to lose the subtlety of this relationship between mission and spirituality. I have heard people talk about the importance of personal prayer and times of retreat as though they were merely an aspect of "self care," a way of ensuring that we do not burn out. But prayer and other spiritual practices have their own value. As in the relationship between husband and wife, there are times when we need to be alone with God just because we are made for union with God and nothing else can satisfy that longing. And then, out of that relationship (whether between God and us or between a husband and wife) grows a deepening awareness of the profound needs of people around us, and so we reach out to draw others in. The more engaged we become in our mission, the more crucial it is to ensure that we stay grounded in the reality of the God whom we serve. We do not engage in spiritual practices in order to prevent burnout—though they can have that effect. It is our prayer, our spiritual practice, and our relationship with God that lead us into mission, and it is our mission that deepens our prayer.

A RUSSIAN DOLL THEORY OF CALL

This leads us back into the heart of who we are as God's beloved. I like to think of our vocation or call to be in relationship with God as being a little like Russian nesting dolls. Children and adults are fascinated with these dolls that come apart in halves. Inside the outermost, largest doll is a smaller one, and inside that a smaller one, too, and so on until one comes to the innermost, tiniest doll. Like a seed, this doll seems to give birth to the larger dolls around it.

If we look at it in terms of the Biblical story, we can situate ourselves in one or more of these nesting dolls:

God Calls the Human Race into Life

At the heart of our faith story and the innermost "doll" is the creation of the world. God created humankind in the divine image and saw that it was good. Everything else about our relationship with God comes from this understanding that we, along with the rest of the creation, are "good" (Gen 1:28, 31).

God Calls Each of Us into Life

But God did not stop with creation in general. God creates each one of us personally, intimately: "It was you who formed my inward parts; you knit me together in my mother's womb. . . . I praise you because I am fearfully and wonderfully made" (Ps 139:13–16). Long before the invention of ultrasound, God saw each one of us being "intricately woven in the depths of the earth" (Psalm 139:15). God loved us so much that we became "the apple of God's eye." Each one of us.

God Calls Us into a Relationship of Loving Intimacy

Within the call of each of us into life is another call, a call to ongoing and deepening intimacy with God: "Come, all you who are thirsty, come to the waters, come buy wine without price" (Isa 55:1–3).

God Calls Us into Relationship with Each Other

Then, within the call to intimacy with God, comes the call to relationship with each other: "Beloved, let us love one another, for love is of God" (1 John 4:7–12). We begin to see how our deeply personal relationship with God leads to an awareness of the need for relationship with others.

God Calls Us into Baptism

Our relationship with God and each other converges in our baptism: "We have been buried with him by baptism into death . . . . So we too might walk in newness of life" (Rom 6:3–11). "Newness of life" is the abundant life that Jesus came to share. Baptism, the entry into the Christian community, allows us to share that with others.

God Calls Us to Specific Roles in the Christian Community

Once we are part of the baptismal community, we are called to exercise the special gifts God has given us: "The gifts he gave were that some would be apostles, some prophets, some evangelists, some pastors and teachers, to equip the saints for the work of ministry, for building up the body of Christ" (Eph 4:1–7, 11–13).

God Calls Us to Repentance and Celebration

In the baptismal service of the Anglican Church of Canada, we renounce evil, we turn to God in Jesus Christ, and then we make specific promises to live out that Christ-life. We promise "to resist evil and whenever we fall into sin, repent and return to the Lord."[8] We are motivated by the promise of unconditional love and forgiveness implicit in the parable of the prodigal son: "This son of mine was dead and is alive again; he was lost and is found" (Luke 15:17–24).

God Calls Us to Reconciliation and Mission

In our set of nesting dolls, the outermost is our mission. When Jesus confronted Peter after the Resurrection, he asked Peter three different times (with slight variations of wording), "Simon do you love me? . . . Feed my sheep" (John 21:15–17). This is our call to mission. And the mission leads back to prayer. A strong mission should produce strong, deep prayer. A deeply rooted life of prayer should give rise to a passionate engagement in mission.

That does not always happen, however, because mission can arise out of our own need to help, or it can get bogged down by the overwhelming needs of those we desire to serve or by a compulsive need to achieve goals and expectations set by ourselves or others. Likewise, prayer can lead to quietism and withdrawal from the needs of the world, so that our spiritual practices become ends in themselves. In fact, though, neither our mission nor our prayer will remain healthy for long if they are separated.

GOD'S LONGING FOR US AND OUR LONGING FOR GOD

It is God's longing for us, and ours for God, that keeps this rhythm rooted. Macarius the Great, one of the Desert Fathers, tells the story about Abba Lot, who went to see Abba Joseph and said, "'Abba, as far as I can, I say my little office, I fast a little, I pray and meditate, I live in peace and as far as I can, I purify my thoughts. What else can I do?' Then the old man stood up and stretched his hands toward heaven. His fingers became like ten lamps of fire and he said to him, 'If you will, you can become all flame.'"[9]

8. *Book of Alternate Services, 159.*

9. *Sayings of the Desert Fathers: The Alphabetical Collection*, trans. Benedicta Ward (Oxford: SLG Publications, 1975) 131.

The point of this story is similar to that of a story which appears in all three synoptic Gospels, of the ruler (or rich man) who asks Jesus what he must do to be saved. After Jesus recites a summary of the commandments, and the man says that he keeps them all, Jesus tells him, "Sell all that you own and distribute the money to the poor, and you will have treasure in heaven; then come, follow me" (Luke 18:18–25).[10]

The story is often interpreted as a commentary on how material wealth can keep us from the Kingdom. But it is much more than that: it is about living our passion, about giving up everything—our possessions, our control over our lives, and the values of our culture, which we absorb like a sponge—in order to be united in a relationship of love with Jesus. The rich young man, had he been able to do what Jesus asked, might have stretched out his hands toward heaven and become "all flame" as well. He might have been consumed in the love of God and been a beacon of that love for others.

This desire for God is an integral part of the biblical tradition, and it reaches its apex in the Gospel of John, who has been called the Apostle of Love. Nowhere in scripture is friendship and intimacy with Jesus expressed so powerfully as in John's Gospel.

In the first chapter of the Gospel, John the Baptizer points Andrew and an unnamed disciple (possibly John) toward Jesus. Jesus asks them, "What are you looking for?" They reply with another question, "Where are you staying?" and Jesus says, "Come and see." The disciples follow Jesus, and John tells us that they "remained" with him that day (John 1:39).

The Greek word for *remain* is the same word that Jesus used in the passage about the vine and the branches: "Remain (or abide, or dwell) in my love." Remaining signifies something more than a mere visit: it signals the beginning of a deep and ongoing friendship. Jean Vanier says of this passage, "In order to follow Jesus and dwell with him, each one of us is called to let go of the search for power, wealth and reputation that our culture tends to impose."[11] This is the tradition of the desert, and it is the journey of every Christian since then who takes Jesus' invitation seriously. We are all called to journey toward union with God.

People often think it is the great mystics who most fully embody the intense longing for God that we find in the life of Jesus and in the early monastic movement, that it is not for ordinary men and women like us.

10. See also Matthew 19:16–30 and Mark 10:17–31.

11. Jean Vanier, *Drawn into the Mystery of Jesus through the Gospel of John* (Ottawa: Novalis, 2004), 41.

On the contrary: the intense desire for God, the call to union with God, is at the heart of who we are as human beings.

In the book *Primary Speech,* psychologists of religion Barry and Ann Ulanov talk of prayer as our first and most basic form of communication, and the only human activity that can satisfy our deep longing for "contact, for connection at the center, that grounding that brings full-hearted peace of mind and soul. We want to be in touch with what lives within everything that matters, with what truly satisfies."[12] Like the Samaritan woman in John's Gospel who meets Jesus at the well, we all have a seemingly unquenchable thirst that can be satisfied only by a living relationship with Jesus.

Another story from the desert monks illustrates in a very simple way how our longing for God is called out by God's longing for us:

> A baby, even though it is powerless to accomplish anything or with its own feet to go to its mother, still it rolls and makes noises and cries as it seeks its mother. . . . And she picks it up and fondles it and feeds it with great love. This is also what God, the Lover of humankind, does to the person that comes to God and ardently desires God.[13]

God calls us into relationship, then commissions us to the work we are called to do. The work we are called to do in turn draws us more deeply into the mystery of God. Mission and spirituality are inseparably intertwined. If our spiritual practices do not lead us into active mission, or if our missional activity does not create an ever-deeper longing for personal intimacy with God, then neither is authentic.

Jesus has the last word here: "Abide in me as I abide in you. Just as the branch cannot bear fruit by itself unless it abides in the vine, neither can you unless you abide in me. . . . As the Father has loved me, so I have loved you; abide in my love" (John 15:4–5, 9).

---

12 Barry and Ann Ulanov, *Primary Speech* (Atlanta, GA: Westminister John Knox Press, 1982), 13.

13. Macarian Homily 46.3, *Intoxicated by God,* pp. 212–13, quoted in Roberta Bondi, *To Pray and to Love: Conversations on Prayer with the Early Church* (Minneapolis, MN: Fortress Press, 1991), 122.

Green Shoots 8
A Free-Spirited Francophone Mini-church

L'Ecclésiole Franglican
Trois Rivières, Quebec

Yves Samson grew up a Roman Catholic in Sherbrooke, Quebec, but left the Catholic Church in 1989 when, as he was preparing for the priesthood, his bishop asked him if he was gay. When he answered in the affirmative, the bishop told him that he could no longer be considered a candidate for ordination.

For a long time, Yves remained unchurched. Then, six years ago, he felt himself drawn to an Anglican Church, specifically to Holy Trinity Cathedral in Quebec City, which has a number of francophone congregants. "I found it quite near to my Catholic roots," he says.

In May 2010, Yves was ordained an Anglican deacon and, the same month, was appointed curate of St. James Church in Trois-Rivières, a two-day-a-week position only, due to financial pressures within the parish. "My responsibility was to serve the existing congregation and to build a new ministry to francophones," he says.

Later that year, Bishop Dennis Drainville challenged clergy and lay leaders of the Diocese of Quebec to initiate new ministries outside of the church walls, including new francophone ministries. This ministry would target people not currently involved in the Anglican Church, including unchurched seekers (those not affiliated with a church but curious about faith), and the dechurched (those who used to belong to a church but had left for one reason or another).

The following week, a few Anglican francophones from the Sherbrooke area asked Yves to join them for a meeting. "We were just four around the table," he recalls. "Keeping in mind our bishop's challenge to do something new and different, we decided to form a group of people who would meet on a regular basis to talk about life and faith, to read Scripture and pray together."

Things began to unfold. In the fall of 2010, Yves participated in a forum focused predominantly on spirituality. One of the speakers was a minister of the Swiss Reformed Church, the Rev. Lytta Basset, who gave a lecture on emergent churches in Switzerland and on the future of the church. She used the French word *ecclésiole*, or "little church," to define a place where people from all walks of life—including those who feel rejected by or excluded from their original churches—are welcomed and may perhaps find healing. "That was the kickoff!" says Yves. "We decided to keep the appellation *ecclésiole*, to which we added *franglican*, a combination of francophone and Anglican." And so, in September 2011, L' Ecclésiole Franglican was born.

Through Facebook postings and notices placed on bulletin boards in parishes, and at the universities of Sherbrooke and Lennoxville, Yves and his colleagues promoted the new group to francophones, Anglicans and non-Anglicans alike.

Today, the small but flourishing group of twelve meets on the second and fourth Wednesdays of each month, at a magnificent private home owned by a member of the group. "We always set an extra place at the table in anticipation of a new arrival," says Yves. Gathering at 6:30 p.m. to enjoy a potluck supper—typically cheeses, delicatessen fare, tossed salad, bread, and sometimes wine—members chat about what is happening in their lives.

The group, whose average age is forty, is independent of the diocese and financially self-supporting. "We don't want to be bothered with a building or structures to follow," says Yves, who acts as pastor on a volunteer basis. "It's a ministry shared by the entire group." He acknowledges that growth has been very slow. "But we don't really care about the number of people around the table. We just want to have a welcoming space where people know they can come. Our motto is 'Come and see.'"

At every meeting, one of the four founders is designated to be host of the evening's discussion, which may begin with a secular topic, such as how to keep a vineyard and what it takes to have a good yield of wine. The topic then segues into a Christian context—in this instance, to John 15, where Jesus says that he is the true vine, his Father the gardener, and we the branches. The Bible is opened, and the group engages in a discussion based on the texts set for the coming Sunday's liturgy at St. James.

"We also try to sing secular or sacred songs, depending on the theme we're exploring. It's all about communication," says Yves, a veteran broadcaster who hosts a radio talk show four days a week. The show covers culture, music, and local events, and the income from it allows him to survive on his part-time salary at St. James.

At L'Ecclésiole Franglican there are no expectations in terms of age or numbers of people. "We want people to know that they can drop in whenever they want," says Yves. The group is a free-spirited haven for disaffected churchgoers and others seeking a place where they can gather with likeminded Christians.

"Some pessimists are saying there is no future for the church. This I do not believe," says Yves fervently. "There *is* a future if we open up new places where people feel freely welcomed and are not bothered with formal membership."

In his view, seekers need a place where they can air their concerns, their questions, and their doubts—a place where they are known and recognized. "Recalling the early church, we know that the building of a community starts with a small group. We need to build companionship, just as Jesus did with his disciples at the beginning of his ministry," says Yves.

He would like to see other similar groups form in the diocese and says that they, too, will have to be "something completely different from the mainstream church as we know it." His advice to similarly minded Christian seekers? "Don't wait for others to do it. Do it yourselves!"

K.J.

Mission is not just rushing off and doing the first thing that comes to hand. If the essence of mission is finding out what God is doing and joining in, then the first step is obviously to find out what God is doing. But how do we do that? We look and we listen. Indeed, looking and listening is always the first posture of a disciple, an apprentice: what is the Teacher doing? What can I learn? Is there something I am supposed to do? Glenn Smith has been learning to look and listen, and helping others around the world do the same, for some thirty years. We cannot do better than begin by learning from what he has learned.

14

Reading Your Community

Towards an Authentic Encounter with a Canadian Context

Glenn Smith

In 1983, I LEFT a ministry to university students to give join Christian Direction, an urban ministry with which I am presently involved in Montreal. It is interesting to reflect back on how a relevant missional theology of the city evolved through that change.

One day, as I was looking out the window from the sixth floor of our office, I asked myself a question that initiated a reflection that continues to this very day. *I wonder what is being done in my city to incarnate the Good News with people who work in the downtown core, Monday to Friday, 8 a.m. to 5 p.m.* Much to my chagrin, I learned that very little was happening. So I began to read about ministry with people in the marketplace and to see the relationship to the needs of urban ministry.

At the same time, I was reading the book of Jeremiah. Having been raised in a family that placed a high priority on the Bible and the church, I am not sure how many times I had read that particular book. But in that cold winter of 1983, the opening words of chapter 29 took on a new meaning:

> These are the words of the letter that the prophet Jeremiah sent from Jerusalem to the remaining elders among the exiles, and to the priests, the prophets, and all the people, whom

> Nebuchadnezzar had taken into exile from Jerusalem to Babylon.... Thus says the Lord of hosts, the God of Israel . . . Build houses and live in them; plant gardens and eat what they produce. Take wives and have sons and daughters; take wives for your sons, and give your daughters in marriage, that they may bear sons and daughters; multiply there, and do not decrease. But seek the welfare of the city where I have sent you into exile, and pray to the Lord on its behalf, for in its welfare you will find your welfare." (Jer 29:1–7)

As God Almighty had called those ten thousand Jewish exiles in Babylon to seek the peace—the *shalom*—of the foreign city, I began to see that I could not easily bypass the social and spiritual needs of Montreal. So began the reflection and the action that have informed my life over this period. The context was shaping how I listen to the Bible. I had to join with others to pursue a contextualized action and reflection.

For a number of years, I have been inviting students, audiences, and readers to join me on the nineteen-kilometre trip that I make every day from my home in the inner suburbs of Montreal to my office in the downtown core. It provides a context for the themes that inform my teaching and writing. Those themes include the social context in which we live our daily lives and the traditions Christians share, rooted in the Bible, Christian history, and theology. Contextual theology done in the framework of a biblical theological hermeneutic seeks to help the community of faith listen to the texts, listen to the context, and pursue mission in an integral, transformational manner.

I walk out the door of my home into an amazingly cosmopolitan neighbourhood called Chomedey. In the homes on my street, I can hear several different languages being spoken, symbolizing a diverse array of cultures. What was once a European immigration has now shifted to a truly global movement. When I first began thinking about my neighbourhood, I was struck by the linguistic plurality. Today, the "Islamisation" of Chomedey is very real. As I stride toward the bus stop, I pass the only Protestant church, and then I cut through the parking lot of the Roman Catholic parish. Forty years ago, both churches were full for weekend services. The United Church had a Sunday school of over two hundred children. The exodus of anglophones from Montreal has decimated that congregation. Today, forty gather on Sunday at 11 am for worship. The Roman Catholic parish once celebrated forty-five masses each week. In 2008, the building was sold to an immigrant Armenian Orthodox congregation. The local mosque is a half a block down the street.

These remarkable religious changes remind me that my neighbours are much more concerned with their own pursuits and the development of a personal value system than with anything offered by ecclesiastical structures. All things religious have been marginalized in Montreal.

A twelve-minute bus ride takes me to the Metro (the subway) where I enter yet another world, the metropolis of Montreal. It is one of the largest French-speaking cities in the world and the hub of a social transformation, known as the Quiet Revolution, that altered the very face of Quebec.

The subway takes me into the heart of the city, but through several different "Montreals." I pass under *student Montreal,* which includes four major universities, thirty community colleges (or CÉGEPS), and forty professional and technical establishments. Montreal has the most students per capita of any city in North America. The population of student Montreal, in and of itself, would make it the thirteenth largest city in Canada.

Montreal is also a *hurting city,* with hundreds of people living with AIDS, 238,000 people on the welfare rolls, and some nine thousand adolescent prostitutes. Harvest Montréal, the organization that orchestrates food distribution among the poor, gives out thirty tons of food a day to 150,000 people a week. If one looks at the issue chronologically, one sees that the salary gap between Montreal and Toronto has been closing since 1960. Yet in 1995, this Census Metropolitan Area (CMA) had the highest rate of poverty in Canada at 27.3 percent, and was still a full 9 percent higher than the rest of Quebec by 2000. With the new so-called Market Basket Measure (2008), Montreal began to show some economic improvement for the poor. My Metro companions seem oblivious to this reality: workers with a secondary school certificate have an average income of $23,562, while a university graduate earns double that amount, $41,277. In a city where more than 50 percent of students drop out of high school, the future does not look bright.

As we swing through parts of *ethnic Montreal,* I am reminded that the two hundred thousand elementary and secondary students in the five school boards of Montreal represent 168 countries.

Then, at the McGill Metro stop, I am literally pushed out of the Metro car. Some 750,000 people call this "home" throughout the working week. This is *business Montreal.* This CMA generates 76 percent of the entire Quebec economy. I arrive at my office full of questions.

Several years ago, I began to do an exercise with my students in a course I teach on urban ministry at l'Institute de Théologie pour la Francophonie (ITF). The class begins by visiting a rather large ethnic grocery store, Inter-Marché, about a kilometre from the faculty building. The store has a huge inventory of foods from several countries, arranged in aisles that represent the continents. Haitian food covers a third of the Caribbean aisle. At one time, forty-five different flags hung from the ceiling, all contributed by the customers of the store. Inter-Marché is a success because the owner realized that Montreal is changing, and that his store had better adapt to new realities. He does a booming business.

However, in the same neighbourhood, we also visit a church building with its English-only sign: "We worship God every Sunday at 11 am." It does not take great teaching skill to guide the discussion that evening on the nature of pastoral leadership in a changing situation. The students suddenly want to know how to "exegete the neighbourhood," in much the same way that they have learned to study a biblical text.

How, then, can we help congregations develop the skills and the attitudes needed to think missionally about the church's work in Canada? Let us look at several principles and practices that can guide us in our learning.

SECTION 1: ORIENTING OUR ACTIONS

Since "discovering" Jeremiah 29, I have learned that this one text would never inform all that is the mission of God in a community. One of my dear friends and doctoral mentors, Harvey Conn, taught me well. I remember him commenting, "Picking one biblical text to sum up my view of urban ministry is an assignment too awesome and dangerous for me. Too awesome, because wherever I turn in my Bible it shouts 'urban' to me. Too dangerous, because the text I select could leave out a piece of the picture too crucial in another text and distort the whole. We need a hermeneutic serious enough to link Genesis to Revelation in the unending story of Jesus as an urban lover and the Church as God's copycat." I realized that I needed to keep studying the biblical texts!

At the same time, several authors, speakers, and teachers began to shape my ministry practice. Many authors invited me to pursue a fresh encounter with our culture, taking the social category of "space" seriously. McGill philosopher Charles Taylor, in particular, introduced me to the term "social imaginaries." This is not the same as the popular idea of worldview, which tends to have a more theoretical focus. "Social imaginaries" refers instead to the deep ideas that inform the life of a social context, and are for this reason critical to pursuing the mission of God.[1] I live in a "place" that is contextually specific. *Place is space with historical meanings, different identities, varied societal preoccupations.*[2] For example, I live in the city where the philosophical term "postmodernism" was first coined and studied as a social and philosophical expression. But I live in a different place than most people who talk about this theme. So the unending story in which we find ourselves always needs to be woven into the fabric of each place a little differently.

The basic purpose of theological and missiological reflection has never really changed. It is the people of God reflecting on God's story in human history, in light of their own circumstances. Missional theology is *God in dialogue with God's people in all their thousands of different situations.* Yet how does a journey through a Canadian community help us to both read our communities and read the narrative of scriptures in our situation?

Two Themes, One Purpose

Some people may take the trip downtown and ask the question, "Where is the church?" and then rush to critique the church's lack of significant involvement in the complexities of the community. In the midst of the plurality and competing social imaginaries that a practitioner runs into on a weekly basis, I would rather ask the questions, "What will the church look like?" and "How will the church reflect biblically about the city, and pursue relevant mission in her context in the years ahead?" As I began to focus on these questions, I soon realized that there are two issues that inform contextual ministry practice and help us to understand what the church will look like: social context and Christian traditions.

---

1. See Charles Taylor, *Modern Social Imaginaries* (Durham: Duke University Press, 2004) and *A Secular Age* (Cambridge: The Belknap Press of Harvard University, 2007).

2. As I am writing this chapter, Montreal is opening a new hall—La Maison Symphonique de Montréal—for the Montreal Symphony Orchestra, inaugurated on 7 September 2011. In the words of the chief conductor, Kent Nagano, "A sense of *place* figures in the hall's success." In talking about the first symphony the orchestra would interpret he wrote, "We felt that the first sounds that were heard in the new concert hall should be Canadian and more than that, they should be Québec" (Montreal Gazette, 7 September 2012). I have been intrigued to watch how a world-class composer, Georges-Hébert Germain, has woven classical music into the fabric of the city. One of his first symphonies was a tribute to the Montreal Canadiens hockey team!

The First Voice: Social Context

First, the theme of *social context with a twin focus*. Many people do cultural studies and wrestle with the sociology of place. On a different track, other practitioners try to understand the demographics that make up their communities. I want to help the practitioner put these two foci together, so that in examining the community as a "place" we are also learning to look closely at the social imaginaries that are reflected in the urban context and in the statistics.

Practitioners need to be able to comprehend the social imaginaries of a community in order to reflect about the spirituality of their particular context. These are "much broader and deeper than the intellectual schemes people may entertain when they think about social reality in a disengaged mode. . . [They are] the ways in which people imagine their social existence, how they fit together with others, how things go on between them and their fellows, and the expectations which are normally met." [3]

Rather than being a theoretical concept held by the elite, a social imaginary is shared by a large group. Generally speaking, social imaginaries are the presuppositions that groups of people hold, consciously and unconsciously, about the basic make-up of the community, relationships, practices, and objects of daily life, whether they are of great significance or of little importance. They are based on the interaction of ultimate beliefs and the global environment within which one lives, and they deal with both the perennial issues of life, such as religion and spirituality, and the answers to even simple questions, such as whether we eat from plates, or how to launder our clothing.

Like the foundations of a house, social imaginaries are vital but invisible.

We should be careful not to confuse social imaginaries with culture, although the two are in constant relationship with one another. Culture is foremost a network of meanings by which a particular social group is able to recognize itself as such, through a common history and a way of life. This network of meanings is rooted in ideas (including beliefs, values, attitudes, rules of behaviour), rituals, and material objects, including symbols, that become a source for identity— for example, the language we speak, the food we eat, the clothes we wear, the way we organize space. This network is not a formal and hierarchical structure. It is defined in modern society by constant change, mobility, reflection, and ongoing new life

---

3. Taylor, *Modern Social Imaginaries*, 23.

experiences. This contemporary reality is opposed to traditional societies where culture was transmitted from one generation to another vertically within the community structures. Modernity still transmits some aspects of culture, like language and basic knowledge, vertically through the bias of the school system, but once this is done, the horizontal transmission of culture through friendship, peers, and socio-professional status and social networking become more important.

Social imaginaries, on the other hand, may be studied in terms of four features: characteristic stories, fundamental symbols, habitual behaviour of the residents, and a set of questions and answers.[4] These features interact with each other in a variety of complex and interesting ways. By studying their intersection, the practitioner can unearth the perspectives of the context under study.

Communities often reveal their imaginaries by the cultural network they produce and constantly reproduce in social interactions, objects, and symbols: from dollars to Metro tickets, from office towers to street-cars, from pottery to poetry, from places of worship to sacred texts, from emblems to funerary monuments, from stadiums to crosses. Symbols provide the hermeneutic grid to perceive how the world is and how we might live in it: they provide a vision *of* reality and a vision *for* it. Symbols describe the typical behaviour of a society and vice versa: the celebration of important events; the usual means of dealing with dissonance; and the rituals associated with birth, puberty, marriage, and death. And for many communities, their symbols and characteristic behaviour are also focused in stories. Furthermore, the answers to fundamental questions such as "Who are we?" "Where are we?" "What are the problems we face?" and "How will we solve them?"[5] give us great insight into the perspectives of a community.

Max Stackhouse helps us understand this first theme—social context—by raising several foundational questions. "How do we know a context when we see one?" "How big is a context?" "How long does it last?" "Who is in it and is out of it, and how do we know?" In reality,

4. I first explored this framework in my doctoral thesis project, "Towards a Contextual Praxis for the Urban French World: A Case Study To Engage Christian Direction, Inc. with Montreal, Quebec" (Northern Baptist Theological Seminary, 1991). A similar schema is employed in N.T. Wright, *The New Testament and the People of God* (Minneapolis: Fortress Press, 1992), 123–124.

5. The first to propose this particular set of questions were Brian Walsh and Richard Middleton in *The Transforming Vision: Shaping a Christian World View* (Downers Grove: InterVarsity Press, 1984), 35.

the complexity of the city means that we must constantly ask these questions. The diagram, figure 1 below, represents different urban contexts and tries to take into account most of the factors that determine what makes a context.

Rather than studying a community with a typical map that might locate neighbourhoods such as those found on the periphery of a wheel, try to see your community as spokes of a wheel. In other words, rather than doing a geographical analysis, think about the functional groupings in a context. This wheel represents many social networks, each with their own world and life perspective within my community. Which ones could you identify in your community?

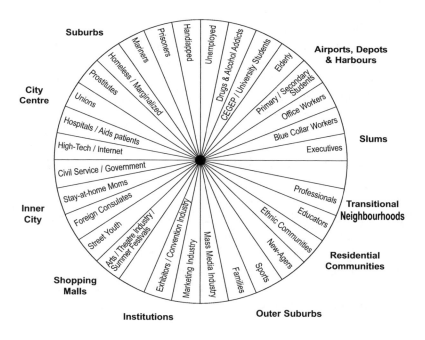

Organizational and Population Segments of an Urban World - Montréal

Figure 1

An attentive practitioner can use a three-step process to analyze the context of a community. I call this a transformational analysis of the social environment. It begins with the social-demographic study. It continues with a contextual biblical and theological reflection. It culminates in specific actions that the community of faith undertakes to pursue the transformation of the context.[6] This analysis allows us to see how social structures and human behaviour interact and influence a community. This method is an excellent tool for the Christian practitioner who desires to study the knowledge and practices of people; the way in which they use their freedom to dominate, transform, organize, arrange, and master space for their personal pursuits so as to live, protect themselves, survive, produce, and reproduce. To do this, one must identify dominant tendencies of the culture so as to grasp where we have come from and where we are going as a society, and what the mission of God in this culture will look like.

The description for cultural analysis that I propose implies that small groups who want to study their context need to take seriously the fact that social activity is culturally and historically specific. Community hermeneutics allows us to decode the polarity between social structure and human agency, which is constantly at work in a metropolitan area. Social institutions—the basic building blocks of a city because of their far-reaching spatial and temporal existence—are used by human agents to create urban systems and metropolitan structures. Human actions are constrained by these structures, but are also enabled by them. In the attempt to understand a city, neither the subject (the human agent) nor the object (society and social institutions) has primacy.

By grasping this geography of spatial functions, we are looking at issues (social dynamics, problems, needs, and aspirations) that are culturally and historically specific. Like the city itself, these issues reflect the prevailing values, ideology, and structure of the current social formation. A useful analytical, social, and theological purpose is served by the empirical recognition that community issues are manifest in geographical space. This implies that the resulting description will detail issues "in" the city as well as issues "of" the city. For example, an issue *in* urban space would include the consequences of population density in a census district in Ville St-Laurent that has 11,536 people per square kilometre versus the Census Metropolitan Area of Montreal norm of 847 per square kilometre. An issue *of* urban space includes attention to the socio-economic factors that go hand-in-hand with such population concentration.

To pursue this kind of analysis, the practitioner will need to bring

6. To see the method explained and applied to Canadian urban issues, see my article, "Community Development in Canada, What Overarching System? What Type of Sustainability?" (Montreal: Christian Direction, 2009)

- a high sensitivity to the local specifics and to micro details in the context;

- a concern for the larger worldview influences;

- a synthesis beyond a simple homogenization of the data; and

- a true appreciation of the differences between cities, regions, and even neighbourhoods, so that one can appreciate the specifics of the area in the light of the mission of the church in that situation.

This transformational analysis can take many forms. As we are seeking the reasons for the spatial differences of human activity in our communities, we will need tools of analysis. One innovative school of thought, The New Urbanism, suggests "transect studies"—intense first-hand observational studies of a neighbourhood by the people studying the community. Within the framework described thus far, it is important to examine Census Canada data on five sets of numbers:

- household revenue (lines 1525–1547 of the 2001 Census data.[7] Lines for 2006 are somewhat different. We use 2001 as the baseline since it was a complete census)

- ethnicity, including immigration patterns (lines 400–734) and language spoken at home (lines 225–380)

- rates of scholarity (lines 1356–1397)

- issues related to family structure: age structure (lines 6–43), birth rates, number of children per household (lines 82–89), marital status (line 45), etc.

- current rates of religious affiliation (lines 1675–1709)

My argument thus far has been that, in order to further the church's mission in our communities, we have to first learn to read those communities. And we have seen that communities evolve within the social imaginaries of the societies within which they are located. Communities are manifestations of deeply rooted cultural processes that encompass economic, social, and religious/worldview elements as well. Now we need to move on to bring our reading of the social context into conversation with a second voice.

---

7. Every five years, Statistics Canada does a census. Every ten years they ask questions about religion. You can consult Christian Direction (www.direction.ca) for help on using the data.

The Second Voice: Christian Traditions

The second theme that informs community research is our *Christian traditions*, meaning our study of history, theology, and the narratives of scriptures. Now the hermeneutical process becomes a true exchange between Gospel and context. We come to the authoritative message with an exegetical method enabling us to understand a biblical theology of place. We ask, "What does God say through scripture regarding this particular context?" This initial dialogue sets us off on a long process in which the more we understand the context, the more fresh readings of the Bible will arise. Scripture illuminates life, but life also illuminates scripture. This dialogue must also include the practitioners' own perspectives and those of the community in which they base their initiatives.

Biblical and social hermeneutics conceived in this fashion represent a holistic enterprise in which the Holy Spirit guides the interpreters to a more complete reading and understanding of scripture and a more complete understanding of their context. There is an ongoing mutual engagement of the essential components of the process. As they interact, they are mutually adjusted. In this way, we come to scripture with the relevant questions and perspectives. This results in a more attentive ear to the implications of the exegetical process, and a resulting theology that is more biblical and more pertinent to the culture. As we move from the cultural context through our own evolving worldview to the Bible and back to the context, we adopt increasingly relevant local reflection and initiatives. As we listen to scripture and walk through our various situations in life, we are faced with a question: how can we hear and apply God's word in our cities and neighbourhoods? In reality, the complexity of our communities means that we constantly ask these questions. Holding text and context together is vital as we continue in an era of rapid urban growth, urbanization, and globalization.

Contextualization and Transformation

The word "contextualization" literally means a "weaving together." For our purposes, it implies the interweaving of scriptural teaching about "place" and the church with a particular human situation—the context. The very word focuses attention on the role of context in the theological enterprise. In a very real sense, all doctrinal reflection from the scriptures is related in one way or another to the situation from which it was born, while addressing the aspirations, concerns, priorities, and needs of the local group of Christians who are presently doing the reflection.

The task of contextualization is the essence of theological reflection. The challenge is to remain faithful to God's revelation and the historic texts of scripture while being mindful of today's realities. An interpretative bridge is built between the Bible and its context to the circumstances of the local group of Christians who are doing the reflection. This is never a simple linear exercise. We approach the texts with humility and deep desire to keep on discovering their meaning. The first step of the hermeneutic exercise involves establishing what the text meant at the time it was written: what it meant "then." The second step involves creating the bridge to understanding the text in meaningful terms for the interpreters today: what it means "now." The final step is to determine the meaning and application for those who will receive the message in their particular circumstances as the present-day interpreters become ambassadors of the Good News: what it means "here." *Contextualization is not just for the one communicating, nor about the content that will be passed along. It is always concerned about what happens once we have communicated—about the ultimate impact of the message on the audience.*

For what purpose does the practitioner pursue contextualization? Why listen to both the present context and Christian tradition, including our study of the scriptures, church history, and theology? Increasingly, we hear the word *transformation* used as a term that encompasses all that the church does as followers of Jesus in God's mission in the city. But what does this mean? What does it entail? Inspired by the South African missiologist John de Gruchy's reflections, I suggest that a transformed place is that kind of community that pursues fundamental changes, a stable future, and the sustaining and enhancing of all of life rooted in a vision larger than mere urban politics. De Gruchy adds that "it is an open-ended multilayered process, *at once social and personal*, that is energized by hope, yet rooted in the struggles of the present."[8]

Because our purpose is to look at how transformation might take root in a Canadian community, we will need some subjective indicators rooted in the social imaginary of Canadians. I would like to propose a model from community faith-based initiatives, rooted in the biblical notions of peace and well-being. (See figure 2.) The model comes from the work of Christian Direction, the urban ministry I lead in Montreal.

8. John W. de Gruchy, *Christianity, Art and Transformation: Theological Aesthetics in the Struggle for Social Justice* (Cambridge: Cambridge University Press, 2001), 3. My italics.

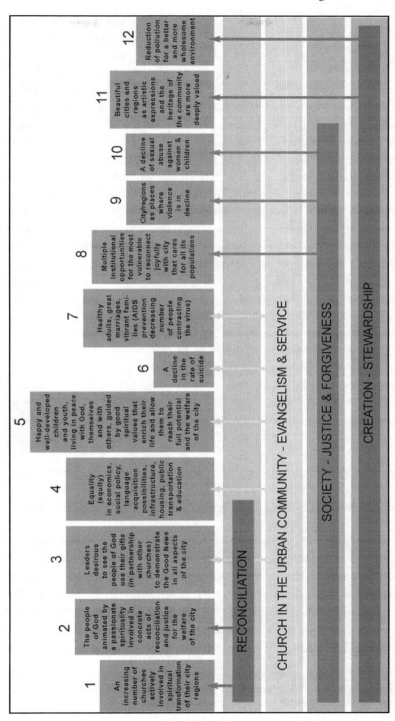

Figure 2

Transformation means that the community is moving with increasing awareness and intentionality toward the vision of peace and well-being represented in the diagram. In light of contextual realities, we at Christian Direction have adopted the following schema and the twelve indicators as a vision of what the transformed city (in our case, Montreal) would look like. These indicators are rooted in four tracks underneath the cityscape. They represent God's concern for all of life, beginning with the congregation that embodies shalom and reconciliation. These communities then demonstrate the Good News in their neighbourhoods in word and deed. They are deeply concerned about justice and forgiveness in society. But as stewards they are also concerned for the whole created order. To measure the vision realistically, we have articulated twelve indicators of the type of transformation congregations are pursuing.[9] These address contextual concerns in our city. Accompanying these indicators are baselines rooted in research on the state of life in the city. Congregations work together to pursue the welfare of the city.

This vision seeks to help congregations participate in the transformation of the city, particularly in an era of broken relationships. Unfortunately, poverty is often viewed and portrayed in purely economic terms. Essentially, poverty is about relationships, not just about economics. Poverty is a broad concept including economic, social, emotional, physical, and spiritual realities. It is often intergenerational. It affects people's identity (social exclusion, absence of well-being and harmony in life) and their vocation (deprivation at every level of life, including the ability to participate in the welfare of the community). The causes of poverty can be traced to *inadequacies in the social imaginary*. These inadequacies are in fact a web of lies beyond the mere cognitive level of deception. This intricate web leads people to believe that their poverty or social status is somehow divinely sanctioned or a result of fate. People sense that they have no choices. The social imaginary is a powerful instrument in perpetuating chronic poverty.

In order to measure these territorial social indicators, we employ objective measures from primary field surveys and from secondary, census-based data sets. So, for example, indicators 4, 5, and 6 in figure 2 can be measured by a blend of documentation from both sources. However, the measures also include subjective social indicators that describe the way people perceive and evaluate conditions around them. So, for example, indicators 7, 8, and 12 are highly dependent on an individual's perceptions

9. These indicators have been inspired by the eight United Nations Millennium Objectives, although this schema lacks the rigour of the Millennium Development Goals' (MDGs) eighteen targets and thirty-two indicators.

of and aspirations about the context in relationship to the indicator. As the reader will see, social imaginary indicators rooted in the religious, spiritual, and transcendent experiences of congregations are included in the presentation. Indicators 1, 2, 3, 5, 7, and 11 touch on these aspects of "the community in the mind"—the subjective views people have about their neighbourhood.

SECTION 2: TWENTY STEPS TOWARD UNDERSTANDING YOUR CONTEXT

To begin the process of reading one's community, let me propose twenty steps. These are best undertaken by teams—usually ecumenical "task forces"—that try to understand their community context. After the "exegesis" or community assessment, it will be important to prioritize the initiatives that congregations will undertake.[10]

These steps can be divided into two sections. The first ten steps allow a congregation to understand its context. They are helpful for starting different types of ministries within the community. Steps 11 to 20 are more useful for those considering various kinds of church planting initiatives.

1. Compile a list of significant historical events that inform the community's identity. These could be specific, historic conflicts that took place, such as a war or dispute; specific unifying events, such as the city coming together to fight a massive fire; specific decisions that leaders made, such as the building of a community centre; or something that happened that gave people hope, such as a person doing something heroic or selfless. These will provide clues to the best way for the church to focus its energy. Begin this step by reading about the community. The local library or historical society is where we always begin.

    Study the growth patterns of the city. One can find this information in libraries, city councils, museums, bookstores, local newspapers, and on local websites.

    - Why is the city growing (or why did it grow)?
    - Who are (and were) the immigrants to the city?
    - Where did they come from and where are they settled?
    - Where are they employed?

10. In Quebec, Christian Direction has worked with congregations in ten different cities and boroughs to implement these steps. To obtain a copy of one of the studies, visit our website: www.direction.ca.

2. Understand clearly the sections or zones that make up the city. For example:

- downtown
- blue collar neighbourhoods
- ghettos
- ethnic neighbourhoods
- industrial zones
- commercial areas

Examine census maps if they are available. Find out from city planners and real estate offices where city populations are expected to move, where commercial and industrial zones will develop, and which areas are slated to undergo major changes. Isolate the sectors of your larger community using the wheel diagram of the city on page 226. This represents the functions of a city.

3. Study the neighbourhoods: their ethnic, social, and economic composition, religious affiliations, occupational patterns, younger and older populations, concentrations of the elderly, young professionals, singles, and problem groups. To understand a neighbourhood you must walk the streets and talk to people, insiders and outsiders. Census data are important, but onsite observation is best. Be aware that people groups crisscross in the community. Probe to discover the dominant influence in a neighbourhood: Is it ethnic identity? Social class? Undertake a participant-observer approach.

What is the extent of social contact between the different people groups? Is social contact increasing? Take time to chat with residents and pedestrians in the area. Ask them what the most significant changes are that they see or experience in the neighbourhood. When walking the streets, watch for the impact of these population shifts on the neighbourhood.

Many congregations use prayer walks as a way to learn more about their community.

4. Determine and analyze the power centres in the community: the political figures, the police department, the business leaders and the Chamber of Commerce, the religious leaders. Who controls the media—TV, radio, the newspapers? Who controls commerce and finance? The schools and the arts? What are the religious and moral commitments of the people in positions of power?

5. Analyze the felt needs of specific people groups within the community. You are looking for indications of receptivity and "keys" which may unlock doors to homes and hearts. Felt needs vary from group to group. In some communities, such things as personal illness; loneliness; physical hardships; insecurity in terms of housing, property rights, and the threat of losing one's dwelling are very real. In other neighbourhoods, the felt needs may be entirely different.

    Once a church has demonstrated a commitment to helping meet people's felt needs, and a bridge of relational trust has been established, there is often a greater openness to a discussion of deeper, spiritual needs, and to Christ who meets all needs.

6. Examine the traffic flow. Just as successful advertisers know where to place their signs, practitioners need to know where to begin their ministries, where they can readily be seen and reached.

    Find out where each of the following is located:

- community service centres
- libraries
- police stations
- fire stations
- city hall
- shopping centres
- sports facilities

7. Seek to discover how news and opinion spread in the community, and in particular groups. Mainly through conversation? By radio or TV? Who are the idea-people, the opinion-makers? Subscribe to the weekly publication in the area. Read it faithfully.

8. Examine the relationship between city-dwellers and the rural, small-town communities outside the city. Do certain segments of the urban population maintain strong ties with their rural cousins? Is there a lot of travel and visiting between city and village? What are the present immigration patterns from the countryside? How might the urban-rural interaction be used for the spread of the Gospel and multiplication of churches? Most of this information is available in census data.

9. Locate ministries and churches in the community on a map. Identify them by denomination, size, and age. What transformational ministries and social services are already taking place through these ministries and churches? Reflect on what the church map shows.

235

10. Analyze the various types of existing churches. Common types found in many communities (depending on their size) are

- "old first"
- cathedral church
- "city-centre" churches
- peoples' churches (with large auditoriums, drawing numbers from all over the metropolitan area)
- university churches
- storefront churches
- ethnic-language churches
- suburban churches
- special purpose churches (use the wheel [figure 1] on page **226** for ideas)
- "renewal" churches, the fastest growing in many countries: usually newer, and often independent
- house or cell churches (sometimes referred to as organic churches).

11. Find out the growth patterns (if any) of the various churches: attendance, membership, and rate of growth. Try to determine the nature of the growth: is it by transfer, conversion, or by births? One can often locate this information by chatting with congregational leaders.

12. Inquire about church planting efforts and church closures in the past several years. Which churches have closed? Why? Who has started new churches, and why and where did they succeed? Learn all you can from them.

13. Who is planning to start new churches? Where, and among which people groups? Find out all you can from church and mission sources as to what is being planned for the community.

14. What strategies have been tried in the past, what have failed, and what were effective in starting churches and stimulating growth? Analyze the information you receive. In the light of recent church growth studies, what has been "done right" in this community, and where ought things to have been done differently?

15. Where are the Christians located (of course, this may not be where they attend church)? Identify areas of the city where relatively few Christians live.

16. Identify Christians in positions of influence in the city: in business, politics, the media, education, entertainment, and sports. Analyze their potential for wider spread of the Gospel and assistance in planting churches.

17. List and analyze the parachurch ministries (if any) operating in and to the community. How might each contribute something to the overall strategy? Are there some you may want to avoid because they might have a negative influence on church multiplication?

18. Make an inventory of all possible personnel resources that might be tapped for the carrying out of your church planting strategy. For example, are there Bible college or seminary students available to help with door-to-door calling? Could interns be borrowed from existing churches to help younger congregations?

19. Evaluate all known methods for church planting in light of what you know about this community—its history, people, existing churches, and particular characteristics. What methods have proven effective elsewhere and appear appropriate for this community—and are within the capabilities of your resources?

20. List and evaluate the community agencies (private, religious, and civic) that are designed to meet particular needs (literacy, overnight shelter, emergency food and clothing, and so on) and consider how their help can be incorporated into your overall strategy.

WHERE THE RUBBER HITS THE ROAD

In 2006, Christian Direction, in conjunction with Roman Catholic parishes and Protestant congregations, published a forty-five-page study of the east end of Montreal—Hochelaga/Maisonneuve—using these twenty steps. This borough is the poorest continuous borough in Canada going back to the 1871 census![11] Together we created the round-table, *Regroupement œcuménique de Hochelaga/Maisonneuve*. Numerous initiatives have been launched as a result of this study. For example, to address the 55 percent high school drop-out rate in the neighbourhood, in collaboration with another social service agency, we started a centre to work with adolescents, their families, and the local schools to promote school success.

11. David Ley, "The Inner City," in *Canadian Cities in Transition: Local through Global Perspectives*, ed. Trudi Bunting and Pierre Fortin (Don Mills, ON: Oxford University Press, 2006) 195.

Together with others in the borough, we advocate with local businesses so they do not employ students during the school day. To address the relational poverty, there are four events each year designed to break the deep solitude people experience. To break the cycle of intergenerational poverty, three "financial capability" projects[12] have been started for young people and their families. In a short time, all three projects were generating income. At the heart of the vision are the key indicators of a transformed community in figure 2 on page 231. This same experience is now being repeated in four other boroughs on the island of Montreal and four other cities in Quebec. Research can *and must* inform transformational strategies.

12. http://www.entreados.ca.

Green Shoots 9
Matching Church to the Needs of Young Families

Messy Church
St. John's, Newfoundland

When it comes to non-threatening opportunities for church and young families to come together, Messy Church is a match made in heaven. No one knows this better than Sam Rose, who was invited in 2006 to join the clergy at St. Michael's and All Angels Anglican Church in St John's to be a mission priest. His task was to develop new models for ministry, as well as plant a new congregation.

"I saw that what we do on Sundays doesn't necessarily speak to children," Sam recalls. And he knew from personal experience that the structure and formality of the Sunday morning liturgy at this traditional Anglo-Catholic destination church was not really what parents needed, either. The stress in his own home on Sunday mornings spoke volumes. "I'm usually up and ready to go, and my wife is feeding the kids, getting them dressed, and rushing off to church, always a bit late and in a panic. And you get there, and the kids have to act like little adults instead of children. So I asked myself, 'Why don't we leave Sunday as it is but create another opportunity for young families to come and be together as families?'"

Sam also realized that for parents and children, a Sunday service was a total disconnect, with children given a bit of conversation up front with the adults and then sent away to Sunday school. This really hit home for Sam when one of his parishioners, a single father, told him, "I only see my daughter on weekends and, when I bring her to church, I want her to stay with me."

About the same time, Sam just happened to pick up a book by Lucy Moore called *Messy Church*.[13] He quickly realized that what the UK-based author was describing was "a kind of condensed Bible school for families," he says. "Most people's lives are not neat and

13. Lucy Moore, *Messy Church* (Abingdon UK: Bible Reading Fellowship, 2006).

tidy. They're complex, and the idea of Messy Church is to embrace that. It's okay to be rushed and it's okay to colour outside the lines. That's what life is like. Life is messy."

In 2007 he began to recruit, focusing on parish families whose children had been baptized in the previous five years. "We wrote them a personal invitation, explaining that this was a Saturday afternoon event with no obligation, just an informal, relaxed atmosphere, and asked them to please come and see," says Sam. Significantly, the invitation emphasized that this was not a drop-off program: parents were expected to stay and take part in the activities with their children. For the opening of Messy Church, Sam set up a corner with toys in the parish hall, "almost like a daycare." There were tables and chairs for craft activities and a coffee area for parents. "What immediately happened was that the kids went to the toys and developed this little community, and the parents were drinking coffee together and asking, 'Which one is yours?'"

Sam left his clerical robes at home. When one parent asked where the priest was, someone said, "Well, that's Father Sam up there in the T-shirt." As Sam recalls, "There was an immediate connection and a little bit of a wall was broken down. I was the guy also drinking the cup of coffee, watching my two kids playing with the other kids."

When the doors opened at 2 p.m., twenty minutes were allotted for "just playing with toys, kids doing what they want to do, parents talking together." Then Sam took the microphone and welcomed everyone to Messy Church. "I am Father Sam," he told the half-dozen families assembled. "We're going to have some fun." He introduced the Bible-based theme for the event: Noah and the ark. The craft, the songs, and the "messy snack" all centred on that motif, using big bowls, bananas, chocolate sauce, blue-tinted Cool Whip for the water, animal crackers, coloured sprinkles, and ice cream to recreate the ark. Even today, Sam's children, who were one and three years old at the time, ask if they can make the Noah and the ark banana split.

For five months, Sam ran Messy Church on one Saturday out of four. Then parents started to ask him for something "a bit more churchy" on Saturday afternoon. "Parents said they wanted it to be a Sunday kind of thing, but on Saturday," he says.

So Sam organized "Saturday Church" on the other three Saturdays, with a 4 p.m. Eucharist, called the Children's Service, in an improvised worship space at the back of the church. Again, there was a corner for toys, and a corner for coffee, donuts, and juice. And after twenty minutes of fellowship, Sam called everyone to worship. A special altar was built on top of the baptismal font, and the liturgy was projected on a screen in easy-to-read PowerPoint. Sam played modern children's music with action songs and used a contemporary liturgy from the Church of England. YouTube clips helped to create a dialogue with the children. And there was always a Eucharist. "Our tradition at St. Michael's was to be a Eucharist-centred parish," he says.

With these new offerings for young families, Sam began to see the blossoming of two distinct fresh expressions of church: one comprising families interested in Messy Church, and the other consisting of those seeking liturgically based, Eucharistic family worship.

By the time of the first Messy Church Christmas service, within four months of its first beginnings, Messy Church had grown to one hundred and ten people. At its peak, Saturday Church had about ninety people in attendance. "Some of these people would have been the same people who came to Messy Church," admits Sam, "but we probably grew [in total] by about thirty-five to forty families."

Jump ahead three years. In 2010, the decision was made to sell St. Michael's and to move to a new building in a new neighbourhood. While the building was going up, Sam held his Saturday and Sunday worship services at an Anglican family-run funeral home in St. John's. At first, he was not sure this would work, but everyone concluded that they "didn't have much choice."

The new church will have a capacity of approximately 325, and that is just the right size as far as Sam is concerned. "Anglican churches are not mega churches," he explains. "They're community churches. These are the real pockets of mission and outreach. When the churches are bigger, people don't get to know each other. It's a real disconnect."

The new church's location is right at the entrance to a 5,000-home subdivision that will house predominantly younger families. Two schools are also under construction. "Every time someone goes to their home, they have to pass by us," points out Sam. His new mission committee is busy discerning ways in which it can serve the new community. "If there's a group of children that need bikes, for example, we can have a bike shop in the bottom of the church, and a child can have the bike for the day and bring it back at the end of the day," says Sam. "We just have to listen to the needs of people and then respond," he adds. "The church has to listen, and listen more, to people who are not part of it."

K.J.

I remember visiting New Orleans a couple of years after Hurricane Katrina had devastated the area. I was struck by the fact that churches that belonged to a denomination had received help from outside, and in many cases had recovered. Independent churches, on the other hand, had disappeared, simply because nobody outside the area knew they were there. It was a lesson in the importance of connection between churches. When it comes to mission, that connectedness means we seek to help and encourage and learn from one another—hence (among other things) this book. On the other hand, connectedness looks different within each denominational tribe. Some will look to a regional office, others to a presbytery or classis or synod or conference. Mainline denominations look to their bishop for that connection. As we seek to connect across denominational lines, a degree of translation will be necessary. Here, then, is one such story about a network of churches—in Anglican terms, a diocese—seeking to become missional. The particularities are unique to the context; the principles, however, can be applied to whatever form of connectedness we prefer.

15

Risky Business

Shaping a Diocese for Mission

Jane Alexander

I BECAME A BISHOP in 2008. Being a bishop these days is not easy—if it ever was. On the one hand, we live in days of declining church attendance, regular budget crises, and pressing controversial issues. However, the church is called to health and growth, as it has always been, and to live in the present without longing for what has passed.

The Anglican Diocese of Edmonton, which I have the honour to lead, was founded in 1913 and presently consists of some sixty congregations (or parishes), twenty of them in the city of Edmonton itself and the rest in a mix of suburban and rural communities.

Since my election, my goal has been to help the diocese move from a culture of maintenance ("Our job is to keep doing what we have always done") to one of mission ("Our job is to work with God towards the re-newal of all things"). For mainline churches, in particular, this is a task which requires learning a whole new language and a new way of thinking and acting—which is always challenging and often uncomfortable.

In these years, we have had some modest successes and some embar-rassing failures. Sometimes we knew we had done the right thing only with the benefit of hindsight: success was not really the result of prophetic imagination, much as we might like to think so. But, as Bishop Steve Croft said when he visited us in 2011, "We're making this up as we go along," and we do have the sense that God is with us—and that is what counts. So if the story of what we have done in this diocese is helpful to others who give denominational leadership, Anglican and otherwise—even if it is sometimes a lesson in what not to do!—we will be very happy.

A MISSIONAL MISSION STATEMENT

When I began, one thing I was grateful to inherit from my predecessor, Bishop Victoria Matthews, was a mission statement with a clear missional focus. (Sometimes mission statements bear little relation to actual "mission"!) Our mission, it says, is, "Proclaiming the Gospel—Making Disciples—Furthering the Kingdom." That is then expanded in our vision statement.[1]

There is always a risk that mission and vision statements remain on paper and never find their way into the everyday life of congregations and individuals. However, they can be called on to justify a new course of action: "Don't you remember, this is what we said in our vision statement? This is who we agreed we are and what we are about." How we have made use of these statements will emerge in the stories that follow.

MY OWN FORMATION

Leaders cannot lead in mission, of course, unless they understand and are passionate about the church's mission. Missiologist Lesslie Newbigin has been a huge influence on me in this respect. I have been particularly influenced by his focus on mission and the unity of the church. A constant theme in his writing is the idea that the message of the Gospel is a gift to the church as a whole and that we, as individual Christians, are called and commissioned to a ministry that at its heart is invitational. This message resonates strongly with me and is central to my own belief. I like the memorable way George Lings, a leader of the Fresh Expressions movement in the United Kingdom, summarizes Newbigin's challenge: "The church has listened to the words of Jesus, 'Come unto me,' but has not listened to the words, 'Go into the world.'"[2] Archbishop Fred Hiltz, Primate of the

1. The full statement may be found on the diocesan website at http://edmonton
.anglican.org/about-the-diocese/the-mission-vision-and-strategic-focus-of-the
-diocese-of-edmonton/.

2. Unpublished lecture, June 2005.

Anglican Church of Canada, has also encouraged me with his reminders that "the Church needs to move away from a culture of membership to one of discipleship."[3]

Between 1984 and 1990, the Anglican Communion, which unites national Anglican Churches around the world, tried various ways to formulate a statement of the church's calling. This has evolved into what are now called The Five Marks of Mission. Each national church has been invited to adapt those Marks for its own situation. I have been helped by the way the National Council of Churches in Australia has summarized the Marks and defined the church's mission:

> Mission is the creating, reconciling and transforming action of God, flowing from the community of love found in the Trinity, made known to all humanity in the person of Jesus, and entrusted to the faithful action and witness of the people of God who, in the power of the Spirit, are a sign, foretaste and instrument of the reign of God.[4]

Mission, then, begins with God the Trinity. The work of mission is focused in the work of Jesus Christ. And the church is the community of those who have responded to God's call through faith and baptism to follow Jesus and take part in God's mission.

I have been influenced by international Anglicanism in other ways, too. Every ten years, all the Anglican bishops in the world gather in England for what is known as The Lambeth Conference. I was fortunate as a new bishop to attend the Lambeth Conference in the summer of 2008 and was particularly encouraged by the presentations on mission and church growth I heard there. From press reports, one could be forgiven for thinking that the main topic of conversation at the conference was human sexuality. In fact, the two official themes were "Strengthening Anglican Identity" and "Equipping Bishops for Mission." I was particularly struck by the address from Rowan Williams, then Archbishop of Canterbury, at the retreat with which the conference opened, on "God's Mission and a Bishop's Discipleship," and the presentation by Brian McLaren on "Changing Contexts: Breaking Open Our Models for Evangelism." Both Archbishop Williams and McLaren, in their own ways, encouraged leaders to have a mission-shaped spirituality that always points to what God

---

3. "Primate Addresses Trinity and Wycliffe Communities," Wycliffe College, January 17, 2008, http://www.wycliffecollege.ca/news_details.php?nid=151.

4. "Mission—The Five Marks of Mission," Anglican Communion, last modified 2012, http://www.anglicancommunion.org/ministry/mission/fivemarks.cfm.

is doing and to the possibilities that are before us. Neither speaker lapsed into an Eeyore-like sense of doom and despair for the future of the church. Christ's body is very much alive.

SEEDING NEW THINKING

We used to assume that people had to think differently before they could act differently. Now we see more clearly that action often comes before thinking, and that fresh thinking can actually emerge from new behaviour. In the Diocese of Edmonton, we have worked with both new thinking and new acting, and the two have informed and shaped each other.

We began with a year of preparation among the clergy, beginning with some missional reading. Clergy read and discussed the book *Simple Church: Returning to God's Process for Making Disciples,* by Thom Rainer and Eric Geiger.[5] The authors are not Anglicans, so there were some struggles over unfamiliar theology and language, but we were eager to be taught by any who have something to teach us, even if they are from a different denominational "tribe." The book helped to stress *focus* over the scattered *busy-ness* that can afflict us in times of change. It was an important precursor to the planning process that followed.

The next clergy conference focused on the topic of mission. This time our reading was more Anglican in flavour: the influential *Mission Shaped Church* report (2004) from the Church of England, the Five Marks of Mission (see page 11, footnote 13), and the Diocesan Vision Statement. We also shared good news stories from around the diocese.

Over these years, we have worked at providing continuing education for our leaders in the area of mission. We have brought in a range of world-class speakers including Caroline Pinchbeck (Canon for Rural Life and Ministry in the Diocese of Canterbury, England), Michael Harvey (founder of Back to Church Sunday), Phyllis Tickle (A Changing World), Lucy Moore (founder of Messy Church), Michael Lapsley (Healing and Reconciliation), Nick Brotherwood (Mission Shaped Ministry training), Claude Payne (the bishop who enabled church planting in the Diocese of Texas), John Franke and Brian McLaren (on Missional Thinking), and Pete Rollins (on "Out of the box theology"). The intent behind hearing from such a diverse group was to stress that there is no one way forward

---

5. Thom Rainer and Eric Geiger, *Simple Church: Returning to God's Process for Making Disciples* (Nashville, TN: B&H Books, 2006).

in mission, no magic bullet. Leaders and their congregations should read widely and see what is most useful in their own contexts.

We also sent people for training to places where new things were happening, to see what they could learn and come back to report and train: the Institute of Evangelism at Wycliffe College in Toronto, the Church Army's Sheffield Centre in England, and various dioceses of the Church of England.

None of us wake up the morning after our ordination or commissioning, miraculously knowing everything we need to know. In fact, I think on those mornings it is more normal to wake up realizing how little we know! The Word of God has not changed and the sacraments have not changed, but the ways we proclaim the Gospel and invite people to receive the grace of God change all the time—and have done so since the days of the first disciples. Just as each of us would expect our family physician to keep abreast of new developments and treatments, so too in the church our training needs to evolve as we strive to find more effective ways of being church in our communities. These forms of training were our attempt to keep up-to-date with best practice in the life of a missional church.

FORMULATING A PLAN

When I returned from Lambeth, I realized we needed a plan to help us move from maintenance to mission. Once again, the church in Australia helped us. I came across an eight-point template put together by the "fresh expressions team" in Melbourne. It was originally intended for a group wanting to begin a fresh expression of church, but we have found it helpful in working towards any kind of missional initiative. Some of the points were fairly intuitive—"Build mission-centred values" or "Listen and pray." Others were more surprising, such as "Prune a little" and "Feed your imagination." We have tried to keep this template in mind as we have considered each step and initiative.

KNOW YOUR COMMUNITY

The parish system, which is part of Anglican and Roman Catholic tradition, assumes that the job of a local congregation is to be the church of and for the local neighbourhood in which it is located. This worked well in a time when communities were more self-contained—when people travelled less, and when there was only one church in a community. The nineteenth-century novels of Anthony Trollope portray this system well, with all its strengths and weaknesses. But as travel has become easier, so the geographical boundaries of parishes have become more porous. So, for example, these days if one does not "like" one's parish church (for whatever reason), one can easily drive to a neighbouring church. And the proliferation of Protestant denominations since the Reformation means there is a choice of churches in most communities—often more than one of them on the same street. This has diminished the sense of "this church for this community."

One of the ways that churches these days are rediscovering their sense of mission is to reconsider the possibility that they are called not just to look after those already inside their doors but to the neighbourhood in which they are set. Newbigin anticipated this over twenty years ago in his call for "local congregations [to] renounce an introverted concern for their own life, and [to] recognize that they exist for the sake of those who are not members." [6]

This realization led us in September of 2008 to offer clergy a presentation on "Knowing our Community," and to ask them to begin exploring the demographics, both of their congregations and of the communities in which they were set. The main tool we used (and are continuing to use) for this is the Mission Action Plan (MAP), again something borrowed from elsewhere—in this case, the Diocese of London, England. [7]

The MAP process seemed to us a tried and tested way of beginning to put flesh on our missional impulse. It helped us identify our strengths and the challenges that faced us, and then to put together a realistic plan for God's way forward. The MAP approach also appealed to us because it did not insist on one correct way of producing a Mission Action Plan (MAP), but was very responsive to the character and needs of any particular parish.

Here is the process as we learned it:

Mission Action Plan

Parish Profile: describe as many aspects of your church as possible, such as styles of worship, a profile of the people who come, church school, church resources, and activities within the church.

---

6. Lesslie Newbigin, *The Gospel in a Pluralist Society* (Grand Rapids, MI: Eerdmans, 1989), 232–233.

7. See www.london.anglican.org/MAP. Reproduced with permission.

Community Audit: compile a profile of your neighbourhood. Include information about local organizations and amenities. Use census data to profile the population. Plot the demography of your parish on a map.

Envisioning Exercise: brainstorm with as many people as possible to come up with new ideas and ventures. Be bold: don't worry about practicalities at this stage.

SWOT Analysis: take the ideas from the envisioning exercise and consider the Strengths, Weaknesses, Opportunities, and Threats for each one. This will help you to think realistically about what might be possible. Remember to include financial and buildings considerations in the process.

Resources: consider what people and skills will be needed to accomplish your objectives. Will local partners need to be involved? Who in the church community might take this forward? What else might be needed?

Prioritize: divide your ideas into three categories: "Quick Wins"—things that can be introduced and make an impact quickly; "Medium range"—things that will require preparation; "Long range"—things that will need an investment of significant time and resources.

SMART Checklist: make sure all your objectives are Specific and Stretching, Measurable, Achievable, Relevant and Realistic, as well as Time-bound and Timely.

Draft: prepare a MAP that sets out your parish priorities and how you intend to achieve them. Be sure this is a collaborative activity so the whole congregation has ownership of the plan.

Launch: celebrate your vision with your community, both churchgoers and those groups and people who have links with your church.

I asked every parish to follow this process and to produce a MAP, so that dreams for their place in the community and the focus of their ministry might become front and centre in all they do. Every parish needs to be clear about what it is trying under God to achieve, and MAPs have helped.

One thing this process did, of course, was to challenge our assumptions about our membership and our ability to reach out into the community. It also helped us realise that we needed to reacquaint ourselves with our neighbours. It is all too easy to feel that we know what our neighbourhood is like simply by looking out at our congregations on Sunday mornings and assuming they are a representative sample of the local scene. To help us see more clearly, quite early on we provided each parish with detailed statistics from a business and marketing service that provided much more detailed demographic information than does Statistics Canada.[8] We encouraged church leaders to look at the spread of people living locally and then overlay that with the spread of people in church. It takes courage to do that, and yet without that kind of close look we make all kinds of assumptions about the type of evangelistic efforts and programs we should be offering.

The information was first shared with the clergy. For many, it was a revealing day as we discussed the figures. Initially, there was some resistance from those who felt that their congregation was a "niche church," unapologetically attracting most of their members from outside the official parish boundaries. However, there were still questions to be asked: how do people know you are here in the first place? If you are not reaching out to people locally and inviting them to know Jesus, then who is?

Most fundamentally, we dared to ask the question, "Who are we here for?"—and tried not to be upset when one of the answers given was "ourselves." Fortunately, the conversation moved on from that point to more productive topics, such as how or why we had limited our hopes for our churches—and even sometimes our expectations of God.

Of course, there were some who argued that "we can't talk about growth until the church has made its mind up on . . ." various issues, ranging from homelessness to indigenous issues to same gender relationships. However, mission is not a secondary activity or an optional extra for the church, and we cannot let distractions—even important ones—stop us. We cannot wait until all questions, all doubts, and all disagreements have been settled before we go out and share the good news of Jesus. This has been a source of some friction for a small group of people.

FINANCIAL RESOURCES

Every church, diocese, and national church institution has of late had to make difficult decisions about the allocation of finances in order to help advance the Church's mission. In Edmonton, we are a small diocese with a working budget of around one million dollars each year. As the Johnny Depp character in the movie *Finding Neverland* says, "Yes, well, we do dream on a budget here."

8. www.superdemographics.com

Like many centralized denominations, each local congregation con-
tributes a percentage of its budget to the running of the central organization. In Anglican dioceses, this is called "apportionment." Like many
other dioceses, we try to keep apportionment to a minimum in order to
leave more for the ministry of the local church. Yet to give leadership in
mission—particularly to fund some new initiatives—costs money. We
decided this was important enough that we should release small amounts
of money from trust funds, though we do not have many of them. However, we did release a substantial amount from the Diocesan Development
Fund—$390,000—to create the Barnabas Initiative, perhaps our most sig-
nificant missional catalyst, which will be described below. This Development Fund was normally used only for bricks and mortar projects, and yet
it was too small to pay for even one new church building, so we decided
to redirect it to people and the support of the existing church's mission.

We have also used the sale money from some disestablished rural
parishes to fund the Rural Ministry Initiative (again, described below)—a
redemptive move with what might otherwise be a rather sad transaction.

All this is rather a leap of faith since the spending is one-time spending. If our vision does not "work" in terms of revitalising and growing the
church, we cannot do it again. Thanks be to God, our preliminary findings
are that it is working. Now we must look for new and innovative ways to
continue funding new ministries that will not hurt existing churches and
make it difficult for them to continue.

TAKING STRATEGIC INITIATIVES

Renewed energy for the church's mission can take many forms. Many will
be in response to unique local circumstances and not replicable in other
places. Others will be a model that can readily be adapted to a number of
places. In the Diocese of Edmonton, the missional impulse has expressed
itself in many ways. Many churches, for example, have embraced the opportunity of Back to Church Sunday. In fact, the first year we tried this,
church attendance on that day across fifty-three churches was up by an
average of 51 percent. Other churches have explored what they can learn
from Appreciative Enquiry. This has enabled them to take a positive look
at their gifts and strategic opportunities for ministry in their communities.
Another fifteen are using Natural Church Development over a three-year
period as a way of reviewing and enhancing their life and mission.

However, we felt that as a diocese there were three particular strategic initiatives which were appropriate for our mission in our unique setting, and which we would therefore promote centrally: the Barnabas Initiative, the Rural Ministry Initiative, and the Indigenous Ministries Initiative.

The Barnabas Initiative

The Barnabas Initiative (BI) was officially launched at our annual Synod in the fall of 2008. In the spirit of Barnabas in the Book of Acts, who was known as "the Son of Encouragement," our goal was to encourage our churches to reach out to the communities around them, so that all may encounter the Gospel of Jesus Christ. If I had to summarise what this is about, I would say that we are helping churches be all that they are called to be—in a word, to be Church.

One practical expression of Barnabas was to begin "building capacity" among clergy by moving beyond the traditional model of "one priest to one parish," and instead sharing the missional gifts of six clergy and lay people (Barnabas Initiative team members) throughout the diocese. They visited congregations in order to lead conversations about mission, they offered coaching in mission and discipleship, and they gave leadership in the planting of new mission endeavours. Two clergy were itinerant, acting as catalysts for new initiatives and serving as cross-diocesan resources. The others were tied to specific parishes or projects ranging from half-time to full-time, and staying a minimum of six months and a maximum of two years. A total of six rural and eleven urban or suburban churches took advantage of these Barnabas resources.

One readily accessible outreach strategy has been Messy Church, new Christian communities ministering to families, usually midweek, not always in a church building, and featuring crafts (messy, naturally), a Bible story and songs, and a meal. In some cases, a simple Eucharist has been added.[9] To date, about one in five of our churches—rural, urban and suburban—have started Messy Church congregations in their community, or outreach programs inspired by Messy Church. Some parishes have kept the name "Messy Church," but for others it has become "Spaghetti Church" and even "Wiggly Church."

Barnabas has also helped to encourage the planting of a new English language congregation at a former Cantonese parish through training a

9. See messychurch.org.uk.

church-planting team of five individuals and providing ongoing support to the congregation as a whole.

Other initiatives catalysed by Barnabas have included the following:

- A New Life Mom's Group, to support new moms struggling with life challenges following the birth of a child.

- The Project, an arts initiative based out of Holy Trinity, Edmonton. This has a double focus: an arts ministry to at-risk, homeless, and street-involved youth, on the one hand, and support for performing artists in the Old Strathcona area of Edmonton on the other.

The Barnabas Initiative has not just been a frenetic whirlwind of new activities, however. The Kingdom is not built by human busy-ness. Rather, there has been a purposeful redirection of energy away from things that were consuming our energy but not contributing to mission. And we have tried to provide opportunities for reflection and learning so that busy people have opportunities to take in as well as give out.

One prime example is an academic partnership that is helping to "equip the saints for the work of ministry" (Eph 4:12). We are fortunate to have Taylor Seminary, originally a Baptist school, here in Edmonton. Part of Taylor's ministry is the E. P. Wahl Centre, which offers programs to train laity and clergy of all denominations for ministry outside as well as inside the church walls. The associate director of the centre is Dr. Myron Penner, a priest of the diocese and a member of the Barnabas Initiative team. This association has provided members of the diocese with numerous opportunities to be nurtured by learning, reading, and reflection.

Two of our younger clergy, Nick Trussell and Thomas Brauer, also put together a program for a day of introductory mission training—Mission Days—based on the United Kingdom tradition of a Vision Day, but adapted for local use. This has been offered on five occasions, and fifteen parishes across the diocese, both rural and urban, have benefitted from it.

Over the course of the first three years of Barnabas, we have seen a total of seventeen new initiatives planned and/or implemented. As well as the initiatives described above, we have seen dramatic transformation in the life of a number of inherited congregations, bringing a new spirit of mission and hope for the future.

The Rural Ministry Initiative

The Rural Ministry Initiative of the Diocese of Edmonton (RMI) was established in 2010 to provide support and specialized training for clergy in rural areas. It also aimed to provide funding for fresh approaches to rural ministry in a few pilot areas. As in many denominations, over time a feeling had grown that urban and suburban ministry were more highly valued than rural, and the RMI seeks to address this issue.

After looking at developments in rural dioceses in the United Kingdom, we adopted the model of appointing a "canon pastor" for rural ministry. The job of the canon pastor is to provide in-person support and training to new rural priests, and to help with planning and visioning in rural parishes. He also helps to address issues around isolation and loneliness and to give leadership to an annual conference especially to address the needs of rural clergy.

The RMI has helped us to invest in rural parts of the diocese where growth is possible but existing parishes cannot afford the needed increase in ministry. For example, the parish of St. Aidan and St Hilda, Rexboro, about one hour west of Edmonton, is in an area showing steady growth. With the closing of the local power plant, and the sale of lakefront land, the community will likely grow still further and become a year-round community. In anticipation of this, the parish has begun year-round services, using a rented space in the town of Wabamun from October to May, and the parish building from May to October. We think of this as our first rural church plant.

Knowing that it will take time to see much substantial development, the RMI has committed support for two years to encourage this ministry. We are also realizing the need for longer pastorates, rather than seeing rural parishes as short-term positions or training grounds where new clergy can "cut their teeth."

RMI has also encouraged the reinvigoration of traditional community services such as Rogation Day services, involving outdoor liturgical processions and the blessing of farmers' fields. We have also joined in sponsoring non-denominational services around local needs such as droughts, or joined in local celebrations by having a presence at stampedes and fairs.

The Indigenous Ministry Initiative

The Indigenous Ministry Initiative (IMI) of the Diocese of Edmonton is presently focused on the development of ministry to First Nations people in the city, although eleven First Nations communities outside the city are within diocesan boundaries. It is headed up by Canon Pastor for Indigenous Ministry Travis Enright, himself a Plains Cree from Central Saskatchewan. Start-up funding for this position came from one of our remaining trust funds.

Travis is able to link the church and First Nations people and to draw us into areas of understanding and commonality. He is a member of the Edmonton Urban Aboriginal Affairs Committee, has attended the Anglican Church of Canada's Sacred Circle, and was instrumental in bringing to Edmonton the "Remembering the Children" gathering to help prepare for the coming of the Truth and Reconciliation Commission.[10] It was Travis who pioneered our first listening circles to help vision our journey.

Through Travis's ministry, we have learned that the face of ministry to First Nations people is changing. Our mission of spreading the Gospel of Christ is taking a new direction as larger numbers of First Nations people move off of the reserves and into urbanised centers. In fact, almost 80 percent of aboriginal people do not live on reserves, and it is expected that by 2016, Edmonton will have the largest urban aboriginal population in Canada.[11] The mission field has moved from isolated communities into the heart of the city. As we follow our call to "go and make disciples of all nations," we are aware that the First Nations people are coming to us. The Indigenous Ministry Initiative seeks to define and strengthen a focus on First Nations ministry, and to commit ourselves to listening and walking alongside them.

CONCLUSION

Looking back over these developments with the wisdom of hindsight, I realize there were some things we "did right" and which I would commend to anyone in denominational leadership trying to lead a group or association of churches from maintenance into mission. To summarize:

10. See http://www.rememberingthechildren.ca.

11. "Canada's Aboriginal Population Tops Million Mark: StatsCan," CBC News, CBC, last modified January 15, 2008, http://www.cbc.ca/canada/edmonton/story/2008/01/15/aboriginal-census.html.

1. Although in the big scheme of things it was probably not the most significant thing, it was nevertheless helpful that we had a Mission Statement that spoke officially of our commitment to mission. A non-missional Mission Statement (unfortunately not an oxymoron) could have hindered us, whereas this one provided an ideological compass.

2. We sought to learn from the experience of our own denomination in other countries and from other denominations at home and abroad. In both cases, some "translation" into our own native language was necessary, of course, but it was worth it. We are not ashamed to borrow: nobody need reinvent the wheel in order to build a new wagon. Or, to put it more theologically, the borrowing is simply benefitting from the gifts of other parts of the Body of Christ.

3. Going to conferences such as Lambeth and the Vital Church Planting conferences gave me (and others) new insights and the opportunity to learn from those who are further down the missional road than us. They also linked us into networks of others who are thinking about the same issues and experimenting with the same approaches—networks about which we might otherwise have remained unaware. And social media, of course, make it far easier to maintain those networks than was possible a few years ago, even when they are scattered in different parts of the world.

4. We worked hard to give our leaders, particularly (but not only) the ordained, resources they could then take back and introduce to folk at the grassroots of church life. New initiatives in church life often come from lay folk—it is significant that 50 percent of fresh expressions of church in the United Kingdom are started by lay people—but sometimes clergy are better placed to encounter new ideas and new resources, and to transmit them to those who are in a position to implement them. If nothing else, those in official leadership can fulfill the crucial role of permission-givers!

5. We realized the importance of sharing the vision at the local level. Change cannot be imposed top-down, as the graveyard of denominational five-year plans silently testifies. Tools like Mission Action Plans have helped local congregations catch the vision, discern the calling of God in their own neighbourhood, and take action.

6. We tried to allocate our resources according to our priorities. Having said that mission was our priority, we moved to reflect that commitment in our budget and our deployment of personnel. We found ways

to provide seed money to innovative projects. By the same token, we found ways to put missionally-minded young leaders in positions where their passion could have an influence. This seems better than the time-honoured strategy of putting them in remote and soul-de-stroying placements where their passion will gradually be destroyed, and they cease to be a threat to the institutional status quo.

7. No church and no denomination can do everything and certainly can-not do too many things simultaneously. So at the same time as seed-ing missional thinking in as many local congregations as possible and encouraging various local responses, we also had to establish some priorities for us as a diocese—the three projects described above.

Michael Peers, Primate of the Anglican Church of Canada from 1986 to 2004, once described how during his lifetime he had seen a con-cern for social justice move from the periphery of the church's life to the centre. Whereas it was once considered the interest of a few eccentrics, these days—at least in the Anglican Church—it is now regarded as an es-sential part of the church's agenda. Without a concern for social justice, Anglican churches are considered a little weird, even irresponsible.[12] Now something similar seems to be happening with the place of mission in the church's life.

In the Diocese of Edmonton, through what some would call a relent-less focus on mission, I believe that we have changed the nature of conver-sation and begun to move mission to the centre of our life. It is easy now to talk about mission and church planting and to know that most of our leaders know what we are talking about. Many smaller congregations are feeling hopeful and encouraged that there is an approach to ministry that they can engage in and feel as though they are vibrant and active members of their communities. Our mistakes, failures, and challenges have only taught us how to do things better. When we started all this, we had pretty much no expertise in church planting or missional revitalization, and we have had to learn it all as we went along.

There is a fresh realization in the Diocese of Edmonton that every church we ever attend was planted primarily to be a sign of the Kingdom in a given community. I am particularly struck by Jesus' parable about the man who sold everything he owned in order to buy "the pearl of great price" that he discovered by accident in a most unlikely place. My hope

12. Elin Goulden, "Moving Towards the Centre: Evangelism in a New Decade: An Interview with Michael Peers," in *good idea!* Newsletter of the Wycliffe College Insti-tute of Evangelism, Volume 9, no. 2, Fall 2002.

for the churches of this diocese is that they become communities where people discover that pearl: a glimpse of God's beauty. My prayer is that in all our churches, in all our fresh expressions, and in all our endeavours, people will catch a glimpse of God's Kingdom so beautiful, so rich, and so inviting that they cannot help but be drawn into the community where it is experienced.

Once again, Newbigin seems to have been prophetic, both about the problems of the church in the West and about the way forward. Commenting on the fact that in Christendom, "missions" and "church" were seen as two separate things, he comments that mission and church "cannot become one until a very deep and widespread change has taken place in the thinking of the Churches about their own nature, until they have come to see, and to express in the ordinary life of the Church, the truth that the Church has all its treasure entrusted to it *for the sake of the world*, and that therefore mission belongs to the very substance of the Church's life."[13]

In the Anglican Diocese of Edmonton, we have not yet achieved that synthesis of church and mission, but we are on the way. The DNA is being reworked. Our priorities are shifting. The structures, the budget, and the leadership are changing in order to support the new life of a missional church. What is required us of now is "a long obedience in the same direction."[14]

13. Lesslie Newbigin, *The Household of God* (London: SCM Press, 1953), 144. Italics added.

14. A phrase of Friedrich Nietzsche, used by Eugene Peterson as the title of his 1980 book.

Green Shoots 10
The Church Has Left the Building!

Destination Church
St. Thomas, Ontario

As Beth Fellinger puts it, St. Thomas is a town with an awful lot of choice in churches—to stay home from, that is. "The city has a population of forty-two thousand, but only one in ten residents goes to church," she says.

So St. Thomas presented a challenge even to this energetic and charismatic pastor, whose successful Christian Reformed (CR) "Destination Church" held its first service in January 2011, and now attracts a Sunday morning congregation of eighty people, with about two hundred adherents overall.

Back in November 2009, Beth, an expert in missional church, was troubleshooting for a Presbyterian church in London, Ontario, mentoring new staff and helping the church to revitalize. Meanwhile, in nearby St. Thomas, the CR Fellowship Community Church, eager to do something fresh and different for the community, posted an intriguing online job description for a church planter. After a gruelling process of questionnaires, psychological assessments, Rorschach inkblots, boot-camp training, and academic credentialing, Beth landed the role of starting a new plant in church-averse St. Thomas.

By June 2010, she was tentatively on her way. "The starting point was asking, 'What should this church look like?'" To answer that, Beth spent June through December speaking with locals in coffee shops, poring over a motherlode of recent demographic statistics, and chatting up everybody from teenagers and business owners to the mayor and city councillors.

"Basically, I asked about a hundred and fifty people to share their stories, so I could make sense of the demographic figures I'd read," she says. "Their stories were very important because the last thing we wanted to do was to create something not needed." For example, demographics showed that St. Thomas had a lower-than-average rate of attendance at post-secondary institutions—thanks in part to a (now-closed) Ford assembly plant and a lot of Mennonite family farms nearby—so to start a church with a university-type ethos would not attract much interest.

Beth's target demographic was simple and unrestricted: anyone interested in attending church. "We were not after an age group but, as it happens, 70 percent of our members are under age thirty," she says. Her congregation comprises single mothers, families, business people, young singles, lawbreakers, and people with addiction problems. Realizing that many of these citizens have had little ceremony in their lives, the inventive Beth baptizes them in her family's hot tub.

Getting down to brass tacks for the launch, Beth set about building a strong team of like-minded people, whose skill sets would complement hers. "I identified my own strengths and also the other strengths that I would need to go along with me," she says.

A good planting team includes visionaries such as "seed throwers, fire starters, grace givers, hope peddlers, and risk takers—people who love God and others, and who are transfixed and mesmerized by Jesus," she says. But to function well, a plant also needs detail people: organizers, administrators, accountants, hospitality planners, IT staff, and marketers.

And even with the most dedicated team, start-up is challenging. Most people in the start-up team come from within an existing church that has a political structure, deacons, and elders. "But a plant runs very differently. This is a very different side of ministry for them," she says.

And even supportive pastors can be nervous: "Are you going to steal all my sheep?" they ask. But, in fact, planting is not about transferring sheep: it is about new growth. Fellowship Church, however, generously offered to give Beth up to ten of its families. So, she spent October to Christmas 2010 getting to know the congregants at Fellowship and gathering her core team, ending up with seven leaders and an additional ten congregants.

As for the church's name, the planters conducted a three-question survey worthy of a hip marketing firm (Beth believes in branding). They drew up a list of names, such as Destination and Common Ground, and asked locals to choose the name that would make them more likely to frequent a) a new coffee shop, b) a new bar, or c) a new church. The people spoke, the name was chosen, and on January 17, 2011, in Rupert House at the University of Western Ontario in London, Destination Church held its inaugural service, with seventeen people in attendance.

In June of that year, it moved into its church offices and began renting a local school gym for services, plus two classrooms for Sunday school. Those premises soon outgrown, Destination now meets in a banquet centre downtown.

As for its guiding vision, that includes connecting closely with and serving the downtown community and working directly with municipal leaders and local businesspeople on downtown projects. "If there's a discussion about anything, we're part of it," she says. "Basically, our vision is about discipleship. It's about a ragtag group of people embracing Jesus, living, laughing, praying, and hanging out together," says Beth. "It doesn't mean seeing heads in the pew in front of me. It's about how we live 24/7."

Beth, whose congregants wear T-shirts printed with the provocative slogan "The church has left the building," likens the established church to a hockey team that never gets out of the locker room to play the game. "It gets equipped and pumped up, but it never makes it to the ice. The crowd has waited so long, it's given up watching," she says. "For us, church begins when Sunday service ends."

For the future, her goal is to impact the lives of four thousand people—10 percent of the population of St. Thomas. "Within four years, if all goes well, we should be branching out into another church in a different part of town," she says. "We'll take out our best fifty and replant them."

Although the challenges of new plants are real, so are the rewards. As one of Destination's leaders puts it, "For fifty-two years, I'd been going to church twice every Sunday and sitting on two committees. Then I'd go home until the next week. For the first time in fifty-two years, instead of being fed, I feel I get a chance to feed someone."

D.S.

16

Help! Where Do I Go from Here?

Resources for the Journey[1]

Jenny Andison

I VIVIDLY REMEMBER MY father's sobering words when I first became a parent: "Jenny, you won't make the same mistakes your mother and I made . . . You'll make quite different ones." And he was right—of course. In so many areas of life, not only parenting, I am on a journey of learning, making mistakes, dusting myself off, and trying to keep going—and my ministry as a parish priest is no different. One area in which I am continuing to learn (and make mistakes) is what it means for the church to be truly the church and to follow faithfully the God of mission.

On this journey of learning, one thing I have come to realize is that the adjective "missional" in the term "missional church" is in fact superfluous. The church is not the church if it does not understand itself as being sent out in the power of the Holy Spirit to make disciples of Jesus and to co-operate in the mission of God.

That very basic theological statement is, of course, not original. My thinking has been shaped and challenged by books that I have read, courses that I have attended, and networks of colleagues with whom I have

---

1. A chapter like this would be difficult for one person to write. I am particularly grateful for the help of John Bowen, Nick Brotherwood and others in compiling these resources.

spent time talking. And that is significant. We cannot go on this journey of learning to be church in and for this culture on our own. We need one another and all the resources of the Body of Christ if we are to have any chance of being adequately prepared to go forward in a healthy way, not blindly repeating the mistakes of the past.

What follows is a brief compilation of some of the resources that are available to help us and our congregations start on that learning journey—or take the next step along the way—so that all of us are equipped for whatever it is that God is calling us to. Because of the nature of this chapter, you may decide not to read it from start to finish, but rather to pick and choose from the smorgasbord offered here. Think of it as "catalogue shopping" for the missional journey.

"WHAT IS THAT IN YOUR HAND?"

Although I will describe some of the programs and media resources that are available, I want first of all to identify a different kind of resource that is actually more important than any of the others. If it does not sound an odd thing to say, God is our most significant resource. I say "odd" because that might sound as though I am suggesting God exists simply to oil the wheels of our grand designs for mission. But what I mean, of course, is that mission is first and foremost the work of God, and therefore if we want to know what we should do in mission and how we should do it, we need to begin by looking to God, especially God as revealed to us in Jesus.

More than this, the Spirit of this same God and this same Jesus is already at work in our world, initiating, prompting, and shaping the work of mission. So our strategy must also begin with being open to the Holy Spirit to direct and enable us. If we want to know what this looks like, we cannot do better than to study one of the best resource textbooks on the topic—the Book of Acts, wherein the Spirit is constantly leading disciples of Jesus into new and unfamiliar experiences in order to further the work of God. That is not a bad place to begin, simply reading through Acts, alone or with a group, asking, "God of mission, what are you saying to us here and now?"

But there is more. The idea of your working within the mission of God may be new to you, but it is not new to God. Indeed, God has always been at work in your life shaping you for this involvement, whether you were aware of it or not. So, as you think about "resources for mission," it is worth making an inventory of the personal resources God has already given you that will not show up in any program, book, or website.[2] Here are some questions that may help you identify what these are. They—and the answers—may surprise you.

- Have you ever worked in a team, either as the leader or convener, or as a team member?

- Have you ever started something new—whether a business, a committee, a charity, a baby-sitting circle, or a Bible study group?

- Are you gifted with internet skills? Have you ever designed or maintained a website? Do you get excited about the networking potential of social media like Facebook and Twitter?

- Are you good at "making do"—creating a wonderful meal out of leftovers or pulling together familiar household objects to create a memorable children's party? Do you get excited about the potential of the ordinary when others do not? Have you learned how to be creative without a large budget?

- Do you enjoy learning from others, not least people of other denominations who are doing creative things in terms of mission? Can you make the kind of connections between people that create the potential for developing new projects?

- Do you sense that you have a special calling to pray? Do you set aside times specifically to pray? Do you keep a "prayer list"? Do you belong to a prayer group?

- Do you have experience at helping people settle their differences and start working together? Do you know how to make people in a group relax, laugh, and open up to one another?

- Do you enjoy meeting friends, new and old, in coffee shops and pubs? In those settings, do you find yourself sometimes involved in deep personal conversations that you never expected?

These abilities are not of a kind the church has always valued. Indeed, you yourself may never have thought of these things as particularly important—after all, they are just "who you are," and you take them for granted—yet they are actually wonderful gifts of God. And in situations where the church is learning to turn outwards to its community, they may well be more strategic than some of the traditionally valued gifts.

---

2. I am grateful for this insight to Nick Brotherwood.

When God called Moses to go and confront the Pharaoh of Egypt, Moses was understandably apprehensive. God's response was interesting. Instead of offering Moses a book on leadership or an assertiveness training course, God simply asked, "What is that in your hand?" to which Moses replied, "A staff" (Ex 4:1–5). And so, empowered by the living God, that familiar, everyday object became the instrument of a tyrant's downfall. When we think about "going missional," the first question to ask is, "What is that in your hand?"

On to more programmatic resources. All of these come from a specific denominational and theological background (where else could they come from, after all?), but all have the potential to be useful to Christians from different "tribes" in a "fellowship . . . of giving and receiving" (Phil 4:15 ASV). In some cases, materials will need to be translated from the language of one tradition into another—but that itself can be a worthwhile and growthful exercise.

I need to add, too, that resources are always changing: old materials cease to serve their purpose and are "retired," and others arise to take their place—and that is as it should be. So this chapter is unavoidably a snapshot in time. Even so, in cases where the resources listed here are no longer available by the time you read this, at least some of the contact information and websites will direct you to whatever is current.[3]

INTRODUCTORY RESOURCES

Many churches are at the point of knowing that "something is wrong," but are not quite sure what it is or what they should do about it. There are resources that seek to engage with people at precisely this point and to help them take their first baby steps in mission. The examples described here happen to be Anglican—maybe because Anglicans are "further back" in the conversation than some other denominations.

Mission Possible

The *Mission Possible* course was developed in the Anglican Diocese of Toronto in 2009 and was first used as a study guide by over fifty Toronto

---

3. The resources discussed in this chapter have been chosen because they are Canadian and are intended to serve the Canadian church in its context. A further range of helpful resources is, of course, available from the USA, UK, Australia, and other countries.

parishes in Lent of the following year. *Mission Possible* is a five-week Bible study, helping people begin to think about who God is, what God's mission is, and how the church needs to be shaped to respond to that call. This course makes a perfect series to work through with a church's leadership team, but it can work equally well for an existing small group or as a special study series during the seasons of Lent or Advent. Some churches have also used it as a basis for a five-week preaching series.

The course can be downloaded free of charge from the website of the Diocese of Toronto at www.shapedformission.ca. Materials available include a leader's guide, a participants' guide, and PowerPoint slides. The course is also available in a Cantonese version.

Vision Days, Mission Days

In situations where a large number of people are asking missional questions, it is often appropriate to organize a one-day event for a number of churches (ideally of different denominations). There is a synergy and enriched learning that happens in such gatherings that are difficult to create in a single-church setting. One way to do this is to invite Fresh Expressions Canada to help you organize a Vision Day, open to all Christians in your area. (The Anglican Diocese of Edmonton has also developed a Mission Day, which takes a different approach in helping people engage with what it might mean to be a church shaped by and for God's mission.) These days usually take place on a Saturday from ten until four, with a simple lunch provided.

The program for these days is fun and interactive. They are an opportunity to reflect on what is going on in our culture, and how and why church no longer connects with a lot of people. Vision Days are also times of celebration of what God is doing and what resources for mission we actually have within the church. From these days, new vision, new ideas, and new relationships feed into a church's ongoing wrestling with questions of mission. People generally leave these days feeling energized and wanting to explore further.

If you would like to explore hosting a Vision Day in your area, contact Fresh Expressions Canada at www.freshexpressions.ca. And for Edmonton Mission Days, check the website of the Diocese: www.edmonton.anglican.org for details.

Reimagining Church

Those who remain hungry for more after a Vision Day or a Mission Day—which is, after all, only a taste of missional thinking—might consider doing a longer course called *Reimagining Church: Shaped for Mission*. Each session includes elements of Bible study, discussion, worship, video, and PowerPoint presentations. *Reimagining Church* is a five-part course which can be taught over five consecutive weeks, or over one or two weekends. It is made up of the following topics:

1. "Brave New World?" considers changes in Canadian culture in the past twenty-five years;

2. "What in the World is God up to?" discusses our spiritual resources—the mission of God (the *missio dei*), the Gospel, and the calling of the church;

3. "The School of Jesus" looks at the nature of evangelism and discipleship;

4. "Changing World, Changing Church" studies different ways in which churches are seeking to connect with their neighbourhoods and with cultures where there is no church; and

5. "Where Do We Go from Here?" asks participants to reflect prayerfully back on the course and all it might mean for their own lives and the life of their congregation.

It is worth adding that the thrust of this course is not so much practical (although there may well be practical results) as imaginative. The purpose is to re-orient our thinking, to sow some new ideas, and to offer some examples of what can be done. This means that leaders will need to be prepared to help churches that have done *Reimagining Church* to explore ways of moving forward from this point.

The materials for *Reimagining Church* can be downloaded from the Fresh Expressions Canada website, www.freshexpressions.ca.

NEXT STEPS

So, if you have successfully begun the "missional conversation" in your community, the obvious question is, what next? Thankfully, there are a number of resources available to help you take the next critical steps.

Natural Church Development

This popular program helps congregations identify their strengths and weaknesses according to the eight criteria that mark growing churches: "In healthy churches leadership is *empowering*, ministry is aligned with *spiritual giftings*, structures *function* well, spirituality *impassions* and guides the rest of life, God *inspires* in the worship, the *whole person* is engaged through small groups, evangelism relates to *the needs* of those beyond the church, and relationships within the parish have a *loving* quality."[4] Churches can fill out a survey that will reveal their strongest and their weakest points and then work to address the weaknesses.

The system has grown in accuracy and sophistication since its inception in 1989. Natural Church Development is based on a growing realization that when new Christian communities are being birthed, they need to have these eight "quality characteristics" built into their DNA in order to enable healthy growth from the beginning. For more information, see the website www.ncdcanada.com.

Two Conferences

Conferences are a great way to be introduced to something new, in terms of being quickly immersed into new content and a new community. Two church planting conferences happen regularly in Canada and serve these purposes. One, the Church Planting Canada Congress (usually just called the Congress), began in 1997 and is held every two years in different cities across Canada. It is organized by people from evangelical churches but is open to friends of all denominations. The website is www.thecongress.ca. The other, the Vital Church Planting Conference, was begun in 2007. It is organized by Anglicans, but it is normal for people from a dozen different denominations to attend and to be involved in teaching and training. Vital Church Planting (VCP) began in Toronto but has also been held in Edmonton, and there is interest in holding similar conferences in other parts of Canada. Information can be found at www.vitalchurchplanting.com.

It is worth adding that the use of the term "church planting" at these conferences does not mean the practice of a previous generation of buying land, putting up a building, and beginning services. Rather, there is a

4. Connie denBok, "Natural Church Development is . . . Still Developing," The Institute of Evangelism, Wycliffe College, April 1, 2009, http://www.institute.wyclif-fecollege.ca/2009/04/natural-church-development-isstill-developing.

widespread understanding that "church planting" these days begins with involvement in the community, listening to God, and building relationships—a much slower and longer-term project.

Both these conferences have an emphasis on theologically-driven praxis rather than theory, and over the years have become gathering places where individuals and teams involved in the creation of new Christian communities can come to learn, to be refreshed, and to network with like-minded friends.

Conferences, of course, though often intense and stimulating, are soon over. While they can be helpful in catalyzing new ideas or providing new energy, long-term change by definition takes longer and needs to be sustained a step at a time. Church traditions that have more experience in "church planting" know this well and have developed helpful resources for this crucial dimension of missional ministry.

Mission Shaped Ministry

Mission Shaped Ministry (MSM) is a course that offers practical orientation in growing new Christian communities. It lasts eight months, usually from September to May, and is adapted for Canada from the materials developed by Fresh Expressions UK. The course is primarily for teams (ideally, lay and ordained together) who are moving towards pioneering a fresh expression of church, as well as for those who are already involved in one.

Over the eight months, the course deals with a wide range of practical issues and strategies. A popular component of the course is the experienced practitioners who participate as guest teachers, share their own experiences, and answer questions. At present, *Mission Shaped Ministry* can only be taken online, though local courses may be added as time goes on. The advantage of the online version, of course, is that it does not matter where you are located in Canada: as long as you have a computer and a good internet connection, you can take the course!

You can learn more about *Mission Shaped Ministry*, including dates of upcoming courses, on the Fresh Expressions Canada website, www. freshexpressions.ca.

Church Planter Assessment

As you pursue some of these options, at some point questions are bound to arise either in conversation or in your mind: "Am I a church planter? Could I start one of these new Christian communities people are talking about? What gifts and experience does it take? What is the difference between a church planter and a church revitalizer, and which one am I?"

If you are asking yourself those kinds of questions, it is worth the time and effort to get yourself properly assessed. There are a number of distinct characteristics that effective church planters display, and there are assessment processes (the shortest takes an hour, the longest four days) to help you discern whether this is what you are being called to do.

Church Planting Canada (CPC), an evangelical network, probably has the most extensive experience in assessment. They have discovered that being properly assessed before you begin—along with having a suitable coach (a topic discussed below)—makes a huge difference in whether your new Christian community will be functioning well and self-supporting after (say) five years of existence. If assessment and coaching are in place, the "success" rate rises from 50 percent to 90 percent. You can check out how CPC does assessments on the website www.churchplantingcanada.ca.

C2C is a newer organization, Mennonite Brethren in origin but pleased to work across denominations. They were responsible for catalyzing Artisan Church in Vancouver, described on pages 93–95 of this book. Their church planter assessment and their training programs are described on their website, www.c2cnetwork.ca.

Some years back, thanks to a generous ecumenical gesture on the part of Church Planting Canada, some Anglicans in the Diocese of Toronto were trained to administer C2C's "Profile Assessment System." After some necessary translation into a different "tribal language," the adapted process has been effectively used among Anglicans who are wondering if they are gifted for church planting. If you are interested in pursuing assessment in a mainline church context, go to the Diocese of Toronto website, www.toronto.anglican.ca, and search for "church planting."

And, if you are not sure whether you are ready to start the process, there are various brief forms of self-assessment you can do online before you decide to check out one of the more extensive assessment processes. One of these can be found in the form of a short survey at www.surveymonkey.com/s/9XXS5B5. A longer "pre-assessment" tool suitable for denominational use allows up to 125 online assessments a year for a reasonable fee. It can be found at www.churchplanterprofiles.com.

ONGOING HELP ON THE JOURNEY

For an individual, going on the missional journey can be challenging, daunting, and sometimes lonely. Thankfully, there are others on the same road, and some who are just a few steps ahead of us and happy to help. Finding someone to coach us as we embark on this journey can be invaluable, and good coaches are worth their weight in gold. In fact, there is pretty clear evidence that whether a pioneer has a coach or not is one of the determining factors in a new project's survival.

Unless you already know a person you would trust to coach you, ask someone in leadership in your denomination or network for suggestions. Or you may know someone in your community whose ministry you admire who could act as a coach. This does not even have to be someone from your own denomination. One Anglican priest approached the pastor of the thriving Mennonite church in her community for help and has benefitted greatly.[5]

Failing that, there are more and more networks of people that can help you find a coach. For example, Church Planting Canada has trained coaches across the country, although, since much coaching can be done by phone or Skype, geography is not an issue. CPC's staff also offer training in how to coach. Contact information for local coaches and information about training are available on their website, www.churchplantingcanada.ca.

If the congregation you are part of is already fairly healthy and vibrant, and wants to make the transition to engaging in missional ministry outside of the church walls, then you may be ready to begin a Missional Transformation Process (MTP). This is a process that takes between eighteen months and two years. It is enabled by coaches from The Missional Network and/or those they train. MTP follows a two-fold track, engaging clergy and missional leaders on the one hand, and lay members of the congregation on the other, in parallel tracks, in order to create new missional DNA for the church. The church as a whole will learn skills for following "what God is up to" both in the congregation and in the neighborhood as they reconnect with it. To find out more, check out The Missional Network at www.themissionalnetwork.com.

---

5. Diana Swift, "Mennonite Mentor Mends Moribund Anglican Church," *The Anglican Journal*, February 8, 2012. http://www.anglicanjournal.com/nc/other/news-items/article/mennonite-mentor-mends-moribund-anglican-church-10446//abp/243.html.

Peer Mentoring

Of course, coaching by a more experienced practitioner is not the only way to get help. Peer mentoring groups are also an invaluable resource, and many are taking shape among pioneering folk in communities across Canada. In such groups, nobody is "the expert," but everyone knows something. Fortunately, people with pioneering instincts tend to find each other through Facebook, blogs, websites, and conferences. At the same time, there are somewhat more formal peer groupings coming together across the country.

Forge Canada describes itself as a network of leaders and churches in Canada committed to training missional leaders. Their peer learning groups are called "Forge Hubs," clusters of missional leaders—some new, others more experienced—who get together to encourage one another, to laugh and weep together, and to pray for one another. Their website, www.forgecanada.ca, describes all of their resources, as well as listing where their "hubs" are presently to be found.

OTHER SOURCES OF SUPPORT

There are many other agencies and networks that provide significant sources of information, support, and advice. Here are some worth checking out:

The Wycliffe College Institute of Evangelism

For more than twenty years, the Wycliffe College Institute of Evangelism has offered resources to help churches of all denominations looking for revitalization. Their website offers articles, printed materials, videos, and podcasts; they also have a variety of speakers who can preach, speak at conferences, and lead seminars and workshops on such topics as evangelism, making disciples, and welcoming newcomers. The Institute can be found at www.institute.wycliffecollege.ca.

Fresh Expressions Canada

Former Archbishop of Canterbury Rowan Williams coined the phrase "the mixed economy." He was summarizing the church's need on the one hand to encourage existing churches—which he called "inherited church-es"—to turn outward and become missional and, on the other hand, the need to encourage the formation of new Christian communities, some-times called "fresh expressions of church." Fresh Expressions Canada is a national organization that seeks to encourage the development of new, culturally appropriate Christian communities, at the same time as encour-aging inherited churches.

Again, there are many effective resources that you can download from the website: stories that will inspire your congregation, training ma-terials, and news about upcoming equipping events that you may wish to attend. Fresh Expressions can also provide speakers for Vision or Mission Days, and it offers the *Mission Shaped Ministry* course online. Check out their website at www.freshexpressions.ca.

The TIM Centre

The Tyndale Intercultural Ministry (TIM) Centre, based in Toronto, de-scribes itself as "Missions Central—your one-stop for missions around the corner and around the world." It is a unique resource for those who want to network with other missional leaders of many traditions and nationali-ties through forums and roundtables. Part of its uniqueness is the training it offers for intercultural ministries. (One example of the effectiveness of their programs is given in chapter 6.) You can also access consultants at the TIM Centre who can help you research your neighbourhood to pre-pare for more effective local ministry. The TIM Centre can be found at www.tyndale.ca/tim.

Outreach Canada

This is an evangelical mission agency with a wide range of helpful pro-grams. The Outreach Learning Network (TOLN), based in Delta, British Columbia, is the training division of Outreach Canada and offers help in areas such as congregational health and revitalization, transitional leadership (interim) ministry, vision renewal, and church planting. Their research department, headed up by Lorne Hunter, is extensive and in-sightful. You can check them out at www.outreach.ca.

EDGE: A Network for Ministry Development

EDGE is a recent initiative of the United Church, with ecumenical scope, intended to foster the growth of missional congregations and to focus resources on the development of new ministries in existing congregations and in fresh expressions of church. EDGE is a network designed to connect leaders to new resources through the following means:

- experienced and trained consultants and coaches who work on-site with ministries;

- web-video peer learning cohorts that come together around the learning needs they are discovering and then connect with various resources, key thinkers, and effective practitioners, as needed; and

- a webinar subscription series that provides online access and conversation with key missional thinkers, writers, and practitioners.

To find out more, check the website www.edge-ucc.ca.

Missional Seminary Training

Twenty-five years ago, Lesslie Newbigin warned that traditional forms of ordination training would not be adequate for the new missionary reality in the West. He wrote, "ministerial training as currently conceived is still far too much training for pastoral care of the existing congregation, and far too little oriented towards the missionary calling to claim the whole of public life for Christ and his kingdom."[6]

Increasingly, seminaries in the Western world are adjusting their training to take account of the new situation. In Canada, three seminaries in particular have changed in this regard in recent years: Tyndale Seminary and Wycliffe College, both in Toronto, and Regent College, in Vancouver. All three have intentionally intensified the missional dimension of all their programs in recent years, but all have also added specific programs and courses to address the growing need.

Tyndale offers what is called the In-Ministry M.Div. This is a part-time program, mainly for people who (as the name implies) are already serving in church leadership. The program happens one day a week, plus one Saturday each semester, for three years. At Wycliffe, students in the so-called "Pioneer Stream" take the same theology, Bible, history,

---

6. Lesslie Newbigin, *The Gospel in a Pluralist Society* (Grand Rapids, MI: Eerdmans, 1989), 231.

and pastoral courses as other M.Div students, but use their electives to take courses specially related to the theology and skills of starting new Christian communities. And at Regent, rather than setting up a specialized missional program, students in all Master's programs are exposed to a missional emphasis, such as the course entitled "Empowering the Church for Re-evangelizing the West." There is, however, the option of a "missions concentration" in the Master's programs. Details may be found on the websites of these schools.

SUPPORTING NEW GROWTH

In recent years, as will be obvious by now, there has been a wonderful proliferation of missional resources springing up across Canada. The Spirit of God seems not only to be calling people to new ministries among the unchurched but also providing the infrastructure within the Body of Christ to support and empower that new life. Why should we be surprised? As a missional leader of a different century experienced, "God's work done in God's way will never lack God's supplies."[7]

What happens next will depend, at least in part, on the response of the denominations to these new things. Some of the smaller, evangelical denominations have for some years been putting more of their resources into reaching out to the growing mission field that is Canada: for example, the Free Methodists, the Christian Reformed Church, the Salvation Army, and the Mennonites. Two illustrations will suffice. One Christian Reformed leader told me that they have been thinking of North America as a mission field since the 1970s and that their present goal is to start thirty new churches a year across the continent.[8] In the early 1990s, the Free Methodist Church in Canada began to make structural changes that enabled it to appoint missional leaders to the national office.[9] As a result, out of their 145 congregations across Canada, fifteen have been started in the last five years, seven of them in Quebec.

At the same time, the older, longer-established denominations are also beginning to recognize and act on the missional challenge. Canadian Anglicans, for example, are beginning to engage with the Five Marks of Mission (see page 11, footnote 13) to guide their future. As Archbishop

7. Leslie T. Lyall, *A Passion for the Impossible: The Continuing Story of the Mission Hudson Taylor Began* (London: OMF Books, 1965), 37.

8. Hilda VanderKlippe, personal conversation, May 2012.

9. Gary Walsh, personal conversation, April 2012.

Fred Hiltz has said, "This beloved church of ours is being renewed by the Marks of Mission—at every level from the parishes and dioceses to General Synod. They are our guiding points of reference in these times."[10] They are also beginning to draw on the resources of their evangelical cousins. Roman Catholics are embracing the Pope's call for a re-evangelization of the West. Cardinal Collins of Toronto, for example, said in an interview with *Maclean's* magazine, "We need to be evangelical, to be on fire, to fire a Pentecost. The Church exploded outward from the upper room, from Pentecost, and we never should forget that."[11]

There appears then to be a growing willingness to make what Rowan Williams has called "a principled and careful loosening of structures"[12] to enable a more nimble institutional response to the missional needs of Canada.

At this point in our history, the words of Isaiah seem particularly appropriate, speaking to us of God's calling and God's provision: "Do not remember the former things, or consider the things of old. I am about to do a new thing; now it springs forth, do you not perceive it? I will make a way in the wilderness and rivers in the desert . . . to give drink to my chosen people, the people whom I formed for myself so that they might declare my praise" (Isa 43:18–21). May we have courage to embrace the "new thing," knowing that God will provide "rivers in the desert" and equip us to declare God's praise across Canada.

10. Personal conversation, June 2012.

11. Brian Bethune, "In Conversation: Thomas Collins: The Archbishop of Toronto on Becoming a Cardinal and Why the Bible is Better on an iPad," *Maclean's*, February 20, 2012. http://www2.macleans.ca/2012/02/20/on-gay-straight-alliances-christian-persecution-and-why-the-bible-is-better-on-an-ipad.

12. Rowan Williams, "General Synod London Sessions, November 15–16, 2005 Archbishop's Presidential Address," The Archbishop of Canterbury, November 16, 2005, http://www.archbishopofcanterbury.org/articles.php/1792/general-synod-london-sessions-15-16-november-2005-archbishops-presidential-address.

Afterword

Colin R. Johnson

"IN THE BEGINNING, GOD . . ." The creation story that opens the Bible (Gen 1:1) describes the origin of God's mission to the world. God is always reaching out. God, who expresses his love and brings into being that which was not, enters into a loving, joyful relationship with his creatures that they may have life in all its abundance. The biblical witness tells us that we creatures have not always (or even usually) responded in love, but have turned away from God—and yet God continually searches us out and finds us. The birth, life, death, and resurrection of Jesus and the sending of the Holy Spirit are the definitive moments in that mission. The final vision and promise is that God will ultimately achieve his goal of reconciling the world to himself, and even now that work is being done.

The Christian faith is never just about Jesus and me: there is always an "us." God's mission is to the whole world, and God invites us to partner with him in achieving his intentions. The Church is the community of those who are responding to his invitation into this life-changing relationship and who join in this mission to the whole world.

After you have read the preceding chapters, I wonder if for you, as for me, two comments from John Bowen's Introduction come back to convey the alternating reactions a reader might have to this book: some chapters will offer "immense and surprising hope," while others will introduce "the troubling voice" that suggests we need to rethink some of our longstanding opinions. I find myself stretched and chastened, encouraged and shaken, affirmed and challenged, intrigued and slightly unnerved by what I have read here. These are Canadian stories, and it is useful to reflect on how the particular context of our geography, our social and political history, and our demography influence how we engage in fresh expressions of church, in ways that are both similar to and different from our

American neighbours and European co-religionists to whom we have so often looked for precedents.

I am an official senior leader of a deeply institutional denomination. There is a great deal of questioning of the Church as institution today: many see it as rigid, narrow, stultifying, boring, controlling, and out of touch. Some have very little respect for, or interest in, institutions of any kind. But institutions also build the infrastructure that provides continuity, accountability, and connections. The fresh expressions experiments push me to think about how much of what I value about my tradition is essential to the proclamation and living out of the Gospel of Christ, and how much is simply an accretion that can be changed. What is a matter of personal likes and dislikes—aesthetics or prejudices or familiarity—and what is of the essence? Who is in front of us, and what resources has God given us for the particular mission in which we are called to participate?

There are some who would love to build a new church, starting with getting rid of all those who currently attend. Unfortunately, faithful missional work starts with those whom God has placed alongside us, not with those whom we wish God had given.

REDISCOVERING PARISH

What I find most notable in the examples in this book is the concern of these newly formed "gatherings" for the surrounding neighbourhood and its needs. The people in these new groups desire to be relevant—not in the sense of being entertained or entertaining, but in being meaningfully engaged in something real. There is such eager willingness to make a difference in people's lives, not only to speak about, but actively to create, the link between Gospel and justice. Is this actually recalling us to our roots in reviving the ancient role of parish, where everyone within the territory, regardless of outward connection to the church, falls within the pastoral care and practical loving concern of the community that gathers for worship?

I believe that the oscillation between respecting the received tradition and rejoicing in the new in-breaking of the Holy Spirit is a genuinely faithful response to God's call. It is more faithful than, on the one hand, clinging obstinately to the "way it's always been" (historically a very questionable point of view), or, on the other hand, a rejection of anything that has come before as "tainted" (the new becomes old surprisingly quickly!). We could benefit from a "both/and" conjunction rather than an "either/or" polarity.

We have centuries of learning gleaned from holy women and men who have prayed, meditated on scripture, conversed with God, reflected on the nature of human life, and discerned faithful ways to respond in daily life. We do not have to recreate this wisdom anew in each age. The role of institutions is to preserve and pass on these values from one generation to the next. But what we must do is to find the appropriate ways to apply this wisdom to the daily demands of life today, in common witness and alignment with the continuing mission of God. Context matters! And God's Holy Spirit is a relentlessly unsettling Bringer of new life.

In the life of Jesus, we meet God who dwells in the midst of the ordinary, and in the particular. God uses the ordinary stuff of life to mediate his presence: flesh and blood, quite ordinary fisherfolk, government officials, flawed people, some bread and wine, a little water, ancient stories and homely anecdotes, wood and nails, a living room, stone and glass, a pub or a coffee shop, a helping hand, a hospital bed, some shared song—these are just a few of the myriad ways our God reaches out to us. Then and now—and tomorrow, too!

God's presence brings healing to a broken world, challenge to a complacent people, reconciliation to a dismembered community. Christ's self-sacrifice for the sake of the world becomes the model for our moving beyond our own self-interests to offer our whole life for the good of others in response to God's love.

UNCOMFORTABLE QUESTIONS

Examination of our call to mission in the context of the society in which we live poses some serious and uncomfortable questions. What is the role of Sunday worship? What is the place of the sacraments, which are a central aspect of the Church's life—Eucharist because it nourishes the people of God with Christ's own life, and baptism as incorporation into Christ and the entrance into the community of faith? How (and, more controversially, when) do these fit into the new missional model? What is the role of the ordained, and what is the preparation required for ministry today? In a tradition like the Anglican Church, how does the newly gathered community link with the wider community, and what are the lines of oversight for accountability, authenticity, and authority?

There is a lot of good work occurring across denominations and the customary boundaries that we have erected. We are witnessing a new ecumenism in practice, perhaps not so much at the official levels as at the grass roots. It is both exciting and challenging for the institution when official policies are being bent by emerging praxis. I believe at least some of it is the work of the Holy Spirit, so that requires me to shift my perspective to fit that of God—an act of repentance or conversion, of turning to God with God's help.

God's missionary action is not always happening where we expect to find it. Sometimes it is in the midst of the most traditional setting, and sometimes it is in what we had judged to be the most barren of spaces. We have been told in the parable that the householder will bring out of his storehouse treasures both old and new (Matt 13:52). Somehow we have not expected it to happen quite like this—until we see it unfolding before our eyes! But this also requires a disciplined discernment, a sifting for what is of God, because not everything that is new and fresh, of course, is good and actually "of God." There is a reason that God endows the community with the gift of discernment!

I find the "Green Shoots" title of this book helpful in imagining this. There is unquestionably new life here but is every expression of the new life of the Church good? Certainly not! Jesus' parable of the wheat and the weeds growing together in a field (Matt 13:24) makes this clear. You cannot pluck out the weeds, he says, until further growth has occurred, and only then can you begin to tell the difference more clearly. You need to "let both grow side by side" for quite a while. Only then can some separation happen. (A wag once proposed that the quick solution to telling the difference would be to mow the whole field down, and whatever grows up again will be weeds!)

The provisional character of fresh expressions of church needs to be respected: some things will flourish, some will not, some germination takes a very long time, and long-term growth is often slow. In a few cases, it may grow with a significant deformity, but in many more of these "Green Shoots," the incipient "marks" of the mature church will enliven and enrich our lives. But it takes patience and perseverance. Maturation is a process.

NO QUICK FIXES

The chapters of this book remind me that we are looking for adaptive leadership and not for technical quick fixes. We cannot simply rely on what we have done before. No single model will provide the magic bullet to revitalize the church or become the best way that the church should embrace

God's mission. This is not a matter of searching for the latest gimmick. The approach must be multifaceted. There has to be a risky (and costly) willingness to experiment. Experiments are by nature unproven; results are guessed at, or perhaps hoped for, but never known in advance. There are no guarantees. Experiments take time and repetition, and they also presume that there will be perceptive observation and careful evaluation. Many experiments fail, but even then there is significant learning.

Finally, let us remember to ask ourselves: what is the purpose of all this? We do this to join in the work of God, in the mission of God to reconcile the world to himself through Christ, that all may have life. This is good news, and it is worth sharing.

Indeed, it is such good news that it is worth pushing out of our comfort zone, trying something new, investing in some creative opportunities, and taking some leaps of faith for the sake of the Gospel. And the stories in this book give us an inkling of what exciting things might happen when the Holy Spirit is at work.